Nelson Multi Media Group
presents

Under Cover

The Promise of Protection Under His Authority

Participant's Guide

A Complete 12-Session Video Curriculum

by John Bevere

with Lee Bozeman, Larry Keefauver, and Neil Wilson
of Livingstone

Under Cover Participant's Guide

Scripture passages taken from:

The Holy Bible, New King James Version (NKJV)
Copyright© 1979, 1980, 1982 by Thomas Nelson, Inc. Used by permission. All rights reserved.

The Holy Bible, New International Version® (NIV)
Copyright © 1973, 1978, 1984 by International Bible Society.

Holy Bible, New Living Translation (NLT)
Copyright © 1996 by Tyndale Charitable Trust. All rights reserved.

The Amplified Bible: Old Testament
Copyright © 1962, 1964 by Zondervan Publishing House. Used by permission.

The Amplified New Testament
Copyright © 1958 by the Lockman Foundation. Used by permission.

Produced with the assistance of The Livingstone Corporation. Project staff includes: Lee Bozeman, Larry Keefauver, Ashley Taylor, Neil Wilson.

ISBN: 0-7852-6628-3

Table of Contents

A Few Words from John Bevere

You say, *"I don't like the subject of authority"*

Well, you're not in a minority. As a matter of fact, the majority in America do not like the subject of authority.

But I believe that as we go through these twelve lessons and you listen carefully, you will find that you will not only like authority, you will also develop a passion to seek it and live it in your own life.

From *Under Cover:*

> In this book I have shared examples of my own failures. I am not a power-hungry leader who desires to beat his sheep, staff, or family into submission. I have a wonderful staff and family. And I am not a pastor. So I write as a man who has made many mistakes or, more accurately put, sins. I served under two international ministries in the 1980s, and from these experiences I draw most of my errant examples. What is most sobering about each incident is that I believed with all my heart I was right in each one when, in reality, I was wrong. I am so grateful to our Lord that His Word exposed my motives.
>
> My heartfelt desire is to see you learn from my hardships and avoid the same mistakes. I pray you'll draw instruction and godly insight from my foolishness, and reap the benefits. For what I later learned as a result of my experiences and the truths revealed in the process was both beneficial and wonderful. Through repentance came safety and provision.

vi

Introduction

Welcome to *Under Cover*, a study of the Biblical principles of authority.

This workbook has been prepared to help you study and apply the principles included in the book *Under Cover* and in the videotaped seminar.

Getting the Most Out of Your Under Cover Study

1. First, read the book, *Under Cover: Your Secret Place of Freedom.* Make notes in the margins, underline key ideas, and mark places where you have questions.
2. Second, keep your Bible open as you read, consulting the Scriptures to make sure you are grasping John Bevere's points.
3. If you are part of a group study, preview each session in the workbook before your group time. Read the chapter summary even if you have read the book and fill out the Warm-Up questions.
4. During the video presentation, open your workbook to the first page of the lesson so you can jot notes in the Personal Notes section.
5. Continually ask the Holy Spirit to give you discernment, particularly in the way the Scriptures apply to your life.
6. Make it your wholehearted desire to get under God's cover in every area of your life, and stay there!

Preparing the Lessons

Read over at least one of the lessons to become familiar with the approach to this study. If you are participating in a group study, make it a point to prepare the first three sections in each study before the group meets. Each lesson includes the following components:

1. *Chapter Summary*—brief summary of the teaching principles in the chapters from *Under Cover* that include the material being studied in the session.
2. *Personal Notes*—space for personal notes during the reading of the book or the watching of the video presentation.
3. *Warm-Up Questions*—topical questions to focus your thinking in preparation for the video presentation.
4. *Teaching by John Bevere*—the 30-minute video session with John Bevere.
5. *Teaching Review*—observation questions to help focus attention during the video session.
6. *Exploring God's Word*—study of each of the main passages used in the session.
7. *Exposing the Truth*—questions to help reach conclusions regarding the Scriptures and insights from the session.
8. *Applying the Lesson*—specific directions for application of the principles in the session.
9. *Checking Your Cover*—a final opportunity for prayerful submission to the truth of the session.
10. *Video Script*—an exact transcript of the video presentation, to which you can refer during your study and discussion.

Under Cover quotes

Several times in each lesson, you will find key quotes from the book that pertain to the subject under discussion.

May the Lord richly bless you and teach you as you discover His cover, and place yourself under it!

Session One

It's Hard to Kick Against the Goads

*"He is my refuge and my fortress;
My God, in Him I will trust."*
Psalm 91:1–2

Summary for Under Cover, Chapters 1 and 2

John Bevere begins his book *Under Cover* with a fact: Life involves continual choices. Where we will live, what type of occupation we will choose, and how we will spend our time are all very important decisions that we will make. As Christians, we have an even greater decision that must be faced daily—Who is in control of our lives? We must continually decide whether or not we are going to let God have control of every area of our lives. We must decide if we are going to stand under His protection or if we are simply going to try and make it on our own.

Why is this decision so difficult for so many of us? The difficulty lies in our submission to authority. More importantly, it is our submission to *the* authority—God. Too often we decide we will not submit to authority unless we agree with the stated principles. With this attitude, we are constantly struggling against the Spirit trying to lead us to the truth. In short, we are rebellious children wanting to do it our own way.

In chapter two, John describes this attitude as "kicking against the goads," a reference to Jesus' words to Paul on the road to Damascus when the Lord knocked him down to get his attention (Acts 9:1–19; 26:14). God will sometimes ask us to do something that we may not want to do. If we resist His will, if we kick against the goads, we are in rebellion. We must realize that God only wants what is best for us. We don't inform Him; He directs us. We are to be His humble servants, submitting to His authority in everything that we do. If we learn this lesson well, we will begin to see how all things work together for the good of those that love Him.

God controls all earthly and heavenly authority. If we understand His authority and learn submission to His will, we will learn how to be submissive to earthly authority as well. God desires His servants to have humble hearts. Our true obedience to God only comes through true and total submission to His authority.

My experience has been that Westerners (dwellers of democratic nations of America and Europe) are some of the most resistant people to truly hearing the Word of God. The reason is fundamental. It is hard to understand kingdom principles with a democratic mind-set. Democracy is fine for the nations of the world, but we must remember the kingdom of God is just that—a kingdom. It is ruled by a King, and there are rank, order, and authority. The laws of His kingdom are not superseded by, or subject to, popular opinion, voting or polls. The laws are not swayed by what we believe to be good for us, as Eve was so cleverly deceived into thinking. Therefore, just as Samuel "explained to the people the

Notes from Chapters 1–2 (Video Session 1)

_____

_____

_____

_____

_____

_____

_____

_____

_____

_____

Warm–Up Questions

1. In what areas of your life do you feel the need for some sort of protection?

   _____

   _____

   _____

2. From where or from whom do you receive protection?

   _____

   _____

   _____

3. What is your general attitude toward authority? Why?

_____

_____

_____

_____

Although they may not be quick to admit it, too many see themselves accountable only to God, and not to authorities. Those who think this way are on a collision course with the very One they call Lord. Recall Jesus' words to Saul (who would become Paul), "It is hard for you to kick against the goads" (Acts 9:5). Farmers in biblical days used goads. A common goad was an eight-foot-long straight branch of oak or other strong wood from which the bark had been stripped. At the front end a pointed spike was used to prod the oxen while plowing. An ox would certainly not resist such a sharp instrument capable of administering a good deal of pain and harm. Hence in Paul's day this proverbial expression was used to describe the futility of resistance to superior authority or power.

Those who resist the authority of God, whether directly, as Paul did, or indirectly to His delegated authority, will find themselves kicking against the goad in God's hands. More often than not this can be a painful experience and lesson too many of us end up learning the hard way, as I did.

John Bevere, *Under Cover*, p.12.

Teaching by John Bevere

Watch the first session video presentation.

Teaching Review

4. Which of the following accurately describe John's use of the phrase "under cover?" (Choose one or more and describe John's understanding)

   Deception _____

   Protection _____

   Freedom _____

   Shame _____

   _____

   _____

5. Bevere points out that in our culture it is hard to understand kingdom principles because we tend to view everything with a _____ mindset.

   _____

   _____

6. According to John, obedience to authority should not simply be an outward act, but should flow from a _____ and _____ heart.

Exploring God's Word

Psalm 91:1–2 *He who dwells in the secret place of the Most High Shall abide under the shadow of the Almighty. I will say of the Lord, "He is my refuge and my fortress; My God, in Him I will trust."*

7. What kinds of people are under God's protection and covering?

_____

_____

_____

_____

_____

_____

Personal Application

_____

_____

_____

Romans 12:2 *Do not be conformed to this world, but be transformed by the renewing of your mind, that you may prove what is that good and acceptable and perfect will of God.*

8. In what ways can we be conformed to this world?

_____

_____

_____

_____

_____

_____

9. As our minds are renewed, how is God's perfect will made manifest in our lives?

_____

_____

_____

_____

_____

Personal Application

_____

_____

_____

Job 36:11–12 *If they obey and serve Him, They shall spend their days in prosperity, and their years in pleasures. But if they do not obey, they shall perish by the sword, and they shall die without knowledge.*

10. How is our prosperity and peace contingent upon our obedience to God?

_____

_____

_____

Personal Application

_____

_____

_____

Romans 13:1–2 *Let every soul be subject to the governing authorities. For there is no authority except from God, and the authorities that exist are appointed by God. Therefore whoever resists the authority resists the ordinance of God, and those who resist will bring judgment on themselves.*

11. What, according to Scripture, is a correct attitude for a Christian to have toward authority?

_____

_____

_____

12. When we resist our earthly authorities, how are we disobeying God?

_____

_____

_____

_____

13. According to this passage, how is God in control of all things?

_____

_____

_____

_____

Personal Application

_____

_____

_____

_____

Psalm 51:16–17 *For You do not desire sacrifice, or else I would given it; You do not delight in burnt offering. The sacrifices of God are a broken spirit, A broken and a contrite heart—These, O God, You will not despise.*

14. In what ways have you offered God what He does not desire?

_____

_____

_____

15. What is it that God desires from us above all things?

_____

_____

_____

_____

_____

16. How can you continually test your own attitudes and
    actions to be sure that you are doing God's will and
    not your own?

_____

_____

_____

_____

_____

_____

Personal Application

_____

_____

_____

Exposing the Truth

17. In the Introduction of the book and the video, John
    discusses the phrase "under cover." How would you
    define this?
    To be "under cover" is to be _____

_____

_____

_____

18. John writes, "the one who is under cover is the one who is under God's authority." How does authority provide us with protection?

_____

_____

_____

_____

19. People often have unpleasant experiences with authority. John points out that, "out of these distasteful experiences has developed a subtle attitude: "*I just don't believe in authority*, or to put it in more adult terms, *I'm just not going to submit to authority unless I first agree with it*." In what ways have your own experiences colored the way you react to authority?

_____

_____

_____

_____

20. In chapter two, John writes, "Too often today, if we don't agree with authority, we can challenge it through complaint or protest. After all, government should be 'of the people, by the people, for the people,' right? This and other democratic mindsets have trickled into our Christianity and marched many down the deceptive path of self-rule." List several results that the attitude of self-rule will have upon the church:

_____

_____

_____

_____

_____

_____

21. Submission to God's authority is one thing, but
    submission to our earthly authorities is something
    else. John writes, "We cannot separate our submission
    to God's inherent authority from our submission to
    His delegated authority." How are these related and
    why is it beneficial for us to learn submission to all
    authority?

    _____

    _____

    _____

    _____

    _____

    _____

22. What insights have you gleaned from John's personal
    testimony of overcoming resistance to his senior
    pastor's authority?

    _____

    _____

    _____

We can make great sacrifices in our lives, serve long hours, labor without pay, give up sleep, seek ways to reach more people, and do all sorts of things because in ministry the list can be endless. Caught up in all this sacrifice, we could easily imagine ourselves and our efforts as pleasing to God. However, in all this activity our core motive could still be deceptively fueled by self-will.

Hear these words: God is pleased with submission that leads to true obedience. The purpose of this book is not only to reveal the importance of submission to God's authority, but also to create a love and passion for obedience to it.

John Bevere, *Under Cover*, p. 20.

Applying the Lesson

As you begin to understand the truth behind submission to authority, you will begin to see God's wisdom in providing leadership in the church. List several ways you see your local church practicing submission to authority:

_____

_____

_____

Submission describes an attitude that requires time and patience to learn. God must transform your mind and heart to enable you to follow His will. List several ways you need to improve in order to have a submissive heart:

_____

_____

Checking Your Cover

As you conclude this session, use the following themes for prayer:

Ask God for a humble heart to know your need for His protection and covering.

Ask Him for wisdom as you examine your own heart and attitudes toward authority and for patience as you endeavor to submit them to His will.

Pray that the Lord will help you submit to His delegated authority with a humble heart and that your actions will be a testimony to all those around you.

Video Script for Lesson 1
It's Hard to Kick Against the Goads

Glory be to God. I'd like you to find two places this morning, Romans 13. And if you'd do me a favor and put a marker in Romans 13. Put your little Bible marker there. Hopefully you've got one. And then also find with me Hebrews 5. And that's where we're going to start this morning.

Now let me say this. You say, *"Under Cover."* What in the world does that mean? Well how many of you know that *Under Cover* speaks of a place of refuge, a shelter, a place of protection?

I remember as a young man, I should say a young boy—I was about five or six years old. When somebody would come up and scare me, I would always hide behind the frame of my mom or my dad. Particularly my dad if he was around. How many of you remember when storms came when you were children and you'd hear the rain beat on your roof like thousands of little hammers? And you'd see the lightning out there and the danger that was out there. But yet you felt safe and secure under the protection of your home. Well how does this apply to us as believers? David makes the statement in Psalm 91:1–2: *"He who dwells in the secret place of the Most High Shall abide under the shadow of the Almighty."* Can you say, "Amen"? "Amen." *"I will say of the Lord, 'He is my refuge,'"*—There's the protection right there.— *"'my fortress; My God in Him I will trust.'"* Now we love to quote this Scripture, don't we, in the church? However, when David says *"He who dwells in the secret place of the Most High,"* a question comes up in my mind. Who is the one who is under the shadow of the Almighty? Who is the one who is under that place or in that place of refuge? Now a lot of people believe that is the person who is born again, or the person who attends church faithfully. But I'm going to show you this morning that it's not the case. That that's not necessarily true. Some people think that it's the person in the

prayer closet. I'm going to show you in these lessons, that that's not necessarily true. I don't know about you, but I want to be the person in "the secret place of the Most High." How about you? Can you say, "Amen"? "Amen."

Now, *Under Cover* speaks of one thing. If we had to summarize it in one word and you're going to see it in these 12 lessons. It speaks of the person that is submitted to divine authority. Everybody say, "Divine authority." "Divine authority." If we look at the garden of Eden, we will find out that Adam and Eve lived in an absolutely glorious place. There was freedom, there was protection, there was great provision. Can you say "Amen" to that? "Amen." And yet when they disobeyed—the moment they disobeyed—they found themselves immediately seeking for that which they voluntarily got out from under through their disobedience. And do you know what that was? To cover themselves. Isn't it amazing? The moment they got out from underneath this cover through disobedience, they are immediately seeking to cover themselves. Now you say, "I don't like the subject of authority. Well, you're not a minority. As a matter of fact, the majority in America don't like the subject of authority." But I believe that when we go through these 12 lessons and you listen carefully, you're going to find out that not only will you like authority, you will have a passion to seek it and live it in your own life. The greatest, most passionate desire of my heart is to know God intimately. Yet I find throughout all of Scripture—and you will see it so clearly—that the ones that really knew God are the ones who understood and were committed to His divine authority. If you look at Moses. Moses knew God and talked to Him face to face. There's a man who understood the authority of God.

If you look at David, it's the same way. You look at

the apostle Paul, it's the exact same way. And that is my heartbeat, that is your heartbeat. I believe that's why you're here today. So, that first and foremost is the reason why I want to know authority. And the reason is this: the reason is because God and His authority are inseparable. If you have truly come to know the Lord, you have come to know His authority. There are many people today in the church that are no different than the children of Israel. The children of Israel came out of Egypt, which is a type of being born again. Isn't that true? Egypt is the type of the world; coming out of Egypt is a type of being saved. Yet God brought them to the mountain and the whole reason He brought them to the mountain—He said that "the whole reason that I brought you out of Egypt was not first of all to bring you into a promised land. The first reason that I brought you out was to bring you to myself." Exodus 19:3–6.

God wanted to have intimacy with them like Moses. And that intimacy was God. And God brought them out and said, "Cleanse yourselves and prepare yourselves because I'm coming down." But when God came down, the children of God backed up and said, "We can't handle it." God said to Moses and Aaron, "You guys come up, I want to talk to you." What the children of Israel did was they stayed down at the bottom and played church. Everybody say, "Amen." "Amen." And what they did is that they created a calf. Now a lot of us in the church would say that we would never do such a thing. But let me tell you this. They created that calf and what they called that calf was Yahweh. That is the holy, sacred name of God which the scribes would not even write. They looked right at that calf and said, "Behold Yahweh who has delivered us from Egypt." They created a god who was a manageable deity. They created a god who would give them what they wanted. And that is literally what idolatry is. The Bible says rebellion is idolatry. Are you with me? Why? Because you created Jesus. A Jesus who saves me. A Jesus who heals me. But that Jesus will give you what ever you want. Jesus makes the statement, "Why do you call me Lord Lord, yet not do what I say?" In other words, "Why bother calling me master when you really live your life the way you want to?" The Bible does not say, "If thou shall confess the Savior Jesus. The Bible says, "If thou shall confess the Lord Jesus yet don't call me Lord unless you do what I say."

The word "Lord" appears over 7,000 times in the Bible. Where does God put the emphasis? God puts His emphasis on Lordship, which means master. Now when it comes to authority we have to understand something. And let me preface it with this: before I say, "We have to say, 'we understand'". I have found "westerners." (When I say "westerners" I mean those of free nations.) The western European nations, as well as the United States and other countries, are some of the hardest people to preach the gospel to in the world. I've preached the gospel in every single continent except Antarctica. I haven't preached to the penguins yet. But we'll see what happens in the next few years. But anyway, I have found that "westerners" are some the hardest people to preach the gospel to. And the reason is fundamental. And that is this: It is hard and—I should actually say it is impossible—to understand kingdom principles with a democratic mind set. You can never understand the kingdom of God with a democracy mind set. You don't even connect. You're not even on the same playing field as God. It is almost like you're trying to play basketball and God's on the football field. You don't even connect. It is almost like trying to plug something into a power source with no power. The power is somewhere else. Are you with me? That is why I have found that people that do not understand the things of God are people that do not understand authority. Because God and His authority are inseparable. When you come to know God, you come to know His authority. If you read through the Bible, you will find the people with the greatest faith, the greatest intimacy with God, who walk in the greatest holiness, are those who knew His authority. Amen. Because Jesus says, "Thine is the kingdom and the power now and forever. Amen." Are you with me? Say "Amen."

Job 36:11–12 says: *"If they obey and serve Him, They shall spend their days in prosperity, And their years in pleasures.*" I'm going to show you in the next 12 lessons that, not only will staying under God's authority protect you, it will also be His provision for your life. It will also be His protection for your life. And I don't know about you, but in these times I'm very interested in that. How about you? Amen.

All right, the freedom that we seek. Now listen very carefully to me. The freedom we seek when we resist authority, is the very thing we lose in our insubordination to it. My wife has a saying that I think is so powerful. My wife says, "There is freedom in submission, there is bondage in rebellion." However, what the enemy does is he gets us to think that what will give us freedom actually is the best thing for us. The rebellion that will give us freedom is the best thing for us. When, in actuality, that's what brings us into bondage. And that's exactly what he did to Eve in the garden.

Now, I want you to go with me to Romans 13. Romans 13 please. Paul says in the first verse, "*Let every soul.*" Now, before I go any further. Does that include you? All right, you're in every soul, I'm in every soul. Amen. "*Let every soul be subject.*" Everybody say, "Subject." "Subject." "*To the governing authorities.*" Keep reading. "*For there is no authority*"—Everybody say, "No authority." "No authority"—"*except from God, and the authorities that exist are appointed by God. Therefore, whoever resists the authority resists the ordinance of God, and those who resist will bring judgment on themselves.*" Now Paul makes this statement, "there is no legitimate authority except from God." And people that resist authority are resisting the ordinance of God. In other words, when you resist authority you resist the one who is given authority. You resist the very one who is instituted and that is God because all authority is from God. I don't know about you, but I don't want to be resisting God, do you? Amen. Now listen to me carefully. This is where people get scared sometimes. They say, "Wait a minute, wait a minute. I don't know if I like that." But let me say this, God is not a child abuser. As a matter of fact, God's love for us is greater than any human being's

love for us, even greater than our own love for ourselves. So when God says to do something, He does it out of love, not out of legalism. Can you say, "Amen"? Unfortunately, there have been people that have beat up people with this Scripture and have gotten legalistic with it. But you're going to find out when you have the heartbeat of God nothing is ever legalistic. What makes the Scriptures legalistic is you losing the heartbeat of it. It's the Spirit that quickens it. Amen. The letter kills but the Spirit gives life. What we must always speak when we're reading the word of God is that we must seek the heart of God in reading it. Amen. Because God is not a God who wants a bunch of rules and regulations and people are being forced or constrained by it. He is looking for people that delight to obey, not have to obey. Let every soul be subject to the governing authorities. There are three things I'd like to point here right away. Number one: all authority originates from God. Number two: God appoints all existing rulers or legitimate authorities. Number three: to rebel against those in authority is to rebel against God Himself. Too many see themselves today accountable only to God and have no authority in their lives. There are people who run around today and say, "I'm spirit filled. Jesus is my Lord. He is the one that speaks to me." However I want to remind you, the very one you call Lord is the very one who set up authorities in the church, in society and in our homes. So if you have that mentality of "I'm-a-Christian-and-everything-I-need-I-can-get-straight-from-God-and-I-don't-need-authority," you may find yourself resisting the very one you call Lord.

Let me remind you what Jesus said to the apostle Paul. He said, "*Paul, it is hard for you to kick against the goads*" or the thorns or the pricks. What was a goad or a thorn or a prick? Actually the better word, the best word was goad. Those goads were long poles about eight feet long that farmers would use. And what they would do is they would use wood like oak or some other hard wood and they would carve those woods. They would take all the bark off that wood and they would make a very, very sharp point at the front of it. And that farmer would use that goad when he was plowing his fields and if the oxen didn't obey that oxen would basically get that goad, that sharp point going right into his hinny. Got it? So there was a proverbial expression in Paul's day that it's hard to kick against the goads. And what that proverbial expression was, was it was used to describe the futility of the resistance of superior power. So that's exactly what Jesus is saying to Paul is "Why are you resisting my superior power? You are kicking against the goads." Now I want to say this, whenever we are resisting His direct authority or His delegated authority, we are kicking against the goads." And let me share with you how my eyes got opened up to that. It wasn't until I was actually in the ministry that my eyes got awakened to the fact that I was kicking against His authority and I didn't even realize it.

Back in the 1980s, I was asked to be youth pastor for a very powerful church in the southern part of the United States. This church had about 7,000 members in it. And I remember when I came to be their youth pastor. It was a move of God. God had spoken to me. I really started seeking God about how to run a youth group. I just didn't want to do it the way everybody else was doing it. The Lord led me to one in particular book of a youth pastor who was having a very successful ministry in Louisiana. They had about 1,250 high school students in their youth group. And I was reading his manual and I really felt this guy had the heart of God for ministering to the youth. So the first two weeks I was at this church after I got hired, I bought a plane ticket and I flew to Louisiana to meet with these pastors who were over these youths. Now I remember when I got picked up on a Wednesday night, they whisked me right to the youth service which met every Wednesday night. Their main youth service was every Wednesday night. And I remember walking into that auditorium. First of all, the auditorium seats 1,500 people and was almost full. What really amazed me is these ninth, tenth, eleventh and twelfth graders we're excited about being there. I thought "This is amazing!" Then when the senior youth pastor started preaching, it wasn't this candy-coated, sugar-coated message about how fun it is to date. It was a gospel of power. He was preaching on holiness and purity. And I thought, "Look how excited these kids are. I'm in the right place."

The next day I met with all four of the youth pastors. I couldn't believe it. This church had four full-time, paid youth pastors. It had two full-time secretaries, paid. And they had their own youth administration building. I mean you talk about a youth, it was a youth group. So I remember sitting down with all four youth pastors and all four of them said this basically, "John, there is one reason for our success here and that is this: our parties." "What do you mean your parties?"

"They're really home fellowship. Every Friday night, 118 home fellowships are going on—we call them parties—all around the city."

He said "John we cannot get people. We can't get them from the high school into the youth service. But we can get sinners into parties." I said, "That's brilliant." So they all talked to me about it. On Friday night, I went to one of their parties. I couldn't believe it. The kids came. They had some music playing, they talked a while, and all of a sudden one of the leaders from the high school students or college students said, "Come on guys. Let's talk." And they all started talking and he led it right into spiritual things. And then gave an altar call and kids got saved. And then they took the kids to the back room and they got their names, addresses and phone numbers. Called them up immediately on Monday and got them into that service by Wednesday and got them plugged into the new believers club for the youth. I thought, "This is brilliant!"

So I remember flying back to the place where I was living and I prayed. Now everybody listen to me. I prayed. I said, "God, do you want me to do this?" And the Lord said "Yes, I want you to do this." Now are you with me? So I said "Lord, what do I do?" And the Lord gave me a plan. He said, "I want you to start a school of leadership. And I want you to start training your young people on leadership, on integrity, faithfulness, loyalty, et cetera." What I did was I started a separate course for the youth what I called the school of leadership. Now we had 250 in our youth group and we had 90 people—kids—coming to that leadership class. And I was very strong with them. I said, "You've got to wear a tie. You've got read through your Bible once a year. You've got to pray." I was very strict. "This is not for the overall youth group. I am training leaders and I'm going to be hard on you." I said, "There's only a certain kind of movie that I'm going to allow you to see." I said, "I don't want you to see any PG-13 or any R rated movies." I said, "We're going to push through God." And you know what? They loved it. I had two of them. They were fourteen-years-old. They were getting up and praying every morning from 4:00 to 8:00, then went to school. And I remember we started teaching them leadership. After about five months, the Lord spoke to me and said, "I want you to choose 24 kids out of that 90 kids and I want them to be your first leaders." So I chose 24 and brought them into another class that I called the discipleship class. Now meanwhile I had seen my pastor, my senior pastor. I had seen him on the parking lot and I mentioned to him what we were doing. I said, "This what we're doing. We're going to start these parties, home groups and all this." And he said, "That sounds great!" And so we continued to go for another two months. And I taught that discipleship class. Meanwhile, my assistant youth pastor and I divided the city up. We broke it down into sections, regions, into smaller zip code areas. We had the curriculum all ready to go. We had the homes picked out. I started preaching the whole vision to the Tuesday night youth group because that's when the main service met for the youth—Tuesday night. And they were all getting excited. I was preaching from the book of Acts about having church in your home. They were all getting excited. They were all thinking, "Who are the first people I'm going to invite to my party?" They were praying for them. They were impassioned about it. You know what I'm talking about? I was excited. My associate was excited. It was a God idea, it seemed to us.

I remember three weeks before we were ready to start the parties, I walked into a pastors' meeting I will never, ever, ever, ever forget. And I remember when I walked into that pastors' meeting, my senior pastor was there along with eleven associates. I was one of the eleven associates. And I remember him walking in there saying, "Gentlemen, the Holy Spirit showed me the direction of this church is not to have home fellowship groups. So I want all of you to cancel your home fellowship groups." After eight months of working on them. Now there was a couple's pastor, a senior's pastor, there was a children's pastor, a single's pastor and they all had floundering home cell groups. And I thought that, well, maybe he means just them and not the youth because I had shared with him in the parking lot three months ago what we were doing. So I raised my hand and said, "Excuse me, Pastor, you mean except the youth don't you?" And he looked at me and he said, "John, the Holy Spirit talked to me and said the direction of this church is not to have home fellowship groups." I said, "Pastor, do you remember when I told you about that church in Louisiana, the one with 1,250 kids in it?" He said, "Yes I do." I said, "All four of their youth pastors said the only reason they're doing so well is because they can't get kids out of high school to youth services but they can get them into a party." And I said "They have 1,250 kids and they're growing by one hundred a month." I said, "Pastor, this is a way we can really reach people." He said, "John, the Holy Spirit talked to me and said the direction of this church is not to have home fellowship groups." I said "Pastor, I can't get these kids out of high school and into this auditorium, they're not going to come." I said, "We can win this whole city for the Lord." He said "John, the Holy Spirit told me and said the direction of this church is not to have home fellowship groups." Now I argued with him for 20 minutes. The whole time the steam kept boiling stronger and stronger. I'm looking at my associate youth pastor and his eyes are like this and my eyes were like this. I'm continuing until finally, by the grace of God, I shut up. And I remember the whole rest of the pastors' meeting I didn't hear another word. And I remember when that pastors' meeting was over, I'm doing a beeline to the door. I'm out of there. I'm so upset. When one of the older associate pastors tried to stop me and talk some sense into me. I said, "Leave me alone. I don't want to talk." I got in my car and I drove home. I'm furious. I pull into my driveway. I open up the front door of my house, I walk in and Lisa, my wife is walking right by me. Right by the foyer when I walked into the house. I said, "Honey, you're not going to believe what he's done." She looked at me and said, "Who, and what did they do?" I said "He has just cancelled the parties—the home groups. What we've worked on for eight months, he's just cancelled in one meeting tonight." And my wife looked at me and she said "Well, it looks like God is trying to teach you something." And she walked out of the room. Now I was mad at her. Insubordinate wife.

And all of a sudden, I heard the voice of the Lord. And the Holy Spirit said to me, "Whose ministry are you building? Mine or yours?" I said, "I'm building Yours". He said, "No you're not." I said "God we can't get kids from the high school into the church, but we can get them in . . ." I started to go through the whole bloomin' thing with God as if he didn't know. That's how deceived a person gets when they're in rebellion. And I'm going to show you later lessons that you will think that God doesn't know what's going on. You will think you will bring him down to your level. I am going to show you how this happens. I was going through this whole thing with God. And when I got done with the whole spiel, the Lord spoke to me and said "Son, when I brought you into this church," he said, "I brought you in as an extension of the senior pastor's hands and an extension of his legs. It is because I put one person over a ministry." I have shown how Moses was faithful to all of his house. He then showed me how the apostle James was the senior man in the church in Jerusalem. And if you look at Acts 15, when all these elders came together: Peter, John, Barnabas, Paul. You know what? Barnabas spoke, Paul spoke, Peter spoke, some of the other leaders spoke. But James stood up and said, "I doth judge," and when

James said, "I doth judge," everybody else got up and that's the way they went. He was the man. And the Lord showed me that He put one man over a ministry. He said, "When you stand before me in judgment for this time period that I have you serving in this church, however long it may be." He said, "You first of all will be judged on how faithful you were to the man I put you under." He said, "Son you can win every single young person, high school student, so on, and still be judged by me at the judgment seat for your rebellion to the authority I put you under." When He said that the fear of God hit me.

Then the Holy Spirit said, "Son, if you keep going the way you're going, the church is going to go this way and you're going to lead the ministry this way. You're going to cause a split." And you know what He later went on to say, "That is what *division* means. Everyone say, "*Division*." "*Division*." The prefix *di* means two, two visions. And I saw the church going in one direction and me going another. When I saw that, I started to repent as fast as I could. And I called the senior pastor. I ran to the phone, called the senior pastor to the phone. And I said, "Pastor, please forgive me, God has shown me that I am rebellious with Him. I want you to know that I'm canceling these home groups immediately." And the pastor was so nice. "Oh, I love you so much. Thank God for you." He didn't know what I had gone through those last couple hours.

Then the Spirit of God spoke to me again. He said, "John, what are you going to do? How are you going to tell your leaders?" Immediately, I had a vision of me walking in to my leaders on that next leadership meeting with those 24 leaders. And I saw myself walking into that meeting, and I said, "Guys, you're not going to believe this, what the senior pastor said." And they all said "What, what?" I could see their faces. I said, "I know we've worked on this for eight months, but the senior pastor has canceled the whole group." And I saw all of them go, "Awww, I can't believe this." And all of them were upset with me. The Spirit of God said to me, "Is that what you're going to do?" I said, "No sir." Now I remember I walked into that leadership meeting and I looked at those young people, the 24 leaders. "Gosh, I've got great news!" I had a spark in my eye, a spark in my voice. I said, "I've got great news!" They all looked at me and said, "What?" I said, "Our pastor has heard from God as we have been spared from birthing an Ishmael." I said, "He has said, the direction of this church is not to have home groups, therefore the parties are immediately canceled." And they all went "Yeah!" And that was it. Never heard another thing about it.

I am convinced that if I did not pass the test right there, I would not be standing in front of you today. Somebody says, "What if the senior pastor was wrong? What if he really didn't hear from God?" We'll answer it in the next eleven lessons. Somebody else says, "But well wait a minute. God spoke to you and told you to do it." Oh, we'll answer that one too. We'll get answers to all of these things.

Let me read to you what David said. David made this statement. Psalm 51:16–17. He said, *"For You do not desire sacrifice, or else I would give it."* Listen carefully, church. *"The sacrifices of God are a broken spirit, A broken and a contrite heart—These, O God, You will not despise."* The sacrifices of God are broken hearts. Folks listen to me. Broken is filled with humility. It means you submitted to authority. Broken doesn't mean you're weakened, it means you submitted to authority. Are you with me? I'm going to read a direct quote from the book. "We can make great sacrifices in our lives. We can serve long hours, labor without pay." Are you listening? "Give up sleep. Seek ways to reach more people, et cetera." Because in ministry, how many of you know the list is endless? "Caught up in these sacrifices we could easily imagine ourselves and our efforts as pleasing to God. However, in all of this activity our core motives could still be deceptively fueled by self will." Are you with me? Hear these words. "God is pleased with submission that leads to true obedience." The focus of this book is not only to teach you about submission, but to give you a passion and a hunger to live it. I can tell you this in my life, I have such a passion to live under divine authority. I believe by the end of the twelve lesson, you will too.

Session Two

The Secret Power of Lawlessness

" Whoever commits sin also commits lawlessness,
and sin is lawlessness."
1 John 3:4

Summary for *Under Cover,* Chapters 3 and 4

According to John Bevere, when most people consider the definition of the word "sin," some specific action or thought comes to mind. Particularly heinous sins such as murder or rape are obvious examples, but they are usually a result of a mindset bent toward sinning. What then is sin? Simply put, it is disobedience to God's authority.

First John 3:4 says, "Sin is lawlessness." Whenever we choose to disregard the commandments of God, we are practicing lawlessness and therefore, sinning. We choose to substitute our own will for the will of God. We may find excuses for not submitting to God, but in the end, we will be left out of His blessing if we continually choose our own way.

Certainly there are sins that are obvious to anyone, but it is the subtle attitudes of pride and self-centeredness that are the root of sin. These are the attitudes that God warns us against many times in Scripture. Many are deceived into thinking that their salvation is secured by a prayer they once made. However, Christ said that it is only those who *confess* and *do* the will of God that will be with Him in paradise.

How do we stay alert to deception? John writes, "We must love truth more than anyone or anything else. We must passionately desire His will more than our comfort or lives. Then we will delight in putting our personal desires aside for His wishes. We will take up our crosses and deny our rights and privileges for the sake of fulfilling His will. Why? Because He is our God, our Creator, our Redeemer, and His love toward us is perfect. This alone keeps us from deception."

As we strive for God, He will reveal His Word in our lives and manifest His Spirit in everything we do. As God reveals Himself to us, we can avoid deception. Unlike Eve in the garden, we can overcome sin and deception through the indwelling of the Holy Spirit in our lives. God speaks to us through His Word and as we embrace Him, we learn the truth that can set us free.

Notes from Chapters 3 and 4 (Video Session 2)

_____

_____

_____

_____

_____

_____

_____

_____

Warm–Up Questions

1. How do you define sin? Sin is

   _____

   _____

   _____

2. How do we deceive ourselves into thinking that some
   sins are worse than others?

   _____

   _____

   _____

3. In what ways can believers be deceived in their
   thinking?

   _____

   _____

   _____

The disciples of Jesus asked Him about the end of the
age. He responded by telling them events that would
take place and by describing conditions that would be
prevalent in the days preceding His second coming. One
of the conditions is this: "Because lawlessness will
abound, the love of many will grow cold. But he who
endures to the end shall be saved" (Matt. 24:12–13).

Whenever I ask congregations whether this applies to
our present society, I am greeted with raised hands and
nodding heads; most view our society as sinful. Very
few, if any, question whether this is an accurate assess-
ment. Yet Jesus was not describing society in that statement. He was describing the church!

John Bevere, *Under Cover*, p. 29.

Teaching by John Bevere

Watch video session two on the tape.

Teaching Review

4. First John 3:4 says, "Sin is lawlessness." What is the definition of lawlessness?

   Lawlessness is _____

   _____

   _____

   _____

5. What does God's Word say about the following obvious acts of lawlessness?

   Lying—Ephesians 4:24–25 _____

   _____

   Excessive Drinking—Ephesians 5:18 _____

   _____

   Adultery—*1 Corinthians 6:18* _____

   _____

   Stealing—*Ephesians 4:28* _____

   _____

6. In Matthew 24:12–13, Christ says, "Because lawlessness will abound, the love of many will grow cold. But he who endures to the end shall be saved." To whom is this statement made? (Choose one)

Society _____

_____

Government _____

_____

Church _____

_____

Exploring God's Word

1 John 3:4 *Whoever commits sin also commits lawlessness, and sin is lawlessness.*

7. How is lawlessness an attitude of the heart and not merely an action?

_____

_____

_____

Personal Application

_____

_____

_____

Matthew 24:11–13 *Then many false prophets will rise up and deceive many. And because lawlessness will abound, the love of many will grow cold. But he who endures to the end shall be saved.*

8. The "love" described in this verse is a godly love given by Christ Himself. How does lawlessness affect our ability to love others as Christ loves?

_____

_____

_____

9. What must a Christian do to endure to the end?

_____

_____

_____

10. Christ directs this statement at the church. In what ways do you see deception filtering into believers today?

_____

_____

_____

Personal Application

_____

_____

_____

James 1:22 *But be doers of the word, and not hearers only, deceiving yourselves.*

11. How is a person deceived when he or she hears the Word of God but fails to do it?

_____

_____

_____

_____

12. How is this type of deception worse than unbelief?

_____

_____

_____

Personal Application

_____

_____

_____

> **God is looking for children whose hearts yearn to walk in obedience. No matter what area of life it may touch, we as believers should delight in doing His will. At the close of a life filled with success from obedience and hardship from disobedience, Solomon breathed wisdom to stand for all time, "Let us hear the conclusion of the whole matter: Fear God and keep His commandments, For this is man's all" (Eccl. 12:13).**
>
> **John Bevere, *Under Cover*, p. 32.**

Genesis 2:16–17 *Of every tree of the garden you may freely eat; but of the tree of the knowledge of good and evil you shall not eat, for in the day you eat of it you shall surely die.*

13. By issuing this command, what was God trying to accomplish with Adam and Eve?

_____

_____

_____

14. What is God trying to accomplish with us today through His commands?

_____
_____
_____

Personal Application

_____
_____
_____

James 1:16–17 *Do not be deceived, my beloved brethren. Every good gift and every perfect gift is from above, and comes down from the Father of lights, with whom there is no variation or shadow of turning.*

15. We often look at things of this world as being good or desirable. How can we be certain that something is from God above and not a deception?

_____
_____
_____

16. Why are so many deceived into pursuing the things of this world and neglecting what is from God? According to James, how can this be avoided?

_____
_____
_____
_____
_____

_____

_____

_____

> We must ask two important questions. First, what is the root cause of this deception? Second, why is this deception able to run its course unchecked? To answer the first, the root cause of deception is none other than what we discussed in the previous chapter: disobedience to divine authority, or lawlessness. We are admonished, "But be doers of the word, and not hearers only, deceiving yourselves" (James 1:22).
>
> Sobering! Scripture tells us when a person hears the Word of God yet does not *obey*, deception enters his heart and mind. This person now lives under the conviction that he is on target when he is actually in error. Where there is not true submission to God's authority, which includes the authority of His Word, the door is opened to subtle but great deception.
>
> John Bevere, *Under Cover*, p. 35.

Exposing the Truth

18. John quotes Vine's *Dictionary* in defining lawlessness as, "the rejection of the law, or will, of God and the substitution of the will of the self." In what ways do you see lawlessness in our society? In our churches?

_____

_____

_____

19. In the parable of the two sons in Matthew 21:32, Jesus says, "I tell you the truth, the tax collectors and the prostitutes are entering the kingdom of God ahead of you." How were the Pharisees deceiving themselves concerning their own righteousness?

_____

_____

_____

20. How do we sometimes deceive ourselves into thinking we are doing the will of God when, in actuality, we are pursuing our own desires?

_____

_____

_____

_____

21. In the *Under Cover* seminar, John says, "Ignorance is a breeding ground for deception. God said, 'Therefore my people have gone into captivity, because they have no knowledge' (Isa.5:13). The revealed knowledge of God's ways and His spiritual laws guards us from the enemy's deceptions. The light of His truth exposes and protects us from any lie." How can our knowledge of God's Word and spiritual laws help protect us from deception?

_____

_____

_____

_____

_____

22. What can be learned from Eve's deception in the garden that will enable you to overcome the sin and lawlessness that Satan tempts you with today?

_____

_____

_____

_____

Applying the Lesson

The Scriptures warn us repeatedly that deception will be widespread in the last days. The only way to stay alert and resist deception is to be reading and practicing the Word of God. In what ways do you see your church equipping its members to overcome deception through the knowledge of God's Word?

_____

_____

_____

In what ways are you equipping yourself to be strengthened against deception and sin?

_____

_____

_____

Checking Your Cover

To conclude this session, pray that God will enable you to:

Be daily renewed through reading His Word and through prayer.

Overcome the deceptions of Satan by being grounded firmly in the truth and by the continual strengthening of the Holy Spirit.

Be a pillar of truth in your church and community.

Video Script for Lesson 2
The Secret Power of Lawlessness

Let's open up our Bibles this morning to 1 John. I want to find 1 John 3. Now while you're turning your Bibles there, I want to start out this session with a little game here. Can we play a little game? Can we play the psychiatrist/patient game? I'll be the psychiatrist, you'll be the patient. You sit on the couch. And I've got my pad and I'm going to tell you a word and you tell me the first thing that comes to mind when I say the word. Can we do that? All right. The first word I'm going to say is "sin." Now I'm going to tell you this. I'm going to help you with the way most people relate to that word "sin." Most people, when they think the word "sin," they think of some kind of sexual immorality. And it just seems to be a real prevalent thought that just comes to people's minds. Another thing that people may think about is drug abuse, alcoholism. They may think about rape; they may think about murder. All these things are sins—true—but let me say this, most people's definition of the word "sin" is very, very limited in the church. In other words, we really don't know what the core meaning or the core understanding of the word "sin" is. Now I want to say this: Before I can really, really go into God's delegated authority, I need to first of all talk about His direct authority. All right? That's what I'm dealing with here in this session.

Now to define it. I want to look at 1 John 3:4. John makes this statement in the fourth verse, *"Whoever commits sin also commits lawlessness."* Now look at this: *"and sin is lawlessness."* And everybody say this with me in the church real loud. *"Sin is lawlessness."* The Greek word there for lawlessness is the Greek word *anomia. Anomia* is defined by the Thayer's *Dictionary of Greek Words* as this: "the condition of being without law because of ignorance of it or because of violating it." Simply put, this word means not to submit to the law or the authority of God. This perfectly lines up with what the apostle

John says. Sin is to violate God's authority. It is to disobey God. Now in Luke's gospel chapter fourteen, I'm going to look at the fifteenth verse. "Now when one of those who sat at the table with Him [Jesus] heard these things, he said to Him [Jesus], *'Blessed is he who shall eat bread in the kingdom of God!'"* Verse 16, then Jesus said to him, *"A certain man gave a great supper and invited many."* Now church, that's the marriage supper of the lamb. Is that not true? Can you say, "Amen"? "Amen." Now watch this, *"and sent his servant at supper time."* Now who is that servant? That servant is Jesus. The Bible is very clear in Hebrews 1, that God in times past spoke to us through the fathers, through the prophets. But in these last days, He has spoken to us through His Son Jesus Christ. I don't know if you're a teacher, a writer, a preacher, or whatever you are, when you speak—the Bible commands us to speak as the oracles of God because it is Jesus who is speaking to us. We're only the vessels. Amen. Amen. So that servant is a representation of Jesus. Now watch this. The servant was sent at supper time *"to say to those who were invited."* Everybody say, "those who were invited." Now really, I'm going to modernize this. We're talking about those people in the church who were born again, who were invited to the marriage supper of the Lamb. Are we there? All right. To say to those who were invited, "Come for all things are now ready." Now look at verse 18. *"But they all with one accord began to make excuses."* The first one said to him, I've got a kickin' party to go to and a fifth of vodka and I ask that you have me excused. Verse 19. And another said to him, I just won an all-expense paid trip to Las Vegas and been given $5000 of loan in the casinos, I ask you please have me excused. Verse twenty. Still another said, I have a trip planned next week to go with my secretary to Hawaii and my wife doesn't know a thing about it she thinks it's a business trip, please don't tell I can't come. Is that what it says? No. Can we really read it? Verse 18: *"But they all with one accord began to make excuses. The first said to him, 'I have bought a piece of ground.'"* Now, look up at me please. Is it a sin to buy a piece of ground? No. Absolutely not. I bought one this year. If it was, I'm in trouble. It's not a sin to buy a piece of ground. But when buying the piece of ground is more important than instantly obeying the Word of the Master, it violates the definition of the word sin. Or I should say it lines up with the definition of the word sin? It is disobedience to the divine authority. Are you with me? Now watch this. *"The first said to Him 'I bought a piece of ground, and I must go and see it. I ask you to [please] have me excused.'"* Verse 19: *"And another said, "I have bought five yoke of oxen, and I'm going to test them.'"* Now, would you look up at me? Is it a sin to buy five yoke of oxen or any other business equipment? No, absolutely not. But when buying that business equipment or testing that business equipment or that business becomes more important than instantly obeying the Word of the Lord, it becomes sin because it's disobedience to the divine authority. Are you seeing this? Verse 20: *"Still another said, 'I have married a wife.'"* Look up at me. Is it a sin to marry a wife? No. If it is we're all in trouble. Amen. But listen, if that wife becomes more important than instantly obeying the Word of God, it violates His Word and it's sin. Are you with me?

So now listen. Look what Jesus goes on to say about these three guys that make excuses. Now we wouldn't consider these things to be great sins. I mean all the guy wanted to do was tend to his land. All the other guy wanted to do was take care of his oxen. All the other wanted to do was be with his wife. But yet they did not instantly obey what the Master told them to do. Isn't that true? So look what Jesus says about these guys. Are you ready? Look at verse 24: *"For I say to you that none of those men who were invited shall taste my supper."* Are you here? Is this sinking in? You see folks, sin is simply disobeying His authority or His Word. There's nothing in this parable about prostitutes, about drug addicts, about pimps is there? Nothing in there about these. Huh? Oh yes there is—there sure is. Keep reading. Look at

this. Verse 21: *"That servant came and reported these things to his master. Then the master of the house [became] angry, [and] said to his servant 'Go out quickly to the streets and lanes of the city, and [go] bring in here the poor and the maimed, and the lame and the blind.' And the servant said, 'Master, it is done as you commanded, and still there is room.'"* And verse 23—Read carefully: *"Then the master said . . ., 'Go out into the highways and hedges, and compel them to come in, that my house may be filled.'"* Folks, the highways and the hedges represent the drug addicts, the pimps, the prostitutes, the thief. Are you saying that those people are going to enter the kingdom of God? Why? Because I believe they are going to come to a place in their life when they're saying, "I'm fed up with these drugs, I'm fed up with this prostitution." And they're going to discover the Lordship of Jesus. And they're going to be people who love much because they've been forgiven much and because out of their love they are going to instantly obey. Whereas all these other people who are going to church say, "Well you know I've got this and I've got that. And I'm busy." They're not going to be eating at the supper of the Lamb. That perfectly lines up with what Jesus said, many will say to Him that day, "Lord we cast out demons in Your Name. We did miracles in Your Name. We did wonders in Your Name." And Jesus will say to them, "You did not obey the will of my Father." Sobering.

This perfectly lines up with another parable. Jesus talks about a man having two sons. How many of you remember this parable? A man has two sons. He says to the first son, "Go out and work in my vineyard." The son said "No, I'm not going to do it." But later on what did he do? He repented and he went out and worked in the vineyard. He looked at the other son and said "Son go out and work in my vineyard." And the son said "Yes sir, gladly." But yet he doesn't do it. Probably got busy with his business or something else he was involved in. Jesus then looked at the religious leaders and said "Which one did the will of the father?" And the religious leaders answered correctly. They said "the first one." The one who said no but ended up going out and working. Then Jesus made this statement in Matthew 21:31. He said, *"Assuredly, I say to you that tax collectors and harlots enter the kingdom of God before you."* And this He was speaking to the religious leaders and preachers of His day. Are you with me?

This perfectly correlates with what sin is, its core definition. But then somebody says, "Well, what about lying? What about getting drunk? What about committing adultery? What about stealing and murder? You mean to tell me that those aren't sins?" Oh yes—they're sins—because you want to know why they are sins? They violate God's command. Because God says about lying in Ephesians 4:24–5—Listen carefully: He says, *"Let each one of you speak truth with his neighbor."* Excessive drinking, Ephesians 5:18, God specifically says, *"Do not be drunk with wine."* First Corinthians 6:18 concerning adultery and fornication. The Bible says, *"Flee sexual immorality."* Concerning stealing, Ephesians 4:28: If you're a thief, stop stealing. Murder, 1 John 3:15: *"Whoever hates his brother is a murderer, and you know that no murderer has eternal life abiding in him."* So absolutely those others are sins. And as a matter of fact, the Bible is very specific that those who practice as such will not enter the kingdom of God. However, when our core understanding of sin is just what we call these "big ones," we're going to miss out on the fact that just these little foxes, according to Ecclesiastes, that steal from us. And we can almost become like I was when I was a young man and I was told my sister was sick. But I didn't connect until she was dead. And there are going to be a lot of people who are not going to connect until Jesus looks at them and says, "Depart from me," until they listen to the word of God. That is why Jesus looked at those religious leaders and said, "Hey guys—the harlots, the prostitutes—they are going into the kingdom of God before you. Why? Because you go to your synagogue, you do this, you do that, but you still live by your own self will." Good preaching. I'll help you. Amen.

Go to Matthew 24 please. In Matthew 24, Jesus is speaking about the last days. How many of you know we're living in the last days? Can I see your hands? Absolutely. I think you'd have to be spiritually blind not to know we're living in the last days. Amen. And Jesus said we would know the season. We wouldn't know the day or the hour. Some people try to think the day or the hour but don't even listen to them. We're in the season. Amen. And you know it's amazing to me in this one chapter alone—you know what Jesus says four times about the last days? "Be careful that you're not deceived." In other words, deception is going to run rampant in the last day. Now there's only one problem with deception and you know what it is? It's deceiving. That's the only problem with deception. You really believe you're right when in reality you're wrong. That's exactly the way it's going to be for those people. They come to the gates of heaven, they have done miracles in His Name, they have professed His Lordship, yet He's going to look at them and say, "The part in you did not do the will of My Father." They were living in deception. They believed they were saved when they really weren't. Did you read the letters to the church in the book of Revelation? You will find out there are a few churches that think they are saved and they are not. He says you have a name that says you're alive but you're dead. He says you think you're saved but you're about to be vomited out of My mouth. One of the things we have to wake up to folks in these last days is that the Bible says that there is going to be massive deception. Paul says to Timothy who says, "One of the things that's going to mark the last days is it's going to bring difficult times." The difficult times is—you're going to have people in churches who still love themselves. They love money, they love pleasure, they're unthankful, they're unholy, they're unforgiving. But they're going to have a form of Christianity, a form of the grace of God, but they're going to deny its power. What power is he talking about? The power that changes us from being ungodly to godly. The power that changes us from being unholy to holy, unthankful to thankful, a lover of self to a lover of others. Are you with me? And you know what Paul said? These people are going to be ever learning, but never able to come to the knowledge of the truth. In other words, they're going to go from camp meeting to camp meeting, church service to church service, seminar to seminar. Going to get a massive amount of spiritual knowledge, but they are going to miss the fundamental thing of Christianity. And that is our submission to His Lordship.

Look what Jesus says in Matthew 24:12 about the last days. He says, *"Because lawlessness"*—Everybody say, "Lawlessness." It is the same Greek word *anomia*. Everybody say, *"Anomia." "Anomia."* Which means not being submitted to the authority of God. *"And because lawlessness will abound, the love of many will grow cold."* Will you look up at me? How many of you know that lawlessness is abounding in our society today? Can I see your hands? Absolutely. Absolutely. Let me tell you, it's more normal to rebel than to submit in our society. However, let me make this statement to you. Jesus is not talking about society. He's talking about the church. You say, "Wait a minute—how do you know that?" Do you see the word "love" there in verse 12? *"Because lawlessness will abound the love of many."* Everybody say, "Love." "Love." There are many Greek words translated *love* in the New Testament. Let me give you one of them. *Phileo* which means brotherly kindness. The world has that. The church has that. There's another one, *eros*, which is sexual love between a man and a woman. The world has that. and the church has that. There's *storge* which is the awe kind of love. That's the kind of love that people have for Michael Jordan, Princess Diana, Tiger Woods. The church has that, the world has that. Then there's *agape*. And agape is the love of God that Jesus said will shed abroad on our heart when we're born again. It's the love that the Holy Spirit sheds about on our hearts. It's the love that Jesus said the world cannot receive. In this verse, Jesus does not use the word *phileo*, he doesn't use *storge*, he doesn't use *eros*. He says, "Because lawlessness will abound, the *agape* of many will grow cold." He is talking about the love of God and the only ones to have it are those who are born again.

Look at verse 13: *"He who endures for the King shall be saved."* Folks, let me tell you something. You don't say to someone who hasn't started a race, "If you endure the race will be safe." You don't normally say that. You say that to someone who has already started. Are you with me? He who endures gets the guy who has already started. Are you seeing this? He is saying that one of things that is going to happen in these last days is going to be massive lawlessness. Folks I'm going to say this. I've traveled all over the world and I can honestly say to you I have seen the words of Jesus being fulfilled. You know what most people's attitude of submission is? "I'll submit as long as I agree." Let me tell you something. Submission doesn't even begin until there's disagreement. What submission is there if you submit if you agree? Good preaching. Amen.

Now there's two questions we've got to ask. Number one: what is the root cause of deception? Good question. Would you like to know what the root cause of deception is? How many of you would like to know really? Go to James 1 and you'll see it.

James the first chapter. I want to look just at the first verse here. Everybody, say, "Amen." "Amen." James chapter one, look at verse 22. *"But be doers of the word, and not hearers only"*—Watch this— *"deceiving yourselves."* Man, that is a powerful statement. James says, "When a person hears the word of God yet he does not do it. Deception enters into his heart. Now it's a scary thing to deceive yourself, isn't it?

Second, the question we've got to ask is: why does deception—or lawlessness I should say—go rampant in the last days? Second Thessalonians 2:10 tells us. Listen to me carefully. The reason lawlessness will run rampant in the last days is because people will not love truth. Now let me make this clear. To love truth doesn't mean love hearing it. It means love obeying it. If you go to Ezekiel 33 which I will not do this morning you will find out that God said the people came to hear Ezekiel preach because he was a great preacher. And he said that they all came and they were all saying to one another, "You've got to hear this guy preach. He's tremendous." And yet God said they will come and they will hear your words but they will not do them. Why? Because they loved themselves. The reason deception will run so rampant is because of the love of self. Exactly what Paul said to Timothy. Men will love themselves more than they love truth. Are you with me?

There's another factor involved here and that is found in 2 Thessalonians 2:7. The NIV version says, *"The secret power of lawlessness is already at work."* Paul talks about in that chapter of Thessalonians — a secret power of lawlessness being at work in the last days. Everybody say, "Secret power." "Secret power." Now Paul in the New King James says *"the mystery of lawlessness."* The mystery of lawlessness is in its secret power. Can you say, "Secret power"? "Secret power." There is a power of lawlessness. Paul makes this statement about Eve because you know what? If I look at Adam and Eve and if I study that out, I'm going to find Satan's best shot. Do you understand what I'm saying? Because let me tell you this. He came into a garden where a man and a woman walked in the very presence of God. They beheld His glory, Eve was never oppressed by a boss, she was never abused by a husband or a father. He came into a perfect environment where the presence of God permeated that place and was able to deceive that woman. So if I understand how Satan deceived Eve, I'm going to understand his best shot for us today. Are you with me? Because Paul makes this statement in 2 Corinthians 11:3. Just listen to it and while I'm saying it go over to Genesis 3. Paul makes this statement in 2 Corinthians 11:3, *"But I fear, lest somehow, as the serpent deceived Eve by his craftiness, so your minds may be corrupted."* Did you hear that? Paul wrote to this Corinthian church and said, "I'm afraid that just the way Satan deceived Eve that he's going to do it to you." Are you with me? So we've got to understand how he deceived her. Amen.

Go to Genesis chapter three. Let's go right back to the beginning here. Genesis the third chapter please. Actually, before we read chapter three, let's look at chapter two. And let's look at the sixteenth verse please. God places Adam in the garden and here is the command. *"And the Lord God commanded the man saying, 'Of every tree of the garden you may freely eat.'"* Verse 17: *"But of the tree of the knowledge of good and evil you shall not eat, for in the day that you eat of it you shall surely die.'"* Would you look up at me? God's emphasis to Adam is, "You can freely eat from every tree." Now let me tell you there were a lot of trees in that garden. So do you hear His generosity? Do you hear His goodness? Are you seeing this? God's a giver, isn't He? But yet His authority restrained them. He said, "But there is one tree." The tree of knowledge of good and evil. So the emphasis of the command is, "Look at what you can eat. All these trees." His authority—because He didn't want robots in the garden—He wanted people that could choose to obey Him. His authority said, "Except that one tree." Right? So now watch. The serpent comes along in 3:1: *"Now the serpent was [much] more cunning than any beast of the field which the Lord God had made. And he said to the woman 'Has God indeed said, "You shall not eat of every tree of the garden?"'"* Are you with me? Now would you look up at me? Can I modernize that and make it more in our vernacular? The serpent comes up to Eve and says, "So you can't eat from every tree can you?" So what does the serpent do? He gets her eyes off of all she can eat and gets her eyes on the one thing God has said don't eat. Are you with me? So now watch, so what he's doing is he's trying to bring God's motive into question. What he's trying to do now is to pervert the character of God in her eyes. Are you with me? He's trying to make God look like a taker instead of a giver that he really is. By getting her eyes off of all she could eat and looking at what she can't eat. Why do you think the Bible says over and over again, "Be thankful, be thankful"? Because it keeps your eyes on all that God has given us. But for some reason people may concentrate on what they can't do. Good preaching. Amen. I'll help you. Amen.

Now, she's looking at this and she's thinking, "Wow." Let me tell you something. Psalm 97:2 says, *"Righteousness and justice are the foundation of His throne."* What is the enemy trying to do? He's trying to challenge the very authority of God because His authority is based on His righteousness and on His goodness. Now look at this. The woman corrected the serpent. She looks back at him and look at what she says. The woman says to the serpent, *"We may eat the fruit of the trees of the garden; but of the fruit of the tree which is in the midst of the garden, God has said, "You shall not eat it, nor shall you touch it, lest you die."'"* In the book I go into that and much more. But I want you to notice something. The woman corrects the serpent, but as she does it's very possible that she begins to wonder about the reason behind the command. Isn't that right? She starts thinking, you know. She's looking at this fruit. She's going, "Wait a minute, it looks good. And you know what? It will make me wise." And so the enemy comes right back in while those questions are going on. Everybody say, "Questionings." "Questionings." And I'm going to coin this phrase, "Those reasonings." All right? Everybody say, "Reasonings." She says, "It looks good. It's going to make me wise." She judges the fruit to be good, not evil. Are you with me? He comes right back and he says this—look at verse 4: *"Then the serpent said to the woman, 'You will not surely die. For God knows that in the day you eat of it your eyes will be opened, and you will be like God, knowing good and evil.'"* So now she's got the promise she won't die. And she's looking at this fruit and it looks good. See folks, you've got to understand something. She wasn't drawn to the evil side, she was drawn to the good side. There is a good

that is very rebellious to God's authority. Did you catch that? There is a good that humanity says is good. And what it is, is that humanity has substituted the principle of reasoning for the principle of obedience. She looks at that tree. Now she goes, "Wait a minute, that fruit's good. It's going to make me wise and I'm not going to die. If that fruit's good, then what else is He withholding from me?" His character has been perverted. The foundation of the strong has been shaken in her heart. Are you with me? Now God in Eve's eyes is a taker, He's a withholder. So what's the next step? She eats and she gives it to her husband; he eats.

James chapter 1. This is why James comes along. Many, many, many years later, listen what he says in verse 16. *"Do not be deceived, my beloved brethren. Every good gift and every perfect gift is from above, and comes down from the Father of lights, with whom there is no variation or shadow of turning."* James comes along and says, "Don't be deceived. Don't be like Eve and be deceived. Get it set in your heart right now. There is nothing good outside of the will of God. Settle it in your heart. Let it be established. Nothing is good for you outside of God's authority or His will." But remember Jesus. He was in the desert for forty days. Starvation sets in. If He doesn't get food He's going to die. And what comes forth? The promise or the temptation? The temptation. "If you're the Son of God. He's not taking care. You change that stone into bread." But Jesus endured. If you have it settled in your heart there is nothing good from outside the will of God, you will not be deceived.

Session Three

The Consequences of Disobedience—Part One

"If you do well, will you not be accepted?
And if you do not do well, sin lies at the door.
And its desire is for you, but you should rule over it."
Genesis 4:7

Summary for *Under Cover*, Chapter 5

How often do we minimize the consequences that sin will produce in our lives? Many times, it is easier to look at the potential gains to be made by indulging in sin than to clearly see the affects that will naturally be a result from sinning. We sometimes make the mistake of believing that God will accept us regardless of our actions and attitudes. We lose the fear of the Lord that guards us from sin.

When people fall prey to sin and disobedience, they harden their hearts to God and are enslaved to the deceptions of the enemy. They attempt to make judgments based on their own reasoning and experience. However, God wants us to obey Him. He is not interested in our ability to reason or rationalize. He is only interested in our ability to follow Him with our whole heart and soul.

Sin is aggressive. The enemy is waiting to rule over us and enslave us to the laws of sin and death. It is true faith and obedience that will overcome deception. Some will live their whole lives thinking they are doing what is pleasing to God. They are blinded to the deceptions of the enemy. It is only through a life of constant obedience to God and His Word that mankind can live freely.

Notes from Chapter 5 (Video Session 3)

_____

_____

_____

_____

_____

_____

> Adam and Eve lived before God, completely God conscious. By taking of the fruit of the Tree of the Knowledge of Good and Evil, they found a source of the knowledge that was good and evil outside God. We can identify this as the principle of reasoning. They no longer needed God to govern them; they had a sense of right and wrong within themselves. That was why the first question God asked them after they fall was, "Who told you?" (Gen. 3:11).
>
> Whenever God asks a question, He is not looking for information. He is drawing you into what He is communicating. God already knew they had eaten from the tree and were speaking from their own wisdom. They had replaced obedience with reasoning. He was actually saying, "So you have now found a source of the sense of right and wrong outside Me. You have obviously eaten from the Tree of the Knowledge of Good and Evil."
>
> John Bevere, *Under Cover*, p. 51.

Warm Up Questions

1. How does the modern day theology of God's "unconditional acceptance" affect many people's understanding of sin?

    _____

    _____

    _____

2. How has your own reasoning sometimes led you down paths that are not pleasing to God?

    _____

    _____

    _____

3. In what ways are faith and obedience inseparable?

    _____

    _____

    _____

Teaching by John Bevere

Watch video session three.

Teaching Review

4. Before Adam and Eve's fall, their actions were guided by their (choose one)
   a) knowledge of right and wrong
   b) reasoning
   c) knowledge of God
   d) instinct

5. Cain's sacrifice did not please God because

6. The desire of sin is to

7. The primary characteristic of sin is that it is the desire to: (choose one)
   have extreme pleasure
   take the place of God
   satisfy desires
   be self-centered

Another way to view this would be to compare the desire of sin to the law of gravity. It is a constant force that is always in place and affects all matter. If you step off the top of a building, you will find its law in effect and fall to the lowest point, in fact, very hard. You may not want to fall or have an awareness of or belief in the law of gravity; nevertheless, you will encounter it.

One day scientists discovered yet another law—the law of lift. They learned that the law of lift superseded the law of gravity if conditions were right. Innovative men designed the airplane based on the law of lift. When you fly in a plane, you are on a lever free from the law of gravity and do not fall to gravity's lowest point. Scripture tells us, "For the law of the Spirit of life in Christ Jesus has made me free from the law of sin and death" (Rom. 8:2). What wonderful news!

John Bevere, *Under Cover*, p. 53.

Exploring God's Word

Exodus 20:20 *And Moses said to the people, "Do not fear; for God has come to test you, and that His fear may be before you, so that you may not sin."*

8. How does this passage use the word "fear" in two different ways?

_____

_____

_____

_____

_____

9. In what ways have we as a society lost both of these fears of God?

_____

_____

_____

10. What is happening to our society as a result of this?

_____

_____

_____

Personal Application

_____

_____

_____

> **Genesis 3:17–19** *Then to Adam He said, "Because you have heeded the voice of your wife, and have eaten from the tree of which I commanded you, saying, 'you shall not eat of it': Cursed is the ground for your sake; In toil you shall eat of it All the days of your life. Both thorns and thistles it shall bring forth for you, And you shall eat the herb of the field. In the sweat of your face you shall eat bread Till you return to the ground, For out of it you were taken; For dust you are, And to dust you shall return."*

11. How did sin and death's entrance into the world change mankind's existence?

    _____

    _____

    _____

12. By choosing to sin, Adam chose his own way instead of God's. Why did this simple act bring about such grave consequences?

    _____

    _____

    _____

Personal Application

_____

_____

_____

Genesis 4:6–7 *So the Lord said to Cain, "Why are you angry? And why has your countenance fallen? If you do well, will you not be accepted? And if you do not do well, sin lies at the door. And its desire is for you, but you should rule over it."*

13. In what ways does sin "desire" to rule over us?

_____

_____

_____

_____

_____

_____

14. Cain's anger was born from God's rejection of his sacrifice. Why does rejection of any sort often cause us to be angry and to sin?

_____

_____

_____

Personal Application

_____

_____

_____

1 John 5:19 *We know that we are of God, and the whole world lies under the sway of the wicked one.*

15. Why is it important to understand the reach of the enemy in this world?

_____

_____

_____

16. Why is it important to know that you are "of God" and not under deception?

_____

_____

_____

Personal Application

_____

_____

_____

Romans 8:12–13 *Therefore, brethren, we are debtors—not to the flesh, to live according to the flesh. For if you live according to the flesh you will die; but if by the Spirit you put to death the deeds of the body, you will live.*

17. What does it mean to live according to the flesh?

_____

_____

_____

18. How can the Spirit enable us to overcome the flesh?

_____

_____

_____

_____

Personal Application

_____

_____

_____

Exposing the Truth

19. In John's "Under Cover" seminar, he says, "Faith and obedience are inseparable because obedience is evidence of true faith." Is it possible to have true faith without obeying the precepts that accompany that faith? Why?

_____

_____

_____

_____

_____

_____

_____

_____

20. Many people in our society believe that God will accept them regardless of the things they do. In what ways is this type of thinking dangerous to true belief and faith?

_____

_____

_____

_____

_____

_____

_____

_____

21. Cain's offering to God was rejected because it was not what God desired as a sacrifice. How can we avoid making sacrifices to God that He does not desire and how do we know what we are to sacrifice?

_____

_____

_____

_____

Applying the Lesson

The consequences of sin are sometimes painfully obvious. At other times there is virtually no way of recognizing that sin is in our lives. In order to be aware of the sin that we are constantly surrounded by, it is important that we stay in tune with the Holy Spirit and with the church. The Holy Spirit guides us through the church and through communion with other believers. List several ways in which you have overcome sin in your life with the help of your local church:

_____

_____

_____

_____

_____

In your personal walk, how are you becoming more aware of sin and its consequences for your life?

_____

_____

_____

_____

_____

People both in and out of churches will one day stand before God and be judged for their lawlessness. Yet if you could have followed the course of their lives, you could never have imagined they would end at such a destination. Even now they would never dream themselves lawless, but on the Day of Judgment when truth is revealed, they will wonder, *"How did I drift so far from obedience to the ways of God?"* The sad answer will be, they did not love and embrace the truth of being under His cover.

John Bevere, *Under Cover*, p.56.

Checking Your Cover

Conclude this session by praying that God will:

Enable you to seek His will in your life and overcome selfish ambition

Allow you to see what is a pleasing sacrifice in your life

Help you to always choose obedience and faith over sin and unbelief

Video Script for Lesson 3
The Consequences of Disobedience–Part One

Let's open up our Bibles to Genesis 4 and we've been talking about God's direct authority. "Under cover" means to be under His authority. There are people today that think to dwell in the secret place is in the prayer closet. To dwell in the secret place is be a member of a church or to pray the sinner's prayer. But you will see throughout Scripture that to be "under cover" means that you are submitted to His authority. There are two ways in which His authority manifests. Number one: His direct authority or inherent authority. Or number two: His delegated authority. God has delegated His authority in the social realm—or society realm, I should say—in the family realm, and also in the church realm. But right now what we are talking about is God's direct authority. Let me say this, if you are ever going to be able to be submitted to His authority you must have a revelation of God. Because He and His authority are inseparable. There are people today that I find say, "I know Jesus, I know the Lord." Yet they are not acquainted with His authority. You can't separate the two. You can make a Jesus that has saved you, and manage Him, and make Him give you what you want, but that's not the Jesus at the right hand of the Father. That's exactly what the children of Israel did when they created the calf. They called him Jehovah, they called him Yahweh, the calf. They said "Yahweh, who delivered us out of Egypt." In other words, they still worshiped Jehovah. They did not look at that calf and say, "Behold Baal, who delivered us from Egypt." They acknowledged Jehovah; they just changed the image of his glory. They created a Jehovah that would give them what they wanted. Anytime the church creates a Lord who will give them what they want in a Jesus, what they want—you will find a church that will become very fleshly. Are you with me? Fleshliness only comes out of rebellion because rebellion is idolatry and we will see it today.

Now I want to say this, in these next couple of sessions we're going to get hit with some pretty hard truths. But you know I remember when I was a young boy and I was scheduled to get my tuberculosis vaccine. I did not want to get it because some friends told me the shot really hurt. And I remember it took two nurses to hold me down and they still couldn't get the needle in my arm. Then my mom and dad sat me down and they said, "Son, tuberculosis is very serious, it's a disease." And I was acquainted with another disease because just a year earlier my sister had died of cancer. When that was explained to me then I went in willing—volunteered—because you know what? I wanted a little bit of pain now to avoid the great disease that was going to bring a lot of pain later. And I have found anytime the Word of God gets a little painful or a little strong or a little hard, it's only God saying, "I'm just trying to protect you from greater pain in the future." Can you say, "Amen"? "Amen."

Now there are people today that have done a very foolish thing. They have reasoned that disobeying God, that the consequences they will face in disobeying God will out weigh the benefits they will get in their rebellion. But yet as my wife has said, "There is bondage in rebellion, but there is liberty in submission." I hope that in these next two sessions, that you're going to clearly see what the consequences of sin are and you're going to see that the consequences are much worse than any kind of temporary benefit you'll get from disobeying God's authority. Can you say, "Amen"? "Amen."

Get your Bibles open to Genesis 4, I want us to look at the first verse. *"Now Adam knew Eve his wife, and she conceived and bore Cain and said, 'I have acquired a man from the LORD.'"* Verse 2: *"Then she bore again, this time his brother Abel. Now Abel was a keeper of sheep, but Cain was a tiller of the ground."* In other words, Abel was a shepherd, Cain was a farmer. Are you with me? Verse 3: *"And in the process of time it came to pass that Cain brought an offering of the fruit of the ground to the LORD."* Now everybody say, "An offering." "An offering." *"Of the fruit of the ground to the LORD"* Now an offering speaks of our life's service to God. Can you say, "Amen"? "Amen." Verse 4: *"Abel . . . brought of the firstborn of his flock and of their fat. And the LORD respected Abel and his offering."* Now watch this carefully. Verse 5: *"But He did not respect Cain and his offering."* Now that right there blows the tradition that we have in our churches. I have heard people say over and over again, "God will accept you just the way you are." No, that's not true. God will accept you just the way you are if you repent. Try telling that to Ananias and Sapphira—he'll just accept them the way they are—it's too late. Are you with me? Notice that God not only had had no respect for Cain's offering, but He had no respect for Cain either. Verse 5: *"But He did not respect Cain and his offering."* Now watch this: *"And Cain was very angry, and his countenance fell."* Now listen, that's what happens every time you preach to a religious person. Whenever you confront a religious person with truth, they get angry.

Now let's talk about this situation. Now I'm going to modernize it. I like to bring things to today. We've got two men that are working diligently to bring an offering to the Lord. Now we are not talking about one who is working to bring an offering to the Lord and the other one wants nothing to do with God. We're not talking about one who's coming to church seeking God and the other one sleeping in on Sunday morning. He likes going to the bars, the strip joints and the football games all the time and he wants nothing to do with God. We're not talking about that. We're talking about two men that are both raised in the church. Now remember their mom and dad, Adam and Eve—I'm modernizing this—they're raised in the church and they're both diligently working to bring their offerings to the Lord, right? Now if you really think about it, Cain is working harder. Now I know a little bit about farming and I know a little bit about shepherding, but I know enough to know this: Shepherding is hard

work, but farming is much harder. When you shepherd you have responsibilities early in the morning and late in the afternoon, but in the heat of the day you can sit underneath the palm tree and sip on a cool one. You got it? But farming you have to work through the whole day. You have to bring forth the fruit by the sweat of your brow, the grain by the sweat of your brow. So Cain is actually working harder than Abel. Yet when they bring their offerings, God rejects the one who actually worked harder to bring his offering. Now the question is, why? Why does God actually not show regard for the man who worked harder to bring his offering? The answer is found with their parents. You have to go back to the garden. When God placed Adam and Eve in the garden the Bible says that He crowned them with glory. All right? They did not have physical clothing on, the Bible says they were naked and unashamed. The reason they were unashamed is because literally the glory of God was on them. "He crowned them with glory," psalmists said. And that word "crowned" literally means this: to circle or surround. They were literally clothed with God's glory. However, when they disobeyed God—which we talked about in depth last session—the moment they disobeyed God, what's the first thing the Bible says. They knew they were naked and they sought to cover themselves. Isn't that right? So immediately their senses of their flesh took over. Prior to the fall, the Spirit dominated them. They were completely God-conscious; they were not self-conscious. After the fall—that is when self-consciousness entered the human race. It is amazing to me how many preachers today try to build people's self-conscious, instead of ministering to them of God-consciousness. Jesus came to deliver us from self-consciousness. If you look at the garden, there is no description of Adam and Eve. If you go through the Old Testament you'll find descriptions of people all over the place. David's handsome, Absalom—they talk about his hair, they talk about how beautiful Rebekah is, Sarah is, right? You come to the New Testament and you don't find descriptions of people any more. Why? Because Paul says, henceforth we don't know anyone after the flesh. He said we don't know even know Jesus after the flesh. Jesus came to deliver us from the self-consciousness. Are you seeing this? Prior to the fall—now listen carefully to me—prior to the fall, Adam and Eve were completely God-conscious. Their living was in God. However, when they took of the fruit of the knowledge of good and evil—that tree of the knowledge of good and evil—what did it represent? It represented a source of right and wrong outside of God. Prior to their eating of that tree, all their living was in God. There was no source for right and wrong outside of Him. Their life was before Him because all of His ways were just and righteous. There wasn't any kind of what's right and what's wrong. But when they ate of that tree it represented finding a source for the knowledge of good and evil or a sense of what is right and wrong outside of God. Are you with me? Even though what they ate was good, it still was rebellious to His authority. Are you seeing this? That's why the very first thing that God said to them after they ate that fruit was, "Who told you?" In other words, "You have a source for what is right and wrong now obviously outside of me. You obviously ate from the tree of knowledge of good and evil." When Adam and Eve ate from that tree, what they did is they embraced the principle of reasoning and they forsook the principle of obedience. You see that curse on humanity ever since. Today you have society saying, "This is good, this is right." This is good according to humanity, but yet it is rebellious to God. And yet it has become so perverted, that just as Isaiah said the days would come when they'll call evil, good and good, evil. That's exactly what's happening. But there's levels of that found in everyone. Are you seeing that it's not walking under the submission to God's authority? So when Adam and Eve ate, they then needed to cover themselves. And so God came into the garden and God said, "Who told you?" And then after He dealt with them, He killed an animal and clothed them with the skin of the animal. Thereby showing Adam and Eve what His acceptable sacrifice was. They attempted, first of all, to cover themselves with fig leaves, that's the fruit of the ground. Everybody say, "Fruit of the ground." "Fruit of the ground." But then God said,

"No, I'm going to clothe you with this animal" and I believe it was a lamb. And God clothed them with the skin of the animal and thereby God showed them His way. Now everybody say this, "Adam and Eve were ignorant." "Adam and Eve were ignorant." "Cain and Abel weren't." "Cain and Abel weren't." Cain and Abel knew what God desired. Cain and Abel both knew that it was not the fruit of the ground that God desired. So when Cain brought an offering of fruit of the ground it represented serving God his own way. He is still serving God, he still wants to go to church, he's not sleeping in—remember this—but he's wanting to do it his own way. Are you with me?

So look what God's says to him. Verse 6—Are you there?—"So the LORD said to Cain, 'Why are you angry? And why has your countenance fallen? If you do well . . .'". Now would you look up at me? What is it to do well with God? What has he said over and over and over and over again in the Scripture? "I desire obedience and not sacrifice." So to do well with God is to what? To obey Him. Everybody say, "Obey Him." "Obey Him." You know I wish everyone of us as believers would do a study throughout the Scriptures. And do a study on obedience and obey, just run through the Bible and read them all. You will find out that this is a high priority to God.

Hebrews 5:9 says this, that Jesus is the author of salvation to all who obey Him. Acts 5:32 says this, that God gives the Holy Spirit to those who obey Him. There is a premium placed on obedience. As a matter of fact you will find that God says to the children of Israel, "I'm fed up with your praise and worship, get rid of it. Get rid of your praise and worship, get rid of your musical instruments, quit bringing ram sacrifices to me." And they said, "Why?" He said, "Because when I spoke nobody listened." They were bringing ram sacrifices and God said, "Your lamb sacrifices are like breaking a dog's neck." They were burning incense which is a type of praise and worship in the holy place, and God said, "Your incense that you're burning in the holy place to me, in my eyes, is like offering up something to an idol."

And they said, "God, why are our lamb sacrifices like breaking a dog's neck? Why is our incense that we're burning in our praise and worship like blessing an idol?" And God said, "Because when I spoke nobody listened." So you're going to see this over and over. Listen folks, I'm going to say this to you: The highest form of worship is not singing. The highest form of worship is obedience. If you notice the first time the word obedience appears in the Bible is Genesis 22 and that is when Abraham said, "We will go up and worship and come back." What Abraham was doing was obeying God all the way to completion. All the way to the mountain he was ready to offer up the most important thing in is life. He was obedient even in the most important area and God said, "Now I know you fear me." So you will find out if you really study the Scripture. See, the problem is, we can preach something and teach something for so long that eventually we believe it's true. So that when the real truth comes along we reject the truth for the falsehood that we taught so long. And if you really sit down and talk to people today and you say, "What is true worship?" They'll tell you it's nice sweet music singing songs to Jesus. Now that's not true.

All right, so now let's look at this. So the Lord said to Cain, Verse 6: *"Why are you angry? And why is your countenance fallen?"* Verse 7: *"If you do well."* Everybody say, "If you do well." "If you do well." What God is saying is that "If you simply obey me." Everybody say, "Obey me." "Obey me." What He is saying to Cain, "Listen to me carefully." He's saying, *"Cain, if you do well, will you not be accepted?"* Look at this. Will you not be accepted? In other words, "Cain if you take some of your crops, trade it for one of your brother's flock, bring that to me, I will accept you just like I accepted Abel. I am no respecter of persons. You're upset because I've accepted him and haven't accepted you. Cain don't you realize this has nothing to do with me and everything to do with you. He simply obeyed me, you didn't." Are you with me?

Now watch this. *"If you do well, will you not be*

accepted? If you do not do well"—or in other words, if you do not obey me—*"sin lies at the door."* Everybody say, "The door." "The door." *"And its desire is for you."* Wow! *"But you should rule over it."* Wow, there's a mouthful here. First of all God said, *"its desire is for you."* Do you notice that sin has desire? Let me give you an illustration to show you what He's talking about there. When sin was released into the earth by Adam, it was almost as if a wicked man, a wicked scientist, released some poisonous gas into the atmosphere. The only protection you would have from that gas would be to have the proper equipment on, isn't that right? But that wicked gas would permeate everywhere whether that scientist's presence was there or not. When sin was released into mankind, that sin was released and it has a desire, just like that poisonous gas would have a desire to destroy you. It has a desire even if the presence of Satan is there or not. That is what the Bible means when it says the whole world lies under wickedness in 1 John 5. The whole world is under its influence. But you've got to have the protective gear, isn't that right? Another way of looking at it is like the law of gravity. What does Romans 8:1–2 say? *"There is therefore now no condemnation of them that are in Christ Jesus, who walk not after the flesh, but after the Spirit."* Everybody say, "After the Spirit." "After the Spirit." For the law of the Spirit of life. Everybody say, "Law." "Law." *"The law of the Spirit of life in Christ Jesus has made me free from the law of sin and death."* Now this is good news. There are two major laws in operation today in the realm of the Spirit. There's the law of the sin of death and the law of the Spirit of life. Now the way I like to see it is like the law of gravity. There is a law in the earth and its called gravity, isn't that right? You take anything and you take it up to a certain level and you drop it—that thing's going to its lowest potential energy, isn't that right? Translated, take something up to the top of a building, let it go, it's going down hard. Right? That's the law of gravity. You cannot escape it. It is everywhere, correct? There is no place on the earth where the law of gravity doesn't exist. Any place on the earth you drop something, it's going down to its lowest place of gravity, right? However one day, scientists, engineers discover there is another law and it was called the law of lift. And they found out that the law of lift superceded the law of gravity. Are you with me? Then these two guys came along named the Wright brothers and they figured out how to put this thing into motion. And they began to fly using the law of lift. Because when you created the right air foil and you put enough thrust behind it, you're going to fly. Now last year alone I flew over 200,000 miles to preach the gospel globally. Now I'm going to tell you something. Every time I get into that plane I'm so thankful for the law of lift. Why? Because the law of lift sets me free from the law of gravity, right? And here I am soaring around the earth, right? I'm going to Singapore on the other side of the earth. Go any further, you start coming home. But you go to the other side in 23 hours cruising along at six hundred miles an hour, right? Because of the law of lift. But how many of you know if the pilot shuts off the engines, chops off the wings, guess what? The law of gravity is still in effect and baby, you're going down faster than what you went up. Isn't that right?

Well listen to what the apostle says in Romans. You know what—put your marker right there, you've got to see this. I want you to see this in your own Bible because we're coming back to Genesis. Go to over Romans 8. Are you there? Now look what Paul says, look at verse 2. I quoted it to you and I'm going to read it again. Verse 2 says, *"For the law"*—Everybody say, "Law." "Law."— *"of the Spirit of life in Christ Jesus has made me free from the law of sin and death."* Notice the laws. Laws cannot be changed. I don't care how much you pray, you fast, you weep, you sing—it can't be changed. That's a good thing to know. How precious and cute you are, that law doesn't change because you're cute. Okay, you got it? It's a law. And this is a New Testament law. Are you with me? Now the wonderful news about this is the law of the Spirit of life has set me free from the law of sin and death. Just like the law of lift sets me free from the law of gravity. But if you stop operating the principles of the law of lift,

you're going with the law of gravity because it's still in effect. Are you with me?

That's why Paul comes along and says in Verse 12: *"Therefore brethren"*—he's speaking to believers, not unbelievers— *"We are debtors—not to the flesh, to live according to the flesh."* Verse 13: *"For if you live according to the flesh you will die."* Pretty plain isn't it? Why? Because the law of sin and death is still in operation. Now the law of the Spirit of life in Christ Jesus is also called the law of faith. Everybody say, "The law of faith." "The law of faith." Now if you look carefully in the New Testament, you will find out that Hebrews 11:4 brags about Abel. Because Abel offered a better sacrifice through faith. Everybody say, "Through faith." "Through faith." Now listen to me carefully. Do you notice that God cannot connect His obedient works with the law of faith? Now this is something a lot of people don't understand today in the church. Faith and obedient works are directly connected. See, unfortunately, we spoke a truth but we didn't tell the whole story in some arenas. We told a truth that faith comes by hearing and by hearing the word of God. But my Bible also says whoever hears the Word of God and doesn't do it has deceived himself. There is no faith in deception. Are you with me? Faith and obedient actions are directly connected. The greater the obedience, the greater the faith. The greater the faith—true faith—the greater the obedience. You can ask people—I have great faith—but if they're not obedient to authority, you're showing me somebody who has a lot of mental assent and they have a lot of knowledge but they didn't make the transformation.

Now go back to Genesis 4. God says in verse seven, *"If you do well, will you not be accepted?"* In other words, "If you just obey me like your brother, I'll accept you just like him. *And if you do not do well sin lies at the door."* Now notice this, watch what he goes on to say. *"And its desire is for you, but you should rule over."* How do you rule over the law of gravity? The law of lift. How do you rule over the law of sin and death? The law of the Spirit of life in Christ

Jesus which, folks, is what obedience to the Lordship of Jesus is. He is the author of salvation to all who obey Him. Hebrews 5:9. Now notice that God said, *"Sin lies at the door."* Everybody say, "The door." "The door." Say it again, "The door." "The door." There is a door in the realm of the Spirit in the life of every single human being. Whether you are aware of that door or whether you're not aware of that door does not negate its existence. It's there whether you realize it or not. And that door is the door that gives legal access to sin and demonic power in your life. And God tells us—right from the beginning, right from the sons of Adam, right from the very beginning of the Bible—what opens that door and what slams it shut. Obedience to God slams it shut, disobedience throws it wide open. And when that door is open, you give the devil an inch, he'll take a mile. You crack that door, he'll blast it open. And that's exactly what happened with Cain. Cain opened that door through his disobedience. What happened? Anger entered into his heart. Jealousy entered into his heart. Hatred entered into his heart. And that hatred soon turned into murder and this young man—now listen to me carefully—This young man who started out serving God, and actually worked harder than his brother, ended up killing his own brother. Now if you looked at this situation and you said, "My goodness." And you didn't have the inside scoop that God gives us right here. And you looked at this and saw these two men starting out serving God. And you look at one who ends up being bragged about in Hebrews 11 in God's Hall of Fame of faith. And the other one who's become a murderer, you'd go, "What happened? He's actually working harder than the other one." If God wouldn't have given us the inside scoop we wouldn't have known.

I have traveled to thousands of churches worldwide. I have been traveling nonstop for 12 years. I do not pastor a church, all I do is travel. Every week I'm in another conference or church or Bible school. And it used to baffle me, I would come to church, they would have some of the greatest preachers and teachers of the body of Christ coming through those churches. And yet I would find more people bound to sexual sin, bound to lust, bound to bitterness, bound to jealousy, and envy, and other forms of sin. And I would go, " What is going on, why is this?" Until God opened my eyes to this very truth. They have not walked in the law in the Spirit of life. They have not walked in obedience to the Lordship. You see God gave us grace to empower us to walk in obedience. See most people today, their view of grace is the big cover up. Grace is not the big cover up folks. Grace empowers us to do what truth demands of us. Hebrews 12:28 says, *"Therefore, since we are receiving a kingdom which cannot be shaken, let us [receive] grace, [whereby] we may serve God acceptably."* Grace empowers us to serve Him acceptably. Are you seeing this?

Here is Cain, he murders his brother, and now he becomes belligerent. Everybody say, "Belligerent." "Belligerent." Because God comes along and says, "Where's your brother, Cain?" And Cain says, "I don't know, am I my brother's keeper?" Now first of all, look at the irreverence that enters into his life. He has lost the fear of God. Secondly, he's out of his right mind, he's deceived. How many people would honestly think God doesn't know where Abel is? I mean come on. But that's exactly what happens when you begin to disobey. What happens is you bring God down to your level. You're deceived. And now you think you know as much as and sometimes even more than God. I mean, let's face it folks, Lucifer worshiped right at the throne. But how absolutely ridiculous is the thought that he could exalt himself above God? He brought God down to his level and below. That is the manifestation of rebellion. He lowered the image, the glory and the deity of God and you make him more manageable. And you convey to God by your disobedience, "I know more than You." That's how serious it is and that is why the Bible clearly says deception would run rampant in the last days. The reason being because people would love themselves more than they love God.

I'm going to read to you right from the book.

"Anyone in their right mind would know that God knew where Abel was. But this is what happens when someone turns to reasoning and allows disobedience in their life. They lose touch with the reality of spiritual things. They attempt to lower the image of God to their level and limitations. And imagine themselves as wise as God or sometimes even wiser. They are not in their right mind. Of course this is first seen in Lucifer. Reasoning birthed from iniquity led him to believe he could overthrow God, how foolish, yet he led many in his ways." Can you see the importance of obeying God? Cain ends up a murderer, he ends up belligerent, he's out of touch with the presence of God, he's no longer walking with God. That's why in our own lives we want to pursue obeying God and pleasing Him.

Session Four
The Consequences of Disobedience—Part Two

"But be doers of the word, and not hearers only,
deceiving yourselves."
James 1:22

Summary for *Under Cover,* Chapters 6 and 7

Not all sin begins with a deliberate attempt to ignore the will of God. Sometimes a person will begin with every intention of doing what they know to be right, but end up caught in deception and sin. This type of partial obedience is as equally offensive to God as blatant disobedience. We can learn from the life of Saul and his partial obedience to the commandments of God. He allowed himself to be swayed by reason instead of fulfilling God's commands and, as a result, was bound in disobedience.

When we intend to do something for the Lord or for His cause, we must be certain that what we are doing is within His will and commandments. It is too easy to be caught beneath a veil of deception, justifying our actions and thoughts. Our conscience becomes seared, easily ignoring the prodding of the Holy Spirit. Without a heart that is open to God, our lives begin to become empty and void of the life of God.

God desires that no one be caught in deception and sin and He provides conviction, prophecy and, when necessary, judgment to bring our hearts into submission. It is always our own decision to repent and turn to God or to continue hardening our hearts to His leading. God will not force anyone to accept Him. He only desires that we follow Him and accept the abundant life He has prepared for us. However, if it is necessary, He will allow hardships and trials to bring us to repentance.

God's Word equates rebellion to witchcraft. In our world, the enemy desires that we rebel against God, opening ourselves to Satan's influence, becoming enslaved to rebellion and sin. The worst possible life for anyone is a life of slavery, yet so many are unaware of the spiritual slavery to which they willingly submit through their actions and thoughts. Satan has deceived many into thinking that freedom is found in self-indulgence. However, the truth remains clear; there is only freedom in doing the will of God.

Notes from Chapters 6–7 (Video Session 4)

_____

_____

_____

_____

_____

_____

Jesus made this statement: *"If anyone desires to come after Me, let him deny himself, and take up his cross, and follow Me"* (Matt. 16:24). Some take up the cross and concentrate on its image of suffering as representing a life of sacrifice. However, in these words of Jesus the cross is not the only or complete focus. You can live a life of self-denial and sacrifice and not fulfill God's purpose or will. In fact, you could choose self-denial and sacrifice and still be in rebellion to God.

The focus of what Jesus was saying is *obedience*. The only way we can obey is to take up the cross. For without death to our own agendas and desires, we will eventually have a face-off between the will of God and the desire of man. If we do not lay down our lives, we will find a way of fulfilling those desires contrary to His, and even use Scriptures to back it just as Saul did. We must ask ourselves, "Does service to God include disobedience?" If so, Satan would receive glory from our "scriptural" religious practices or sacrifices since he is the originator and lord of rebellion.

John Bevere, *Under Cover*, p.65.

Warm-Up Questions

1. Why do you think some people start to follow the will of God but eventually turn to their own ways?

   _____

   _____

   _____

2. What happens to a person that has hardened his/her heart to God and is unable to feel conviction? How is this overcome?

   _____

   _____

   _____

3. In what ways has God allowed hardship in your life to bring you back to repentance?

_____

_____

_____

Teaching by John Bevere

Watch the fourth video session, using the space provided above for any notes.

Teaching Review

4. How would you define "partial obedience" and why is this considered rebellion?

Partial obedience is _____

_____

_____

_____

This type of obedience is rebellious because

_____

_____

_____

5. What happens when we justify rebellious actions and turn our backs on true repentance?

_____

_____

_____

_____

6. List the three-step process God uses to reach someone in disobedience:

_____

_____

_____

7. How does God use judgment to bring someone to repentance?

_____

_____

_____

8. To what does God equate rebellion?

_____

One of the most interesting principles I learned about occultic practices was this: when initiating an individual into a coven (a group of individuals practicing witchcraft), the leaders encouraged him to take drugs, drink, engage in illicit sex, steal, and carry out various other acts that defied the laws of God or our land. I was uncertain why until God opened this truth to me: "Rebellion is witchcraft."

They were taught, the more you rebel, the more power you obtain, and they seek power. This is true because rebellion is witchcraft. The more they rebel, the more they give access to demonic powers that influence, control and empower their lives. By rebelling against the order and laws of God and His delegated authority, they knowingly grant legal access to the controlling demonic realm.

This idea is reflected in what sorcerers call their satanic Bible. A few years ago, while changing channels in a hotel room after a service, my wife and I came across a network special on Satanism and witchcraft. I was about to flip the channel, which ordinarily is wise to do, because I believe all we need to know about spiritual warfare should come from the Spirit of God. However, I felt impressed to watch it a moment. The show discussed the satanic bible. The journalist reported the number one commandment: "Do what thou wilt."

John Bevere, *Under Cover*, p. 68.

Exploring God's Word

1 Corinthians 10:11 *Now all these things happened to them as examples, and they were written for our admonition, upon whom the ends of the ages have come.*

9. How can the experiences of others, particularly the people of Scripture, help us avoid sin and deception?

_____

_____

_____

_____

Personal Application

_____

_____

_____

James 1:22 *But be doers of the word, and not hearers only, deceiving yourselves.*

10. What is the difference between knowing and
    practicing God's Word?

    _____

    _____

    _____

    _____

11. How is a person deceived when they fail to do what
    they know?

    _____

    _____

    _____

    _____

Personal Application

    _____

    _____

    _____

1 Corinthians 11:30–31 *For this reason many
are weak and sick among you, and many sleep. For
if we would judge ourselves, we would not be
judged.*

12. Why is a life of personal reflection and repentance
    important?

    _____

    _____

    _____

    _____

    _____

13. Why is it sometimes so difficult to see our own faults?

_____

_____

_____

_____

_____

14. What can be the result if we fail to carefully examine ourselves?

_____

_____

_____

Personal Application

_____

_____

_____

Matthew 16:24 *If anyone desires to come after Me, let him deny himself, and take up his cross, and follow Me.*

15. A life of self-denial is foolishness to the world. How is our salvation dependent upon it?

_____

_____

_____

Personal Application

_____

_____

_____

2 Peter 2:19 *While they promise them liberty, they themselves are slaves of corruption; for by whom a person is overcome, by him also he is brought into bondage.*

16. How can the pleasures of this world begin to control a person?

_____

_____

_____

_____

_____

17. How can the virtues of the Christian life, such as prayer, fasting and alms giving, help a person overcome slavery to sin and corruption?

_____

_____

_____

_____

Personal Application

_____

_____

_____

_____

1 Samuel 15:22–23 *Behold, to obey is better than sacrifice, And to heed than the fat of rams. For rebellion is as the sin of witchcraft, And stubbornness is as iniquity and idolatry.*

18. Why does God desire obedience over all else?

_____

_____

_____

_____

_____

19. In what ways can our reasoning sometimes be contrary to true obedience?

_____

_____

_____

_____

20. Why does the Scripture equate rebellion and stubbornness with witchcraft and idolatry?

_____

_____

_____

Personal Application

_____

_____

_____

Exposing the Truth

21. In *Under Cover,* John writes, "The moment a person disobeys the Word of God clearly revealed to him, a veil goes over his heart, and that veil distorts and obstructs his view. It is deception." Once deception covers a person's heart, why is it difficult for that person to follow God's leading?

_____

_____

_____

22. Often, when we are convicted of sin, we try to justify our actions. What does this type of reaction say about us and how will this affect the way we deal with sin in the future?

_____

_____

_____

_____

23. John writes in *Under Cover,* "I have met many churchgoers who for some reason or another live in an almost constant state of disobedience. Most are unaware of its severity because they have been numbed by a lopsided teaching of grace that downplays the importance of obedience. One crisis follows another in their lives . . . these problems consume their time, energy, and livelihood. Somewhere an access has been legally given to demonic oppression or influence. Their disobedience has made them vulnerable." How can obedience to God's Word help people in this situation?

_____

_____

_____

_____

_____

_____

_____

_____

_____

Applying the Lesson

One of the only ways to combat deception and disobedience is through accountability to other mature Christians. In what ways does your local church help provide accountability for its members?

Our church provides accountability through:

_____

_____

_____

Below, write a brief statement committing yourself to the truth and obedience by avoiding justifying, rationalizing or ignoring sin:

_____

_____

_____

_____

_____

I have seen this with entire congregations, families, and individuals. I have met many churchgoers who for some reason or another live in an almost constant state of disobedience. Most are unaware of its severity because they have been numbed by a lopsided teaching of grace that downplays the importance of obedience. One crisis follows another in their lives. There is always some problem or sin over which they just can't seem to gain victory. They escape one snare to find themselves entrapped in another. Each scenario seems progressively worse. These problems consume their time, energy and livelihood. Somewhere an access has been legally given to demonic oppression or influence. Their disobedience has made them vulnerable.

I have watched their marriages suffer or, even worse, end in the broken state of divorce. Others are passed over for promotions or, worse, lose their jobs. Some fall prey to theft, financial crisis and tragedy. Frustrated, they frantically look for someone to blame. Many times they blame the treatment they received from parents, pastor, boss, spouse, children, government or anyone else available who doesn't agree with their reasoning.

John Bevere, *Under Cover*, p. 77.

Checking Your Cover

End this session asking the Lord to enable you to:

Overcome deception by complete obedience to His Word

Humble your heart to be able to feel conviction

Combat rebellion and stubbornness in your life

Video Script for Lesson 4
The Consequences of Disobedience–Part Two

Welcome to lesson number four and I want you to open up your Bibles to 1 Samuel 15. First Samuel 15 please. Now let me say this, in our last session, what we talked about was Cain and Abel. We learned very clearly that Cain brought an offering that was disobedient, Abel brought an obedient offering. The result, God said to Abel, if you would do just what is right, He said, you would be accepted just like your brother. But God said, "If you do not obey Me sin lies at the door." We discovered that there is a door at every person's life. And that door gives legal access to sin and demonic power. And that door is there whether you realize it or not. We learn what opens that door: disobedience. And we learned what shuts it closed: obedience to God. Is that true? Cain unfortunately did not listen to God's wisdom. Cain persisted in his own way. Sin entered into his life in the form of hatred, anger, strife, resentment, jealousy. It eventually turned him to murder. And this young man who started out serving God ends up murdering his own brother.

We are going to look at another very similar incident found in 1 Samuel 15. Now let me tell you what's happening here in 1 Samuel 15. We have two major personalities. The first one is king Saul. He is the first king of Israel, correct? The second personality in this chapter that is a major personality is Samuel. And if I can say it like this—that Samuel is the senior prophet of Israel, okay? The scene opens up in verse one with Samuel coming to the king, King Saul, and giving him the Word of the Lord. Samuel said to Saul, "Thus sayeth the Lord. 'I want you to go and gather your armies. And I want you to go and attack the nation of Amalek. And I want you to destroy every man, every woman, every child. And as a matter of fact every animal that they own. Everything that breathes, put it to death with the edge of the sword.'" This was a command. Now I want to make a very strong point here. When

Samuel gave Saul that command. Saul did not look at Samuel and say, "Are you crazy? I'm not going to do that,"and turn and walk away. That is what we call rebellion. Nor does Saul say to Samuel, "Okay, I'll do it," and later not do it because it wasn't important to him. We might call that disobedience. I want you to be fully aware this morning that Saul gathers his armies and they go attack the nation of Amalek. Saul kills tens of thousands of men, women and children. As a matter of fact, I can be safe to say close to a hundred thousand men, women and children. He also kills thousands of animals—goats, sheep, oxen, etcetera. But, he spares the finest animals to give to the people so they could offer animal sacrifices to the Lord. Are you with me? Saul kills hundreds of thousands of people. But he does something. He spares one man. And that is the king of Amalek. Why does Saul do that? Because back then, whenever you conquered a nation, for you to take that king of that nation captive was like taking a living trophy. Are you with me? Every time you saw him as a slave in your palace, he reminded you of your victory over his nation. Are you with me?

Now Saul does all this and I want you to notice what God says to Samuel. Look at Verse 10: *"Now the word of the LORD came to Samuel, saying, 'I greatly regret that I have set up Saul as king, for he has turned back from following Me, and has not performed My commandments.'"* Now God later goes on to say he has rebelled. Are you with me? Listen carefully. Saul has done 99.9% of what he was told to do. When you kill all but one person that is 99.99%. Amen. But God says, "He's rebelled, disobeyed." So this shows us something right away: that partial obedience is not obedience at all. As a matter of fact, we can go on to say that partial obedience usually can end up being—and usually is—rebellion. Well somebody said, "Why didn't you look at everything I did do? Why did you have to look at the little I didn't do?" Have you ever heard somebody say that before? Especially kids. Are you with me? "Well look at all the room that I did clean up. Just don't look at the part that I didn't clean up." How many times have you heard that one? But listen to me carefully. God is not that way. God focused in on what Saul didn't do. Because God says, "Saul's not obeying me, even though he's done 99.9% of what he was told to do." Now I want you to notice what happens. Look at Verse 13: Samuel goes out to Saul the next day and Saul said to him, *"Blessed are you [with] the LORD. I have performed the commandment of the LORD."* Now would you look up at me? Saul sees Samuel coming out the next day after this campaign, this war. And Saul goes running to Samuel and says, "Praise God, Samuel! I have done everything I was told to do." Well, that's not what God said to Samuel the night before is it? So how do we account for the difference of opinion here? God says he's rebelled, and Saul believes with all of his heart he's obeyed. The answer is found in our Scripture that we've brought up time and time again. James 1:22. "Let's be doers of the word, not hearers, deceiving your own selves." Deception is when you really believe with all of your heart you're right. When in reality, in God's eyes, you're wrong. A person deceives himself. The reason Saul believes with all his heart he really obeyed is because he did not obey the Word of God. He was deceived. Deception entered into his life. Are you with me?

Now when deception enters into our lives—I want to read to you straight from the book. "At this point the person may fall away from any semblance of godliness or, more frequently, they continue with a form of godliness but live religiously under the curse of the knowledge of good and evil." That's what usually happens, folks. When people get into a pattern of disobedience. Now let me say this very carefully—this was a pattern in Saul's life. This is not the first time he disobeyed. But you go back and you'll notice that he had a pattern of it. And I have found that every time you disobey, what happens is that a veil goes over your heart and the veil is called deception. Do you remember the first time you

sinned by, let's say, speaking out against somebody? And the moment you spoke out against that believer, you felt like a knife hit your gut? Remember that? Right? Your heart was tender to the Holy Spirit. Right? You felt like a knife. Well, what I'm saying is right, it's true, it's accurate. Well, you can be 100% right, but be wrong. Are you with me? So a veil over your heart is called deception. Right? Then what happens? You speak about somebody again and now you don't feel a knife, you feel a pinch. Are you with me? But you go, "But I'm right." So another veil goes over your heart. Then the next time you speak about somebody you don't feel a pinch, you feel a tingle. But you go, "But I'm right." Another veil goes over your heart. Then the next time you speak about somebody you don't feel a tingle, you don't feel a pinch, you don't feel a knife, you don't feel anything. What's happened? Your conscience is now seared. When you sear something it is beyond feeling. Are you with me? At that point you are seared and God will have to send a messenger to you, and usually it is a prophetic messenger. It could be a prophet, it could be a pastor, a teacher, or it could be a friend. And they will come and help you see the error of your ways. That is why James says, "Let anyone who has wandered from the truth and somebody who has come and shown him the way, he has saved that person from a multitude of sins." Are you with me?

What I have noticed is that God has a three-step process. First of all, he tries to get your attention in your conscience. But if you have repeated disobedience, after disobedience, after disobedience, what happens is he has to send a messenger to you. If you don't listen to the messenger, then judgment comes. Remember what David said, "Before I was afflicted, I went astray." Let me tell you something. Hardship will come to people's lives; affliction will come to people's lives because of not obeying. Are you with me? It is not God that does it. He has protected me and loved, and you will see what happens is you are now a target for the enemy. Are you with me? And we are going to see that clearly. But what happens is people—most of the time—still have a form of godliness. They still come to church. And now they are living on the letter of the law. They are living based off of the principle of reasoning, not off the principle of obedience. Are you with me?

So listen to what else I've said in the book. "His sense of right and wrong is now drawn from a source other than the Word of God breathed by the Holy Spirit into their hearts. They live by the deceived dictates of their hearts. It could be the letter of the Scripture which kills or it could be with what society deems as right and wrong. Either way they are out of touch with the living God. Now the only way they can be reached is by God sending a prophetic messenger to them." Are you seeing this?

Samuel is that prophetic messenger for Saul. Samuel comes and basically confronts Saul. And you know what Saul does? He says, "But I have obeyed." And Samuel says, "Then what's the bleating of the sheep? And what's the lowing of the oxen I hear?" And Saul says, "But it's the people, it's the people. They wanted to offer a sacrifice to God." Now let me tell you when you're in real trouble. When you believe you can serve God through your rebellion— that's when you're in big trouble. I don't care if you can find it from the Bible. Saul could have found that from the Torah. And he could have said, "But Samuel, I'm doing exactly what Moses said to do." *He did not obey God.* Let me tell you. I have learned that people find what they want to find in the Scriptures. And that is how they enter into perverted lifestyle—because perverted means twisted. And that is when you take what God says and you twist it to your own advantage. I have the Spirit of God speak this to me one day. He said, "Son, do you know what a religious spirit is?" And I've learned that whenever God asks me a question, He's not looking for information. Are you with me? In other words— some of you are not getting it, I'm seeing your faces—God was not looking for me to go, "Yes, I know what a religious spirit is. It's this and this and this." "Oh, John, thanks I really needed to know that." Now when God asks you a question, He asks

you that question because you don't know the answer. Now I've written on it, I've preached on it, I've heard other men preach on it, I've read other men's writings on it. When God spoke to me that few years ago and said, "Do you know what a religious spirit is?" I real quick said, "No, I don't know." And the Lord spoke to me. As soon as I said, "Lord, I don't know." He said, "Son, a religious spirit is one who uses My work to execute his own desires." I will never forget that. And immediately Saul came to mind. Saul won favor with the people. He gave them those animals. And while they're offering those animals, I'm sure those people are going, "Wow! What a godly king we have. He always puts Jehovah first. He got that king so he could have a trophy in his house." Are you with me?

So Samuel confronts him, "What's the bleating of the sheep?" And Saul says, "The people . . . ", and Samuel says, "Wait a minute—*you* Saul." He backs right into the corner with the Word of God. And then finally watch what happens. Look at Verse 22: *"So Samuel said, 'Has the Lord great delight in burnt offerings and sacrifices, as in obeying the voice of the* Lord?'" Everybody say, "Obeying." "Obeying." *"'Behold, to obey is better than sacrifice.'"* Can you say, "Amen"? "Amen." Now watch this. Verse 23: *"'For rebellion is as the sin of witchcraft.'"* Now those of you with the King James Version and the New King James Version will you notice please with me that in this verse, verse 23, the words *is* and *as* are in italic type. Do you see that? So rebellion *is as, is as* in italic type, the sin of witchcraft. The reason they are in italic type is because they do not appear in the original text. The translators added it for clarity. However, I went back to the interlinear Bible, I went back to the books that have every single Hebrew word with every English word above it and I found out that this is not an accurate translation. Now let me tell you the accurate translation. Are you ready for it? "The rebellion is the sin of witchcraft." Now it's one thing to be like witchcraft, it's a completely different thing to be witchcraft. Now to get an understanding of this the Hebrew word there for witchcraft is the Hebrew word *qesen.* And I went back and studying out this word and I found out that this word doesn't really implicate a kind of occultic practice. What it really indicates is the goal or the effect of witchcraft. Now listen to me carefully. What is the goal of witchcraft? To control. Let's look at an extreme case. Why does a witch put a curse on somebody? She wants to control their life through demonic power. The goal of witchcraft is to control. What God is saying here is rebellion is to be controlled. Are you seeing this? Now this can operate even with people being totally unaware of it or with people in occultic practices or Satanists being totally aware of it. Are you with me?

Now listen. A few years ago, my wife and I came into a hotel room after a meeting one night. We flipped on the television and we were on one of the major networks, either NBC, CBS or ABC. And they were having a special on Satanism. Now when I saw that I went to turn the channel because I don't care to get any information about spiritual warfare outside of the Bible. That's just me personally. But the Holy Spirit checked to me. And it felt like the Lord said, "Watch this." They were talking about the number one commandment of the Satanic Bible. Does anybody here know what it is? Did anybody come out of the occult? What's the number one commandment? That's exactly right. The number one commandment of the Satanic Bible is, "Do what thou will."

If I remember, when they said that I screamed on the inside of me. That's a perversion. What did Jesus say? He said "I did not come to do My will but the will of Him who sent Me." And then when I was a youth pastor, we had a lot of occultic practices in the area where I lived. We had a town right outside of San Diego called Casadega. Which means house of the devil. And they had seances there, and witches and warlocks, and all this other stuff over there. So there were a lot of kids who dabbled in the occult in our high school when I was youth pastor. And a lot of them would come into our youth services and were getting saved. So we started interviewing them and we found out something. When these kids joined witches' cults, you know what their leaders

tell them to do? The first thing they tell them to do is to drink, take drugs, commit illicit sex with one another, and steal. They tell them to break all the laws of God, society and of their parents. And they teach them, "The more you rebel, the more power you get." Well isn't that true? Rebellion is witchcraft. Rebellion is to be controlled. Rebellion opens up the door legally and gives Satan access. They do it because they want more power. However, it works either way.

Listen to what the Bible says. Second Peter 2:19, New Living Translation. *"They (those leaders want leaders who encourage insubordination) promise freedom."* But listen to this. *"But they themselves are slaves to sin and corruption, for you are a slave to whatever controls you."* Romans 6:16, The Living Bible. *"Don't you realize that you can choose your own master? You can choose sin or else obedience. The one whom you offer yourself, he will take you and be your master and you will be a slave."* Listen to me, folks. What we live speaks louder than what speak. You can confess, "I'm a Christian," until you're blue, pink, yellow, in the face, but until you live it, your lifestyle speaks louder than what you speak. That is why Jesus comes along and says, "Most assuredly"—John 8:34— "Most assuredly, I [think] whoever commits sin is a slave of sin." Why? He opens up the door, the demonic power gets legal access into his life. Are you here?

Samuel warns Saul, correct? He warns him. But Saul doesn't heed. He doesn't truly repent from his heart. Why? Because Saul says, "I have sinned, but yet now honor me." In other words, he's more concerned about being embarrassed than he is he hurt the heart of God. And you know what the Bible says right after this? The Bible says, "The Spirit of the Lord lifted and an evil spirit came." That door was opened and that evil spirit came into his life and he caused Saul—look, Saul had done things he never would have done in his own right mind. If you would have looked at Saul as a young man— Remember when he was humbled before he became king?—and you looked at him and said, "Saul, one day you're going to kill, you're going to murder in cold blood 85 of God's ministers, their wives and their children in cold blood." He would say, "You're crazy, I'd never do that." Yet he did it. That spirit, that sin, got access into his life and caused him to do things he never would have done in his right mind. If you would have looked at Cain when he was a young man and say, "Cain, one day you're going to murder your brother." He would have said, "You're crazy." But what did Cain end up doing? He gave legal entrance to sin into his life.

Go to Numbers 23 please. Remember, we are talking about in these last two lessons the consequences of sin. Some people foolishly think that they can disobey God. And the temporary reward or benefit they get out of their disobedience will outweigh the consequence. I hope that after you did these last two sessions you will say it will never outweigh it again. And you will never ever have a desire to disobey willfully again. I'm hoping it puts the fear of God in you. We need the love of God and we need the fear of God. Can you say, "Amen"? "Amen." The love of God makes me want to run and jump in his lap. The fear of God has me approaching his throne with trembling and also staying as far away from disobedience as I can. Are you with me? We need them both.

Numbers 23—are you there? Let me tell you what's happening here in Numbers 22, 23 and 24. There is a man—two men—in these chapters again that are major figures. The first guy's name is Balaam. Everybody say, "Balaam." "Balaam." Balaam is a prophet, he is a prophet of Jehovah. As a matter of fact, his prophetic ministry was so powerful that it reached the ears of kings. One king in particular who knew about Balaam was a king named Balak. Everybody say, "Balak." "Balak." Now Balak was the king of the Moabites and also he ruled the Midianites as well. Now listen carefully. In Numbers 22 it opens up with Balak the king seeking to hire Balaam to come and curse Israel. Why? Because Moab and Midian were nervous. They knew Israel destroyed the most powerful nation in the world, Egypt. And now they [the Israelites] were camped on

Moab's plains and they [the Moabites and Midianites]were concerned that what they did to Egypt they were going to do to Moab and Midian. So the king says, "I've got a brilliant idea. I will hire this prophet because I know whoever he blesses is blessed and whoever he curses is cursed. I will have him come and curse this people." Are you with me? So Balaam consents and he comes. The next morning they go up to the high places of Moab and Balaam says to the servants of king Balak. "I want you to build seven altars." They built seven altars. Balaam goes and opens up his mouth to give the oracle, and what he does, he ends up blessing Israel and not cursing it. King Balak goes nuts, he says, "What are you doing?" Balaam says, "Maybe we need to go higher." So they go another level higher. So he builds seven more altars and he opens up his mouth to curse and he blesses. The king gets furious, "What are you doing?" "Well maybe we need to go higher." Now this goes on for four levels. And each level he blesses them. I want you to hear what he says on the second level. Look at Numbers 23:23. This is one of his oracles. He says, *For there is no sorcery"*— Everybody say, "No sorcery." "No sorcery"— *"against Jacob, Nor any divination against Israel."* Now can I communicate that in today's words? There is no witchcraft against the Church, nor is there any divination against God's people. Let the witches chant their chants, burn their candles, do whatever they want, they cannot touch the Church of the living God. Amen. Amen.

Proverbs 26:2 says, *"Like a fluttering sparrow or a darting swallow, an undeserved curse does not come to rest."* Listen to what David says in Psalm 64:7-8. David is talking about people who put curses on him. He said that *"God shall shoot at them with an arrow; Suddenly they shall be wounded, So [God] will make them stumble over their own tongue."* Alleluia. That's why Balaam in one of his oracles, Numbers 23:8, says, *"How shall I curse whom God has not cursed?"* Are you with me? He could not curse them. Now listen. He goes up four levels and basically tells the king, "I can't curse when God's blessed." The king of Moab is furious, right? And so the king looks at Balaam and says, "You know what? I was going to give you a lot of money. But you're not getting a dime. Not even a penny," and he starts walking away furious, right? Now Balaam wants the money, right? So Balaam goes, "Wait, wait come back here." The king goes, "What?" And Balaam goes, "Listen, I can't put a curse on them, but I can tell you how to get them under a witchcraft curse." The king goes, "How?" Balaam said, "It's simple. Send your women into their kingdom, tell them to bring their idols. And when they begin to rebel and sin against God, they will come under a witchcraft curse. Because rebellion is witchcraft." See folks? Listen. Do you remember Jesus made the statement? Listen. Remember, Jesus made the statement. Revelation 2:14. Listen. He said that Balaam had taught Balak to *"put a stumbling block before the children of Israel, to eat things sacrificed to idols, and commit sexual immorality."* Listen to what Moses says in Numbers 31:16. Moses says, "Look, these women caused the children of Israel [to sin] through the counsel of Balaam, to trespass against the LORD in the incident of Peor." Everyone say, "The counsel of Balaam." "The counsel of Balaam." What he [Balaam] did was say, "Balak, I can't curse them. But I can tell you through counsel how to get them under a curse. Get them to sin. Get them to disobey."

Now his oracles are finished at the end of Numbers 24. Are you with me? The very last blessing that he gives Israel is after Numbers 24—it's between 24 and 25. He gives the counsel. Now look at 25:1. *"Now Israel remained in Acacia Grove, and the people began to commit harlotry with the women of Moab. They invited the people to the sacrifices of their gods, and the people ate and bowed down to their gods. So Israel was joined to Baal of Peor, and the anger of the LORD was aroused against Israel."* Wow, would you look up at me? Know what happens as a result of this? A plague breaks out. And this plague, this curse of a plague that breaks out is so powerful that you know how many people die? Twenty-four thousand people. Look at verse 9: *"And those who died in the plague were twenty-four thousand."* And would you look up at me please? Their disobedience

brought them under a curse right? Let's stop the curse. You may guess this. Radical disobedience started it, radical obedience stopped it. Look at verse 7: "Now when Phinehas who was the son of Eleazar, the son of Aaron"—in other words, this is Aaron's grandson— "the priest, saw it, he rose." Because what happened? Watch this, verse 6—let me let you see what's happening. *"And indeed, one of the children of Israel came and presented to his brethren a Midianite woman in the sight of Moses and in the sight of all the congregation of the children of Israel, who were weeping at the door of the tabernacle."* This guy flaunts his rebellion in front of Moses and the whole church. Right? Watch what Phinehas does, Aaron's grandson. Verse 7: *"Now when Phinehas the son of Eleazar, the son of Aaron the priest, saw it, he arose from among the congregation and took a javelin in his hand; and he went after the man of Israel into the tent and thrust both of them through, the man of Israel, and the woman through her body. So the plague was stopped among the children of Israel."* Radical obedience stopped the plague. And you know what God said about this young man? He said, "I will give him the covenant of my peace forever because he's radically obeyed me." Look at this—verse 10: *"Then the LORD spoke to Moses, saying:"* Verse 11: *"Phinehas the son of Eleazar, the son of Aaron the priest, has turned back My wrath from the children of Israel, because he was zealous with My zeal among them, so that I did not consume the children of Israel in My zeal. Therefore say, Behold, I give to him My covenant of peace; and it shall be to him and his descendants after him a covenant of an everlasting priesthood, because he was zealous for his God and made atonement for the children of Israel."* How did he make atonement? Through obedience. How does Jesus make atonement for us? Through His obedience. He was obedient to the point of death. Let me tell you something folks. God loves radical obedience. Why do you think God says, through the prophet Jeremiah, why do you think He says, "Where are those who have abolished the truth on the earth?" It's easy to go along with the crowd, it's another thing to stand out and obey authority. Let me tell you something. If you don't obey authority, you're going to be a minority today, not the majority. I'm talking about in the Church.

Galatians 3 please. Now Paul is writing here in Galatians 3. He is writing the church of Galatia. He is not writing the city of Galatia, correct? All right. Listen to what Paul says, Verse 1: *"O foolish Galatians! Who has bewitched you?"* Would you look up at me? Who has bewitched you? You know what bewitched means. It means brought you under a curse of witchcraft. Now look up at me. He's speaking to the Church. Somebody says, "I thought there's no witchcraft against the Church. There's no witchcraft to the obedient." That's right. Paul writes to this church and says the whole Church is under a curse of witchcraft. Look what he said, *"Who has bewitched you that you should not obey the truth, before whose eyes Jesus Christ was clearly portrayed among you as crucified?"* Would you look up at me?

This is a specific incident that gives us a universal truth. Are you with me? The specific incident is this: God had revealed, clearly revealed—Everybody say, "Clearly revealed." "Clearly revealed"—to this church that you have been saved by grace, not the works of the law. Now listen carefully to me. It's not what He has not clearly revealed to us but it's what He has clearly revealed to us: That we come under a curse if we don't obey. Are you with me? That we open that door if we don't obey. Here's what Paul is saying. The universal truth is this. What God clearly reveals to us is that we willfully disobey—that brings us under a curse. Why? Because we open up a door. Folks, Jesus made a statement. Let me say this to you. Jesus said in John 14:30. He said the ruler in this world comes. Listen. *"But he's found nothing in Me."* Why did he find nothing in Jesus? Because Jesus said in the next verse, *"As the Father has given Me a command so I do."*

Session Five

Does God Know Who Is in Charge?

*"Let every soul be subject to the governing authorities.
For there is no authority except from God, and the authorities
that exist are appointed by God. Therefore whoever resists the
authority resists the ordinance of God, and those who resist
will bring judgment on themselves."*
Romans 13:1–2

Summary for *Under Cover*, Chapter 8

Understanding and following God's direct authority is
usually something that can be recognized and obeyed.
However, following God's appointed authority is often
much more difficult for people. Scripture clearly indicates
that all authority on earth is delegated and appointed by
God. Why then does God appoint certain leaders that are
corrupt or even hostile to good people?

The plans and wisdom of God are beyond our
understanding, but we can know and believe that all things
work together for good. God allows corrupt leaders to gain
authority in order to carry out His will in people's lives.
Throughout history we can see the hand of God moving
through situations and events to bring people to
repentance and salvation. God never allows hardship to be
meaningless.

Today, our culture tells us to resist authorities that we
disagree with. The Bible however reminds us that humility

and longsuffering, even in the face of hardship, are the virtues of the Christian life. God wants to redeem us even if it means we have to face suffering. We can see numerous examples of godly men and women that suffered for their faith throughout scripture. Men such as Joseph and the apostles had to suffer so that God's will could be worked in their lives. There is so much we can learn from these examples if we are willing to humble ourselves and accept what it is God has given us.

> Not only Egypt, but the whole earth came to know of Jehovah as the true and living God. That knowledge was a direct result of His humbling the most powerful nation on the earth. God gave the nation wisdom through Joseph, which positioned it to be the greatest—only to later be defeated by Israelite slaves. The defeat had a much more profound effect on the watching world than if slaves had defeated a poor and weak, or even an average, nation. God made such an impression on the whole earth that after years of Israel's wandering in the desert, the nations still feared Him and trembled before Israel.
>
> John Bevere, *Under Cover*, p. 94–95.

Notes from Chapter 8 (Video Session 5)

_____

_____

_____

_____

_____

_____

Warm-Up Questions

1. Why is it often difficult for us to submit to an authority that we do not respect?

   _____

   _____

   _____

2. Why do you think God wants Christians to always maintain an attitude of humility and submission to authorities? What does this show the world?

   _____

   _____

   _____

3. In what ways have you seen God use difficult situations for good?

   _____

   _____

   _____

Teaching by John Bevere

Watch video session 5 after reading the review questions below.

Teaching Review

4. List the four divisions of delegated authority found in the New Testament:

   _____

   _____

   _____

   _____

5. What is the nonmilitary definition of the word "subject" found in Romans 13:1?
   To be subject is _____

   _____

   _____

   _____

6. Complete this sentence: When we oppose delegated authority, we are opposing

   _____

Exploring God's Word

Romans 13:1—2 *Let every soul be subject to the governing authorities. For there is no authority except from God, and the authorities that exist are appointed by God. Therefore whoever resists the authority resists the ordinance of God, and those who resist will bring judgment on themselves.*

7. Who is to be subject to authority?

   _____

8. Why is it important to understand that God raises up, or appoints authorities?

_____

_____

_____

9. How can our lives take on meaning and purpose with this proper understanding of authority?

_____

_____

_____

Personal Application

_____

_____

_____

Exodus 9:16 *But indeed for this purpose I have raised you up, that I may show My power in you, and that My name may be declared in all the earth.*

10. How does this verse confirm to us God's control over all things?

_____

_____

_____

_____

11. Why is it important for Christians to know that it is God and not Satan that controls those who are in authority?

_____

_____

_____

Personal Application

_____

_____

_____

> **Genesis 45:4–8** *"I am Joseph your brother, whom you sold into Egypt. But now, do not therefore be grieved or angry with yourselves because you sold me here; for God sent me before you to preserve life. For these two years famine has been in the land, and there are still five years in which there will be neither plowing nor harvesting. And God sent me before you to preserve a posterity for you in the earth, and to save your lives by a great deliverance. So now it was not you who sent me here, but God."*

12. How did Joseph's faith and belief in God help him to trust God no matter what situation he was in?

_____

_____

_____

_____

_____

_____

13. In what ways can the life of Joseph help us understand God's divine will in our lives?

_____

_____

_____

_____

Romans 11:33–34 *Oh, the depth of the riches both of the wisdom and knowledge of God! How unsearchable are His judgments and His ways past finding out! "For who has known the mind of the lord? Or who has become His counselor? Or who has first given to Him And it shall be repaid to him?"*

14. Why are God's ways unsearchable to us?

15. When you fail to understand God, how do you generally react?

Personal Application

1 Timothy 2:1–3 *Therefore I exhort first of all that supplications, prayers, intercessions, and giving of thanks be made for all men, for kings and all who are in authority, that we may lead a quiet and peaceable life in all godliness and reverence. For this is good and acceptable in the sight of God our Savior.*

16. According to this verse, how are we to pray for authorities?

_____

_____

_____

_____

_____

_____

_____

17. As we pray for those in leadership over us, how does God reward us in return?

_____

_____

_____

_____

Personal Application

_____

_____

_____

_____

Exposing the Truth

18. In the *Under Cover* seminar, John says, "If we learn to obey God, we will have no trouble recognizing God's authority in another. Are there times when we will have to choose between God's direct authority and His delegated authority? Yes! But not as often as most believers think . . . the issue here is that most Christians think obedience is the exception and personal free choice is the rule. Following this type of reasoning can lead us into a course of destruction." How can submission and obedience to authority spare us the pain of a wayward life?

_____

_____

_____

_____

_____

_____

_____

_____

_____

19. John also says, "We must remember God's priority is not for us to have the comforts and enjoyments of this world—His priority is redemption." How are people being deceived by our modern culture into believing God wants them to be prosperous more than righteous? What is happening to Christianity as a result of this?

_____

_____

_____

20. In *Under Cover* we read, "In His wisdom, He never allows suffering without purpose, even when we are not able to see the purposes at the time. However, eternity reveals them. In His goodness, He never allows harm to us within the scope of eternity." How can being eternally and spiritually minded enable us to deal with physical suffering here on earth? How does God use suffering to help us grow?

_____

_____

_____

_____

_____

> In His wisdom, He never allows suffering without purpose, even when we are not able to see the purposes at the time. However, eternity reveals them. In His goodness, He never allows harm to us within the scope of eternity. You may argue, "But harm, much harm, has come to people at the hands of corrupt leaders." This is true in the physical sense, yet God judges the spiritual world above the physical. Abel's death appeared vain, but it wasn't because his blood still speaks (Heb. 11:4). Thousands of Christians were put to death by corrupt leaders during the Inquisition and persecutions that preceded and followed, yet their blood was not shed in vain. Their blood still speaks.
>
> John Bevere, *Under Cover*, p. 97.

Applying the Lesson

The authorities in our churches are in a position to minister to those that are in need. They have the unique opportunity to bring meaning and purpose to people's lives. In what ways do you see your church teaching appropriately on authority?

_____

_____

_____

For you personally, having a correct attitude toward authority will bring blessings on your life. Evaluate your own attitudes on those in authority over you and, if necessary, list several ways you can improve your attitude to be more godly. Make these notes to yourself specific and practical.

_____

_____

_____

Checking Your Cover

End this session praying with the following themes. Ask God to:

Accurately reveal your attitudes toward authority.

Enable you to see God's ordinances in all authorities.

Have the humility and faith to see how all things work together for good.

Video Script for Lesson 5
Does God Know Who Is in Charge?

And I'd like us to go tonight to Romans 13 to our foundational Scripture. We discussed God's direct authority and the protection that is involved in it. Now listen to me carefully. Authority in the kingdom of God speaks of divine protection, it speaks of provision, and it speaks of His presence. Can you say, "Amen"? "Amen." Now tonight, I want to show you that His authority extends beyond Himself directly. God has delegated His authority and if you are in Romans 13, I want to read the first and second verse. Paul says under the inspiration of the Holy Spirit, *"Let every soul."* Everybody say, "Every soul." "Every soul." Now let's go through this again. Does that include you? Yes. That includes me, that includes every soul, amen. *"Let every soul be subject to the governing authorities. For there is no authority."* Now read these words like you have never read them before. There is absolutely no authority, no legitimate authority, *"except from God, and the authorities that exist are appointed by God. Therefore whoever resists the authority resists the ordinance of God, and those who resist will bring judgment on themselves."* Now notice he says, "Those who resist, resist the ordinance of God." God and His authority are inseparable. If you come to know God, you come to know authority because He and His authority are one in the same. Amen. And God so plainly says through the apostle Paul, and I want to make this clear— This was not written by a power-hungry preacher, it was not written by a pastor trying to beat people into submission—This was written under the inspiration of the Holy Spirit and I have found, and, listen, this is always true, God always speaks for our protection. Can you say, "Amen"? "Amen." God is not a child abuser. So when He gives commands that don't look so comfortable we've got to find the wisdom of God in them because there's always the wisdom of God which perfectly lines up with His character. And let me tell you something, folks, God is love. He doesn't have love, He is love. He is the very definition of it. Amen? Amen. So God says, whoever resists the authority resists the ordinance of God. In other words, to resist appointed authorities is to resist God Himself. This is usually where people start having a little problem.

Now before I go into those little problems, let me make this mention. This is a specific Scripture spoken about civil authorities. Let me say this to you. There are four areas of authorities that the New Testament speaks of. There are civil authorities; which is your governors, your mayors, the president, the congressmen, the king if you're in a kingdom, et cetera. Next is church authorities. We all are very familiar with church authorities. The apostle, prophet, evangelist, pastor and teacher are sent into the church by Jesus Himself. They carry His authority. Next is family authority which was the original. Before there was a church, before there was a civil authority, there was family authority. Amen. And we know that to be the husband is the head of the home, et cetera. And we talk about the wife and the children obey their parents and honor their parents. Next in the order is social authorities—what I like to call social. That's your jobs, your bosses, your teachers, coaches, et cetera. Are you with me? Now God says, *"Let every soul be subject to the governing authorities"*—even though He is specifically speaking about civil authorities in these verses. Most times when the Lord speaks about authorities in the New Testament, it transcends all four areas. In other words, the wisdom or the command will not only apply to the civil, but to the family, to the church, to the social as well. So that is the case with this verse as well. God says, "Every soul is to be subject because there is no authority except from God." Everybody say, "No authority." No authority except from God. Now right here is usually where walls begin to go up in people. In this verse, *"Let every soul be subject to the governing authorities."* Everybody say, "Subject." "Subject." The Greek word is hupotasso. It is a Greek military term meaning to arrange troop divisions in a military fashion under the command of a leader. And in nonmilitary uses this word was used to define a voluntary attitude of giving in, cooperating, assuming responsibility, and carrying authority. Now let me put it to you simply. Simply put, this word used in this verse, exhorts us to voluntarily place ourselves under submission to authority with the full intent of obeying him. Now, *"Let every soul be subject to the governing authorities, For there is no authority except from God, and the authorities that exist are appointed by God."* Everybody say, "Appointed." "Appointed." Appointed is the Greek word *tasso*. This word means to assign, ordain, or set. Now listen carefully. In no way does this word have a "by chance" implication, it is a direct appointment. So, are you getting the emphasis of what Paul is saying here? Authorities are specifically appointed by God and God expects us to submit to them with the full intent of obeying them. Amen.

Now as I've been trying to get to, this is where walls go up with a lot of people. Because they will go, "Well, we have seen leaders that are harsh and actually downright cruel. How can you tell me that our loving God, our loving Father could appoint leaders like that?" Well, in order to answer that question I want to go to an extreme case. I want to talk about a leader in the category of a Hitler or a Stalin. Because I don't know about you, but I can't think about two more cruel leaders in the past hundred years than Hitler and Stalin. Would you agree with me on that? I want to talk about somebody like that, so let's talk about this man named Pharaoh. Now Pharaoh was a man who beat the children of Israel—suppressed them and afflicted them and mistreated them to the point where they lived in slums. They had stripes on their backs and literally killed thousands of their babies—their men babies—when they were born. He was a man who was a murderer, he mistreated God's people and, as a matter of fact, I should say brutally treated them. Where did his authority come from? Well, if you go over one or two chapters, over

to chapter nine in the book of Romans. Look at the seventeenth verse. I want to read just the first half of the verse. *"For the Scripture says to the Pharaoh, 'For this very purpose I have raised you up.'"* Now this is a direct quote from Exodus 9:16 where Moses speaks about the Spirit of God to Pharaoh "for this [very] purpose I have raised you up." So there's your two witnesses and out of the mouth of every two witnesses, every word is established. Now, Pharaoh was raised up by God, but let's ask a question. How did Abraham's descendants get underneath him? Did you ever wonder about that? Well in order to look at that, we've got to go back to Abraham.

When God cut covenant with Abraham, and God did this in Genesis 12, God said to Abraham, "I want you to leave your family, depart and go to the land where I'm going to show you." Abraham was obedient, he left his family, and once God saw his obedience, (in Genesis 15) God came along and cut covenant with Abraham. When the covenant was being cut, the Spirit of God came on Abraham and God spoke to him and this is what he said. Genesis 15:13 and this is out of the New International Version. God says, *"Know for certain that your descendants will be strangers in a country not their own, and they will be enslaved and mistreated four hundred years."* Now the New King James Version says *"they will be enslaved and afflicted four hundred years."* Now I don't know about you but that's not a prophecy that I would to get too happy about. Abraham's son's name was Isaac and, as a matter of fact, if you look at his life in the book of Genesis you'll find out he's a very godly man. Isaac fears God. God gives him a godly wife and they have two sons. One's name is Esau and the other's name is Jacob, correct? God said about Esau, He said, "I hated him." And He said about Jacob, "I love him." Jacob has a little bit of a rough start because he is a little bit deceptive, but yet he has an encounter with God that could heal. And when he wrestles with God, God changes his name to Israel which means "prince with God." And you talk about a change in this man's life! He looks at his family, he tells his family, "Put away your idols, purify yourselves, we're going to go dwell at Bethel, the place I've met God," which means "house of God" in the Hebrew. He takes his family to Bethel and the Bible says the terror of God is upon them as they travel. He's a godly man, you do not see deceptiveness out of him anymore. Now Jacob, or Israel, has twelve sons. The eleventh son is the most godly son, his name is Joseph. Israel favors Joseph—gives him a robe of many colors—and Joseph's brothers don't like that. Now one night, Joseph goes to sleep and God gives him a dream and shows him he's going to be a leader, and, as a matter of fact, his brothers are going to serve him. He wakes up the next morning and shares with great excitement with his brothers his dream, but they don't share his enthusiasm. He goes to sleep again and has another dream. Now his brothers are just plum mad and want him gone. So he's coming out to see his brothers while they're feeding the sheep far from home. And when he comes, the brothers say, "Okay, this is the dreamer, this is Mr. Man with the call of God on his life. He's going to lead us. Let's kill him and see if he ever leads us." Nice brothers, huh? So you know what they do? They take him and they strip his robe and they throw him into a deep pit and they're going to let him starve to death in that pit. Now pit, for those of you who don't know, stands for Preachers In Training. Are you with me? So they've got Joseph in the pit, they're all happy about it now, but all of a sudden, a few hours later, a caravan of Ishmaelites is coming down the road to go to Egypt and do slave trading. Judah, the fourth born son says to his brothers, "Hey guys, what are we doing? Let's sell him, we'll make money off him. He'll be as good as dead if he's sold as a slave." Because if you're sold as a slave, your wife's going be a slave and your children are going to be slaves when you're sold to be a slave to another nation. Hence all the brothers say, "Great idea, let's get some money out of this." So they sell him, he's brought down to Egypt and he serves as a slave for ten years. Now ten years, he is faithful to God. We don't find any evidence of complaining, but yet something very bad begins to brew. The master Potiphar, who is an officer of Pharaoh's; his wife gets the hots for Joseph. She wants to commit adul-

tery. She begins to come to him not once, but daily, the Bible says, and I love the way this young man fears God. Every day he says, "No, no, no." Finally, she catches him by the robe one day when they're alone in the house. She's says, "Lie with me. Nobody will know it, we're alone." He said, "God forbid I sin against God and your husband," and he does what the Bible says. He flees sexual immorality. He is an obedient young man. I mean, listen, folks. No church, no brethren, nobody to fellowship with for ten years, and yet he's still obeying God like this. I love the way this man fears God. He runs from sexual immorality. The robe tears, he runs out of the house naked. She's a scorned woman and she screams, "Rape!" Now the very thing he's fleeing from, he gets thrown into the dungeon for. Now he's thrown into the dungeon, and, let me tell you, Pharaoh's dungeons are so much worse than our prisons today. Our prisons could be compared like country clubs to Pharaoh's dungeons. He's in that dungeon for over two years, yet we still don't find any evidence of complaining. Do you see how godly this young man is? Are you with me? He's in the dungeon and Pharaoh has two men, a butler and a baker, that are sent to prison. Both of these men have a dream. And in their dreams, God shows them specific things about themselves. They wake up and are very afraid about it. Joseph interprets by the Spirit of God their dreams. And exactly what he interpreted came to pass. The butler was restored, the baker lost his head. All right? Later, God gives Pharaoh a dream. Now, here's where it starts getting good and pay attention —this is where it really gets interesting. A little bit after this, God gives Pharaoh a dream. Pharaoh is troubled by this dream. None of his magicians can interpret it. But the butler says, "I remember this Hebrew boy in the dungeon. He interpreted my dream and it came to pass." Pharaoh said, "Make haste and bring him here." They bring Joseph before Pharaoh, Joseph interprets Pharaoh's dream. He says to Pharaoh, "God has given you this dream, and God is showing you what is about to come on the earth. There's going to be seven years of great harvest and then there's going to be seven years of famine." Pharaoh listens to Joseph and he realizes that this is the interpretation. And Joseph says to Pharaoh, "This is what you must do. Store up the grain. God is showing you this because you should store up the grain so that when the seven years of famine come you will have enough. Not only for you but for others." Pharaoh loves Joseph and makes him the second in command. The nation and world go through seven years of great harvest. Now listen carefully—The famine begins and when the famine begins, because the only one who had knowledge of the famine was Pharaoh, now all the nations of the world have to come to Pharaoh to buy grain.

Jacob, or Israel, who is godly, who is the covenant man of God, doesn't know the famine's coming. God didn't give the dream to Jacob. He gave the dream to Pharaoh because it was His way of doing two things. Number one: making Egypt the most wealthy, powerful nation in the world, and number two: causing Jacob to come to Pharaoh to have to buy. Because that would be the vehicle, he would get Abraham's grandchildren underneath Pharaoh's rule. Are you seeing this?

Now God makes Egypt the most powerful nation, because all of the nations are having to buy from them. Now eventually, two years into the famine, Jacob has to send his sons to Pharaoh to buy bread. When they come they meet up with Joseph, Joseph recognizes them but they have no idea it's Joseph. After two meetings, Joseph finally reveals himself to his brothers. When he does, his brothers are horrified because they think, "He's going to kill us."

I want you to go to Genesis 45 and I want to show you something. Look at verse 4. This is when Joseph reveals himself to his brothers. Genesis 45:4: *"And Joseph said to his brothers"*—Watch this—*"'Please come near to me.' So they came near. Then he said: 'I am Joseph your brother, whom you sold into Egypt. But now, do not therefore be grieved or angry with yourselves because you sold me here; for God sent me before you to preserve life.'"* Notice he said, "God sent me." For these two years the famine has been in the land and there are still five years in which there will be neither plowing nor harvesting. Now look at Verse 7: *"'And God sent me before you to preserve a posterity for you in the earth, and to save your lives by a great deliverance. So now it was not you who sent me here, but God.'"* Now you think, "All right, the guy is deranged. The dungeon obviously got to him, he's been out of church for too long. What do you mean God sent him there? Joseph was the most godly of all twelve sons. Do you mean to tell me that God would actually not only allow,, but plan Joseph to go through all that suffering of slavery for ten years, then a dungeon for over two years?"

Well let's see what the psalmist says. I'm going to read what Psalm 105:16–19 says. *"Moreover [God] called for a famine in the land."* Who called for a famine? God. *"He destroyed all the provision of bread."* He did it for a reason, he wanted to make Egypt the wealthiest nation in the world. *"[God] sent a man before them—Joseph—who was sold as a slave."* Now listen carefully. *"They hurt his feet with fetters. He was laid in irons. Until the time that his word came to pass, the word of the lord tested him."* Notice he was hurt with fetters and chains. Notice that it was God who sent him. Now folks, I've heard a lot of people try to walk around that one, but when I've got two witnesses, the psalmist and Joseph, both saying that God did it I'm going to have to believe it. Are you with me? Now why would God allow this godly young man to go through such suffering at the hands of authority? Well there's a reason in this. If you go to Exodus 9, go with me there, we're going to see it.

Exodus 9:16 says—this is the word of the Lord from Moses' mouth— "But indeed for this [very] purpose. Everybody say, "For this very purpose." "For this very purpose." *"I have raised you up, that I may show My power in you, and that My name may be declared in all the earth."* Folks look up at me. Up to that point, the only ones who knew who God was, were Abraham, Isaac, Jacob, and their descendants. What is the thing that Moses has said to God when God said, "Go command Pharaoh to let my people go"?

Moses said, "Who shall I say sent me?" Isn't that right? What is the first thing that Pharaoh said when Moses said, "Thus sayeth the Lord, 'Let my people go'"? Pharaoh said, "I don't know this God, who are you talking about?" Nobody knew who God was prior to this except for Abraham, Isaac, Jacob, and their descendants. Let me tell you something folks. When God got through destroying the most powerful nation in the world by a bunch of slaves, all the world knew that He was God. It first started out with Egypt. Once the plagues started, listen to what the Bible says in Exodus 9:20. It says about the Egyptians, it says, *"He who feared the word of the Lord among the servants of Pharaoh made his servants and his livestock flee to the houses."* Already some of the Egyptians are seeing He's God.

In Exodus 10:7, they were pleading with Pharaoh, the citizens of Egypt. Listen to what they said. *"Let the men go, that they may serve the lord."* Even the magicians of Egypt said to their king in Exodus 8:19, *"This is the finger of God."* Their newly found knowledge of Jehovah became quite evident as we read Moses was very great in the land of Egypt and in the sight of Pharaoh's servants and in the sight of the people. They greatly respected the people because Exodus 12:35 says, they gave them articles of silver and gold. The Egyptians gave to the slaves articles of silver and gold. You don't do that with slaves. Chapter 9: 27 even shows that Pharaoh finally said, *"The lord is righteous, and my people and I are wicked."* When God got through with Egypt, all of Egypt knew He was the Lord. But let me tell you, not only Egypt knew He was the Lord, but all the earth. Because folks, let me tell you something. Even after 40 years of walking aimlessly through the desert. When Joshua sent the two spies into the nation of Jericho, they went to a harlot's house who lived on the wall who's name was Rahab. And I want you to know what Rahab said to these men.

Rahab said in Joshua 2:9–11—write these verses down— *"I know that the LORD has given you the land, that the terror of you has fallen on us, and that all the inhabitants of the land are fainthearted*

because of you. For we have heard how the Lord dried up the water of the Red Sea for you when you came out of Egypt, and what you did to the two kings of the Amorites who were on the other side of the Jordan." And she goes on to say this. She says, *"As soon as we heard these things, our hearts melted; neither did there remain any more courage in anyone because of you, for the LORD your God, He is God in heaven above and on earth beneath."* This is a prostitute of a foreign nation, Jericho. She said, "The LORD your God, He's God on earth and God in heaven." What happened as a result? This prostitute gets saved. She ends up becoming the great-grandmother of David and her entire household gets saved. Now let me answer the question for you. Why would God allow His people to go through such suffering? This is what a lot of people, especially in the churches in America, do not know and understand and that is this. This is the point I've been getting to this entire lesson: God's first priority is not our comfort. It's not His first priority. His first priority is redemption. If we can get this in our spirits, does God want us to prosper? Absolutely. Does God want us to live in peace? Absolutely. Does God want us to live a life of joy? Absolutely. But His first priority is redemption. If you go to the Christians of the inquisition and you tell them—I'm talking about the ones that were martyred in Europe for their faith by wicked and corrupt leaders—If you tell them God's priority for their life is comfort and success they'll laugh you right out of the room. They spilled their blood but their blood was not spilled in vain. Their blood spoke and brought many into redemption. This is the thing we've got to settle into our spirits and I hope that this one lesson—I've taken this whole time on this one lesson just to get this point across and that is this: God knows who He appoints. And any position of leadership, God is never taken by surprise by any appointed leader. He knows who has been appointed because He plans it. And this is the kind of thing we've got to understand. He is always way ahead of what's happening. It may not make any sense to us at the time we're going through it. Just like it made absolutely no sense for the children of Israel to be enslaved for four hundred years. And let me tell you something, it meant redemption for many of the nations in the world because all of the world knew he was God. Are you with me?

If you look in the Bible you will find out that the apostle Paul makes a statement to us which I think a lot of people sometimes avoid and that is this. It's found in the book of Romans. He says, "Therefore God has mercy on whom He has mercy and He hardens whom He wants hardened." *"Oh, the depth of the riches of the wisdom and knowledge of God! How unsearchable are His judgments and His ways past finding out! 'Who has known the mind of the LORD. Or who has become His counselor?'"* Now listen to this statement. "But who are you oh man to talk back to God?" Paul makes it so clear that God's wisdom sometimes comes to a place where it's beyond finding out at the moment. There are times in which God will reveal what His wisdom is in a situation and there are other times when God says, "I expect you to take Me by the hand and walk through this knowing that I'm going to lead you to a good place." Would God ever allow any harm to come on any of His people? No, but you must remember He does not look at harm in the physical sense, He looks at harm in the spiritual sense. Not one of those believers that spilled their blood in the inquisition were harmed spiritually. As a matter of fact, they were refined and are gloriously in His presence right now. However, they did experience harm physically. And they experienced harm in the hands of leaders.

Folks, I need to make this clear to you tonight. We can affect leaders over us by the fact of our prayers and humility. Paul says in 1 Timothy 2:1–2, "I exhort the prayers, supplications, petitions, and thanksgivings He made for all men and for those who are in authority." For kings, why? So that we might live a quiet and peaceable life in all godliness and honesty. Our prayers, the prayers of the Church, can affect leadership over us to the point where it can even affect their appointment. I believe that the appointment of the President of the United States in this last term was because America got down and

prayed. But now listen carefully to me, it's not always the case. Because if you look at the apostles, nobody prayed like them. But let me tell you, they had some wicked kings over them. There was a king named Herod Agrippa. Now you've got to understand there were many Herods. Herod was a title given to these kings that were over the land of Samaria and Judea. Herod Agrippa was the king who was king when Peter and James were arrested and when James had his head cut off. Are you with me? Herod Agrippa was a very, very political man. He helped Claudius get into office. After Caligula was murdered, he helped Claudius get into office. He was a very political man and when he got into office Claudius rewarded him for what he had done by giving him more land. And so he had more territory than anybody except for Herod the Great, his great-grandfather. However, when he got into office, he saw that there was a division between the Jews and the Christians. And he, being a political man, picked the majority—he picked the Jews. So what he did, he went out and arrested James to make the Jews happy. And you know what he did? He cut his head off. Was the Church godly? Yes. Was the Church praying? Yes. But then the Church really started praying once he did it, because he arrested Peter and was going to do the same thing to Peter. Are you with me? But because of the Church praying, God sent an angel and delivered Peter out of the prison. Isn't that right? Herod got up a few days later and allowed the people to call him a god and he was eaten by worms. Was he a wicked leader? Absolutely. Was he judged by God? Absolutely. Was Pharaoh judged by God? Absolutely. But listen to what the Bible says right in that chapter when he cut off James' head. *"The word of God grew and multiplied [greatly]."* You see folks, when we get that into our spirit that God has got a plan, that he never allows any leader in your life over you by accident, then we will be free and we'll be able to seek God and see the counsel and the focuses of God in the things we're going through, instead of complaining like the children of Israel.

Session Six

Honor the King

Honor all people. Love the brotherhood. Fear God.
Honor the king.
1 Peter 2:17

Summary for *Under Cover*, Chapters 9 and 10

We read many times in the gospels that we are to practice honor and submission to those in authority over us. Christ taught His disciples, and they in turn taught those they ministered to, to live a life of reverence and humility. For us today, this message should still be in practice as we, too, live under authorities ordained and appointed by God.

The difficulty we face daily is the cynicism and self-centeredness of our culture. No one is respected. No one is taken seriously. We have leaders that blatantly corrupt the offices with which they are entrusted. It is easy for the Christian to become cynical and lose the respect for authority that Christ has commanded us to have. How then should we as Christians think about and respond to authorities? We should continually remind ourselves that God has ordained each leader for the position they are in.

It is the fundamental fear of the Lord that breeds honor in a person's life. No matter what the actions of a leader may be, we are to maintain a fear and respect for God's authority and for those on whom He places leadership. Our culture praises those that are able to slander or criticize our leaders. Christians must resist this behavior if we are to be a light in this world. God has called us to a higher calling; one that isn't influenced by what we see and hear, but by our faith in the Lord Jesus Christ.

This mentality and spirit of reverence and humility begins in our homes, our churches, and in our schools, as we raise children to know and understand respect and honor for God and authority and carry it throughout their lives. Our society will then be transformed by people that have been shaped by the fear of the Lord.

Many times we are guilty of having a critical spirit when it comes to authority. God wants us to be renewed in our minds and understand that He is the creator and sustainer of life and that all authority rests in Him. As we begin to live in the fear of the Lord, we become witnesses to His wisdom and love for all mankind.

Notes from Chapters 9 and 10 (Video Session 6)

_____

_____

_____

_____

_____

_____

_____

_____

_____

I've heard numerous believers gripe about the taxes they pay. I've met people in churches who have figured out ways of not paying taxes. They claim it is their constitutional right. To them, I argue, "Your exhortation from God supersedes your supposed constitutional right. God says to 'pay taxes.'" I then say to these people, "Who is paying for the roads you drive on? Who is paying for the policemen, firemen and lawmakers who protect you?" I have listened as accountants tell me how believers cheat on their taxes by trying to cut corners. It is heartbreaking. I told our accountants, "I don't want any gray areas; I don't want to cut corners." Paying taxes is an opportunity to give back to the government that serves us. We can't be stolen from if we choose to give! When are we believers going to revel in this truth?

John Bevere, *Under Cover,* p. 109 - 110.]]

Warm-Up Questions

1. How have you been taught to honor and respect those in authority?

   _____

   _____

   _____

2. Write down the first thought that comes to mind for each of the following:

   The President _____

   Police officers _____

   Your father _____

   Your pastor _____

3. Looking at your answers to the previous question, explain why you feel the way you do about these authority figures.

_____

_____

_____

Teaching by John Bevere

Watch video session 6 on the tape.

Teaching Review

4. Define the word *honor*. To *honor* is to

_____

_____

_____

5. In what ways does the fear of the Lord breed honor in a person's life?

_____

_____

_____

_____

6. According to 1 Timothy 2, what are the three actions Christians are to take concerning leaders?

_____

_____

_____

_____

7. When a person bestows honor on their parents, what two blessings does God promise?

_____

_____

_____

8. To whom are we to give "double honor?"

_____

_____

_____

Exploring God's Word

Ephesians 6:5–8 *Bondservants, be obedient to those who are your masters according to the flesh, with fear and trembling, in sincerity of heart, as to Christ; not with eyeservice, as men-pleasers, but as bondservants of Christ, doing the will of God from the heart, with goodwill doing service, as to the Lord, and not to men, knowing that whatever good anyone does, he will receive the same from the Lord, whether he is a slave or free.*

9. Why is it important that we sincerely obey the authorities placed over us?

_____

_____

_____

_____

_____

_____

10. When we honor and obey an authority, who are we truly obeying and honoring?

_____

_____

Personal Application

_____

_____

_____

1 Peter 2:13–17 *Therefore submit yourselves to every ordinance of man for the Lord's sake, whether to the king as supreme, or to governors, as to those who are sent by him for the punishment of evildoers and for the praise of those who do good. For this is the will of God, that by doing good you may put to silence the ignorance of foolish men—as free, yet not using liberty as a cloak for vice, but as bondservants of God. Honor all people. Love the brotherhood. Fear God. Honor the king.*

11. According to this verse, what is the will of God?

_____

_____

_____

_____

_____

12. How does God want us to use our freedom?

_____

_____

_____

_____

_____

13. By following this submission to authority, what will be accomplished?

_____

_____

_____

_____

Personal Application

_____

_____

_____

Isaiah 11:3 *His delight is in the fear of the LORD, And He shall not judge by the sight of His eyes, Nor decide by the hearing of His ears.*

14. When we delight ourselves in the Lord, how does our perception change?

_____

_____

_____

_____

_____

_____

_____

_____

15. Why is it dangerous for us to judge out of our own understanding and reasoning?

_____

_____

_____

_____

_____

Personal Application

_____

_____

_____

1 Timothy 5:17–18 *Let the elders who rule well be counted worthy of double honor, especially those who labor in the word and doctrine. For the Scripture says, "You shall not muzzle an ox while it treads out the grain," and "The laborer is worthy of his wages."*

16. Why is it important for Christians to be especially respectful to authorities in the Church?

_____

_____

_____

_____

_____

_____

17. According to this verse, how are laborers in the Church to be taken care of?

_____

_____

_____

_____

_____

_____

_____

Personal Application

_____

_____

_____

John 13:20 *Most assuredly, I say to you, he who receives whomever I send receives Me; and he who receives Me receives Him who sent Me.*

18. How does this verse clearly portray God's ordinance in the authority of the Church?

    _____

    _____

    _____

Personal Application

_____

_____

_____

Exposing the Truth

19. In *Under Cover,* John writes, "It is difficult to submit to delegated authority if we have yet to encounter the authority of God. The harder we try to obey, the harder it becomes if we fail to see true authority." List several areas of your life in which you have surrendered authority to God and describe what you have learned from this submission:

Area	*Lesson Learned*
_____	_____
_____	_____
_____	_____

20. Again in *Under Cover,* John writes, "Those who fear God are those who keep before them the Lord of Glory's high and lofty position. They have met with and been consumed by His far-reaching authority. They esteem what He esteems and hate what He hates. Firmly implanted within their lives are reverential fear and respect for all in leadership because God has His delegated authority." How has modern Christianity been affected by the loss of an appropriate fear of God? In what ways can we say we esteem what God esteems and hates what God hates?

_____

_____

_____

_____

21. John goes on to say, "Many times God will send us what we need in a package we don't want. This very presentation will manifest the true condition of our heart, exposing whether we are submitted to His authority or resistant to it." How has this truth been made manifest in the struggles of your own life? How were you able to overcome your resistance?

_____

_____

_____

_____

God actually promises a child two distinct blessings when he honors his parents. First, it goes well with him. A person who does not honor his parents cannot count on life going well for him. He is under a curse.

The second promise is a long life. What a benefit for honoring your parents! You may think, *Wait a minute. I've known children who honored their parents, yet died young.* I know for sure that the Word of God says this is the first command with a promise. We get in trouble when we allow what we see around us to negate the promises of God. Consider this: our Father promises complete freedom from fear to those who are His. In His words, "In righteousness you shall be established; You shall be far from oppression, for you shall not fear" (Isa. 54:14). Yet precious Christians live in fear. If the promises were automatic, why do so many live under this torment? The answer to this questions is: they are received through prayer and won by the good fight of faith.

John Bevere, *Under Cover*, pp. 110–111.]]

Applying the Lesson

Learning to honor those that God has placed in authority over us can be a difficult task. Consider people that are in authority over you in the four areas of delegated authority. List their name and describe your attitude toward that person:

Social _____

    My attitude _____

Family_____

    My attitude _____

Church _____

    My attitude _____

Civil_____

    My attitude _____

As you consider your attitude, pray that God will enable you to see His divine ordinance on that person and enable you to honor them for the Lord's sake.

> I have been in developing world nations and nearly wept when I saw the way the churches treated me. Monetarily, it may have been small by American standards, for I'd received much larger offerings at some of the churches that were indifferent in America. What touched me the most was the love behind the gift of these grateful people. It was no different from the widow Jesus said gave more than all the rest, even though the amount that she gave was the least. She honored God with her gift. These precious saints honor and appreciate the servants God sends to them. Let this permeate your heart. Seek to honor the men and women who labor among you in the Word of God.
>
> John Bevere, *Under Cover,* p. 127.

Checking Your Cover

Conclude this session in prayer, asking the Lord to:

help you see His authority

humble your heart to be able to honor those in authority.

Video Script for Lesson 6
Honor the King

First Peter 2:13, are you there? Peter says, *"Therefore submit yourselves to every ordinance of man."* Everybody say, "Every ordinance." *"Of man for the Lords's sake, whether to the king as supreme, or to governors, as to those who are sent by him for the punishment of evildoers, and for the praise of those who do good."* Verse 15: *"For this is the will of God, that by doing good you may put to silence the ignorance of foolish men."* Verse 16: *"As free, yet not using liberty as a cloak [of wickedness], but as bondservants of God."* Verse 17—very important verse: *"Honor all people. Love the brotherhood. Fear God. Honor the king."* Everybody say, "Honor the king." The king is the one who is in authority over you. In specific terms, the king that Peter is talking about there is the king who actually beheaded James. Are you with me? Now, I want to get to a point here. How in the world can you honor a guy like Herod Agrippa I, who killed the apostle of the Lord just to win favor from people? The only way you can do that is to see beyond the man and see the authority on the man. There is where many believers miss it. What they do is they will submit to authority if they like their personality, if they like their leadership style. In other words, as long as that leader's treating me nice I'll be submissive to him and I'll honor him. But if he doesn't treat me the way I like to be treated, I'm not going to give pastor the time of day. You really don't fear God unless you submit to authority. You can tell me all day long until you're blue in the face, "I fear God," but if you don't submit to authority you don't fear God. Because you don't even respect the authority of those delegated standing right in front of you, that you can look at and touch in the flesh. How can you tell me that you fear God whom you don't see then? Now, notice he says, "Honor the king." The Greek word for honor there is the Greek word *timao*. And this is what it means to honor, to hold in honor, to revere, to venerate. It is the exact same Greek

word that Jesus used in John 8:49 when He said, *"I honor my father."* Are you with me? Webster's *Dictionary* says this word means "to revere, to respect, to treat with deference and submission and to perform relatives duties to." You got it? Are you getting that, getting a hold of it?

Now, I had a heartbreaking interview about a year ago. I was on a radio interview program in a very large city in the southern part of the United States. We were talking about one of my books. And I remember this radio interviewer—it was a live program. We talked for about twelve minutes and then we went into a station break. Now when we went into the station break it was like the volume went down a level. I remember that they were doing commercials and then this man comes on and starts talking about the weather and he said it's going to be so cold in this particular northern state that it's going to freeze the governor's lips so he can't open up his mouth to say anything stupid. Now I couldn't believe what I had just heard and I'm sitting there going, "This is a Christian radio station, right?" You know because these people that have me do interviews always send me these sheets and maybe I thought this isn't a Christian radio station. But then I covered myself with the thought maybe this is piped in by the UPI or the AP or somebody like that. And I thought, "You know, it can't be, it just can't be the guy on this radio station." And so I remember that when the guy came back on we went back to talking about this book and I was answering him about having the heart of God. And I said, "Like in this situation like just happened in the break." Now mind you this is live radio. I said, "Like what just happened in the break." I said, "Now this is a Christian radio station, right?" And he goes, "Yes." I said, "Well, obviously this announcement must have been piped in, but this is not having the heart of God. When you speak about a governor, one of the 50 governors of the United States, about not being able to open up his mouth and saying something stupid." I said, "Now this is not having the heart of God, if somebody had the heart of God they would speak with respect about this man. Even though his behavior in life probably doesn't deserve respect." And the man said, "The person who made that statement was me." And I said, "Okay." And he said, "But you know what? There's nothing wrong with having a little bit fun." I said, "Not at the expense of what God tells us to honor." I said, "God says, 'Don't speak against the ruler of your people.'" I said, "We must honor what God honors and not at the expense of Him are we going to be making fun." And I thought, "How many thousands of people are affected by this man's irreverence towards authority? Is he releasing the character of Christ or is he furthering the mystery of lawlessness?" That's what kept going through my spirit.

You see folks, let me tell you something. The Bible says in Isaiah 11:2–3 about Jesus, *"The Spirit of the LORD shall rest upon Him, The Spirit of wisdom and understanding, The Spirit of counsel and might, The Spirit of knowledge and of the fear of the LORD."* Now listen to this. *"His delight is in the fear of the LORD, And He shall not judge by the sight of His eyes, Nor decide by the hearing of His ears."* That is speaking about Jesus. Out of the fear of the Lord, Jesus did not judge by the sight of the eyes or the hearing of the ears. So when you see the authority of God on somebody, you respect that and you don't judge by the seeing of the eyes and the hearing of the ears. This is the way Jesus was.

Second Peter 2:10–11 says, *"God is especially hard"*—(this is out of the New Living Translation)— *"especially hard on those who follow their own evil lustful desires and who despise authority."* Everybody say, "Despise authority." "Despise authority." These people are proud and arrogant, daring even to scoff at glorious ones without so much as trembling. They lack the fear of God and they speak about people in authority as if they were nothing. This is not having the heart of God.

In the Bible we are told—let's go to Romans 13. I'm going to continue to read where we left off at verse 2. So let's read from verse 3. Paul says, *"For rulers are not a terror to good works, but to evil. Do you want to be unafraid of the authority? Do what is good and you will have praise from the same."* If you don't want a speeding ticket, don't speed. But if you get caught and he writes you a ticket, don't blame him. I've received a couple speeding tickets in the past seven or eight years. And you know those policemen when they pull me over they start writing the ticket and I let them write it out and they hand it to me. I say— you know I've done this with every one of them—I shook their hand and say, "Thank you, officer, for doing your job. I was guilty and I deserve this, and I appreciate the service that you give to our community." You should see their faces. As a matter of fact, the second to the last guy was a little bit kind of hard on me—excessively hard on me. And when I made that statement to him he softened up so much I could almost tell he almost wanted to take the ticket back. Now I didn't do that to get him to do that. I did that because I wanted to honor him. When God is in your heart, when Jesus lives in your heart, let me tell you, there is a respect for authorities. You want to be unafraid of them. Do what's right you won't have to worry about them. Watch this, verse 4. *"For He is God's minister."* Everybody say, "God's minister." "God's minister." That governor that radio talk show host made fun of—he's God's minister. That policeman is God's minister. Watch this. *"For he is God's minister to you for good. But if you do evil, be afraid: for he does not bear the sword in vain,"* that's talking about the ticket amongst other things. *"For he is God's minister, an avenger to execute wrath on him who practices evil. Therefore you must be subject, not only because of wrath but also [because of] conscience' sake. For because of this you also pay taxes, for they are God's ministers attending continually to this very thing."* Why do you pay taxes? To help God's ministers out. You like giving to your pastor don't you? You like giving to ministers don't you? Well guess what? They're ministers too. Verse

7: *"Render therefore to all their due: taxes to whom taxes are due, customs to whom customs, fear to whom fear, honor to whom honor."* You know there are actually Christians that I have met that have gotten out of paying their taxes? They have found a loophole and have stopped paying taxes. I had a conversation with one of those men and I said, "I want to ask you a question. Who's paying for the roads you're driving on? Who's paying for the President to make the decisions for your country? Who's paying for the military that's protecting your wife and children?" I said, "Why are you letting other people pay that?" "Well there's a loophole." I said, "So you just want to drive on those roads and have everybody else pay for you?" He didn't like that very much. You know I was in a church up in the state where the governor was being made fun of and the pastor was sharing with me that this church is experiencing a tremendous amount of growth. And every year I go back, this church gets huge. And the pastor was sharing with me—not the last time, but the time before that when I was with him—how that God put this Scripture in his heart. And he went to the city and found what the city's greatest need was. And what it happened to be was that they had a volunteer fire department and they needed one of those masks where the firemen could see through the smoke with that mask and find the victims and pull them out. But the mask was way ahead of their budget for that year, it was $25,000 for one mask. So this pastor went before his church and at that time they were only running about five or six hundred people. He went before his church and said, "Folks we need to minister to these guys. They are ministers attending to us, the city." And he said, "This is the greatest need of our city right now." So he said, "I want to take an offering. I want all of you to be able to give towards this mask." Do you know that he raised over $25,000 in that one offering? He took the check, went to the city, presented it to the city, and said, "You know what? We appreciate your service towards us. We appreciate you being ministers," and showed them with the Word of God where they were God's ministers. And he said, "We have gotten together and we've given you this check for $25,000, please go buy one of those masks." He said, "John, you wouldn't believe the way this has touched this city." He said, "These guys are so used to people griping about paying taxes." He said, "We chose not to gripe, we chose to give. Why pay taxes when you can give? And as a result, when we dedicated our new building, which was just about a year ago—John, you wouldn't believe the number of city officials that came to that service." And he said, "Now, many of them still attend this church regularly." They are literally touching that city just simply by honoring the authorities that God has put over them. How many times I've heard Christians complain about paying taxes. How many times I've heard them complaining about the police or the fire department or the about the mayor or about the governor, when really we have the opportunity to bless. What is really going to set us apart, folks, is when we choose to live above the standards of this world. Are you with me? Alleluia.

Now let me say this, this authority issue extends to every single authority area of the four levels. I want to show it to you. Go to Ephesians 6, it stars the family authority. I am going to go through a lot of Scripture here in this session. Ephesians 6:1 - 2, says, *"Children obey your parents in the Lord, for this is right."* Verse 2: "Honor." Everybody say, "Honor." "Honor." *"'Honor your father and mother,' which is the first commandment with a promise."* Man this is powerful, there's two promises actually. Number one: *"that it may be well with you."* And number two: *"that you may live [a] long [life] on the earth."* God guarantees and promises if children will believe and receive this promise, that a child who honors his parents two things. Number one is it will go well with you and number two you will live a long life. God promises you that you will not die prematurely if you honor your parents.

Deuteronomy 27:16 says, *"Cursed."* Everybody say, "Cursed." "Cursed." *"Cursed is the man who dishonors his father and mother."* Now what do you want—a blessing, a long life, a good life, or a curse? Take your pick. In speaking about social authorities—

Are you there? First Timothy 6:1 says this, *"Let as many bondservants"*—which say employees—*"as are under the yoke count their own masters [or bosses] worthy of all honor."* Everybody say, "All honor.' "All honor." Do you want to know how to really, really minister to your boss? Go honor him when he doesn't deserve it by his action. Go honor him just because he's your boss. Watch what happens to your job. See folks, this is what it means to be a Christian. This is what Jesus meant, if they want you to go a mile, go two. The Roman soldiers would say, "Take my horse one mile." And what Jesus said, "You want to live the way God lives, you want to walk in that kind of character? Just look at him and say you know what? You're not taking from me anything because I'm giving. I'm going to go a second mile. If they want your shirt, give him your coat. You're not stealing from me, I'm going to give this to you. That's when you enter into the high life." Are you seeing this?

Now as far as church authorities, what does God say? Look at 1 Timothy 5:17, *"Let the elders who rule well be counted worthy of double honor."* Everybody say, "Double honor." "Double honor." Isn't that powerful? God says to honor all the other areas but when it comes to church authorities give them double honor. Powerful isn't it? Why does God tell you to honor church authorities—for their sake? Yes, but more, much, much more so for your sake. Because when you honor the authorities that He sends into your life, you open up yourself to receive from Him.

There was a woman in the Bible named Hannah. Hannah had a husband named Elkanah. Now Hannah was barren, so Elkanah took a second wife named Peninnah. Peninnah was filling his house. Hannah may have filled his heart, but Peninnah was filling his house. She was barren, Peninnah was having kids all the time. Not only that, Peninnah was severely persecuting her rival, Hannah. Making fun of her because she wasn't having children. Every year they would go to Shiloh where the ark of God was, where Eli the priest was. And Elkanah would bring his two wives and Peninnah would have children and Hannah would have none. Hannah's heart was being broken. Not only that, she was constantly being persecuted and tormented by her rival. So Hannah one year goes to that place where Eli was and Hannah makes a vow to the Lord. She says, "God, if you give me a son, I will give him back to you. He'll be yours forever." She is praying so passionately that Eli, the head pastor, is sitting there watching her. And you know what he says to her? First Samuel 1:13–14 [Eli saw] her lips moving but, hearing no sound, he thought she had been drinking. And he said to her, "Must you come here drunk?" He demanded, "Throw away your wine!" Now, isn't this amazing? Hannah leaves the presence of her adversary Peninnah only to walk into a priest who calls her a drunk when she's really pouring her heart out to God. Now can you just imagine what many people would have done today if a head pastor said that to somebody who was praying? Can you imagine the thoughts, "He calls himself a man of God. Doesn't he realize that I'm fasting and praying and crying out to God? What kind of church is this?" That would probably lead to an outburst of, "You call yourself a pastor? Don't you realize that I'm praying? I'm leaving this church, I'm going to another place." Now can you just imagine that?

Let me show you the way Hannah responded to Eli, the man who called her drunk. The fifteenth verse says, "Oh no sir," she replied. "I am not drunk, but I am very sad and I was pouring out my heart to the Lord. Please don't think that I'm a wicked woman." So she actually takes it back on her, "For I have been praying out of anguish and sorrow." Isn't it amazing? She actually takes it back on herself. But she says, "No, I'm praying to God." Verse 17, Eli's response is, "In that case cheer up. May the God of Israel grant the request that you have asked Him." And you know what she says? And it says in the eighteenth verse. "Oh thank you sir," she exclaimed. Then she went back to eat again and she was no longer sad. You know what happened? That year she got pregnant and she gave birth within a year's time to the person who would bring revival to the whole nation. She birthed revival in her nation. And you know what amazes me is God used that insensitive priest to speak the words that brought her prayer to pass. "Go your way and may the God of Israel give you your request," he said. Because she honored him when actually his behavior didn't deserve honor, she received the thing that she was crying out for. That is why God says, "Give them double honor." He says it even more for your sake. Are you with me? Are you together with me?

Folks, let me tell you something, Jesus made it really clear. Now I'm going to say this, this may really hit some of you. He said in Matthew 7, he said, *"Many will say to Me in that day, 'Lord, Lord, have we not . . . cast out [devils] in Your name, and done many wonders in Your name.'"* And He's going to say, *"Depart from Me, I never knew you workers of iniquity."* We always look at the side of those people that are going to be turned away because of their iniquity. And have you ever thought about the flip side? Did you ever realize that those people really did cast out demons in Jesus' name and had ministry in Jesus' name? And that people really did receive genuine ministry from them. See folks, do you realize that when Jesus sent out his 12, he sent Judas? That Judas cast out devils and Judas healed the sick and he was one of the 12 that came back and rejoiced and said, "Even the demons are subject to us"? And do you know that Jesus knew that he was a demon? Because in John 6 he said, "Didn't I choose all 12 of you and yet one of you is a devil?"

Now let me make this clear. Scripture does make it clear to us that when a man has sin in his life, it's openly exposed. And what I mean by openly exposed is there are two or three witnesses that have evidence. And evidence doesn't mean here—say it means actual evidence that could hold up in a court of law. Because the Bible says, "Do not receive an accusation against an elder except by two or three witnesses." If something comes out into the open . . . Let's say a man is in homosexuality or he is in adultery and he refuses to repent—that's when the Bible says, "Get out from underneath his umbrella. Don't

drink from his fountain any longer." But until it is made openly known, don't sit there and walk around saying, "I've got the sign and I think this person's acting like this and I think this person's got sin in their lives and all this." Because you're going to be harming other believers around you. God will make a leader's sin known in its time. Even Jesus knew through true discernment that Judas was a devil, but he still sent him out to minister to people. Are you with me? This is so important that we understand this. Hannah understood something that Jesus later said. Jesus said later in John 13, *"He who receives whomever I send receives Me; and he who receives Me receives Him who sent Me."* In another words, when Jesus said "When you receive the person that I send, you're receiving My authority, which in turn you're receiving the father's authority." Are you with me?

Jesus came to the city that was looking for the Messiah. They were preaching about His coming, they anticipated the time of His coming. But yet the Bible says, *"When He came to this city called Nazareth,"* in Mark's gospel it says, *"In that city, He could not do any mighty works."* Now that's mind boggling to me. It doesn't say that He would not do any mighty works. Now if it would have said, "Would not" I could have received that a lot easier, but it said, "Could not." Do you realize the Son of God who has the Spirit of God without measure was refrained from doing any mighty works? Do you realize that? That's amazing to me. Why could He not do any mighty works? The reason is, He didn't come the way they expected Him to come. They knew from the book of Isaiah that Isaiah said, *"Unto us a child is born, a Son is given. The government shall rest upon His shoulders and of its kingdom there will be no end."* So they were looking for the Messiah to come and set up His earthly kingdom and deliver them from Roman rule. But when Messiah came, when Jesus came—Listen, a carpenter with a bunch of fisherman and tax collectors following—they said, "This is not the way we want it." Not only that, He was brought up in their town so there was that familiarity. So that was two strikes that they had to deal with. The Messiah's not coming the way they expected and they've got that familiar thing, "He's Joseph's son. He made my table that's in my house right now. Who does he think he is?" And the Bible says, "He could not do any mighty works." He was refrained because they expected Him to come differently than He came, which tells me this folks: Many times God will send you what you need in a package you don't want. Can you give double honor to that package that you don't necessarily want?

And let me tell you one other thing. If you go in and study it out, you will find out in the Amplified [Bible] it makes this very, very clear. Let me read this to you. It says, *"Let the elders who perform the duties of their office well, to be considered double worthy of honor and a financial support, especially those who labor faithfully, preaching and teaching."* The double honor he's talking about is financial as well as honoring him as a man of God or woman of God. I'm going to tell you this. I've traveled all over the world wherever I find churches that take care of their pastors, I find the businessmen in those churches prospering greatly. Wherever I go into churches where the people there skimp with their pastors, I find them constantly complaining about the economy. Not only that, I find this in overseas nations. Folks, let me tell you something, I've gone into churches. When I go into those churches they have a beautiful fruit basket in my room, they have flowers in my room. When you come there they receive you and the whole time you're there they say, "Do you need anything? Do you need this, do you need that?" I feel like a broken record, "No, no, no I'm fine." But I realize what they're doing. And you know, those are the easiest churches for me to preach in. But I go to some places and I think, "Why did you even ask me?" And I've gone to those churches and you know what? They let me grab my own luggage—which is fine—I can carry my own luggage, I don't care. They

come in a jalopy and all this stuff and they kind of throw in a hotel, give me twenty bucks, and say, "Here go get yourself something to eat if you're hungry." And you know when I leave the hotel, my white sweat socks are charcoal black from the dirt that's on the carpet of the hotel. You can't use the e-mail because it doesn't work. And you're just sitting there, "Okay, it's fine." But you know what I notice is that they don't receive. Now let me say this to you. I've gone to overseas nations. I've gone to places like Ukraine, Indonesia, other places. Well you know what? You know these people are making about fifteen dollars a month and they walk up and they give me twenty-five cents U.S. and my heart is just absolutely bursting with gratefulness. Other places give me an offering that is far less than what some other American churches would give me. But I knew it was their biggest gift. I knew they were honoring the servant and because of that miracles happen. Things happen all over those places. It's not about how much, it's about the fact that they just honored the man that came. Because they said that God sent this man or God sent this woman and, because of that, they receive Jesus and in turn they receive the Father and they are blessed because of it. Amen? Amen. Don't ever, ever, ever, ever stop honoring men and women of God that God sends into your life. When you honor them, you will receive what God has to give to you, to your family, through those men who He sends you. And let me say this, I have no other agenda in saying this other than the fact that it's for your sake. Because I've left the hotels with the black socks and all that other stuff and God's turned around and taken care of me some other avenue. God's going to take care of me because I'm His servant. God's going to take care of preachers because they're His servants. But I'm saying this for your sake tonight and I hope you're getting it. Amen.

Session Seven

Obedience and Submission

"Obey those who rule over you, and be submissive,
for they watch out for your souls, as those who must give
account. Let them do so with joy and not with grief,
for that would be unprofitable for you."
Hebrews 13:17

Summary for *Under Cover,* Chapter 11

Often, when we are confronted with the word
"submission" we immediately feel a certain amount of
hesitation or even resistance. In our sinful natures, we are
not naturally inclined to submit to authority on any level.
We can begin to misunderstand the nature of submission
and ask questions like these:

Is obedience unconditional?
What if I don't agree with my leader's decisions?
What if authority is making bad decisions?
What if authority tells me to do something wrong?
Where do I draw the line?

The Scriptures tell us repeatedly that God judges the
condition of a person's heart. Once we begin to understand
the difference between an attitude of submission and the
action of obedience, we can learn to follow the precepts of
God and avoid sinning through obedience to authority. We
must always remember that our submission is to God and
not to man. The only time that we should resist obedience
to an authority is if we are being asked to directly violate

the Word of God. Even then, our attitude should remain respectful and our actions should represent the Lord.

Notes from Chapter 11 (Video Session 7)

_____

_____

_____

_____

_____

_____

_____

_____

_____

Again the command of God reads, "Obey those who rule over you, and be submissive." As I previously stated, people often ask me with all sincerity, "Where do we draw the line? Does God expect us to obey authorities, no matter what they tell us to do? What if I am told to do something that is sin?" The Bible teaches unconditional submission to authorities, but the Bible does not teach unconditional obedience. Remember, submission deals with attitude, and obedience deals with fulfillment of what we are told.

The only time—and I want to emphasize the only exception in which we are not to obey authorities—is when they tell us to do something that directly contradicts what God has stated in His Word. In other words, we are released from obedience only when leaders tell us to sin. However, even in those cases we are to keep a humble and submitted attitude.

John Bevere, _Under Cover_, p. 135.

Warm-Up Questions

1. Why do you think people in today's society find it so
   difficult to have an attitude of submission?

   _____

   _____

   _____

2. In what ways do you see a submissive attitude in the
   life of Christ?

   _____

   _____

   _____

3. List several ways people are sometimes misled into
   sinning even though they are practicing an attitude of
   obedience:

   _____

   _____

   _____

Teaching by John Bevere

Watch video session 7.

Teaching Review

1. The writer in Hebrews 13:17 exhorts us to do what
   two things?

   _____

   _____

2. Obedience deals with our _____ toward authority.
   Submission deals with our _____ toward authority.

3. What is the only exception to obeying authorities?
   We are not to obey when _____

   _____

4. How did each of the following people obey God's law rather than man's? For assistance, see Daniel 3, 6 and Acts 4:1 - 22.
   Daniel _____

   _____

   _____

   _____

   Shadrach, Meshach, and Abed-Nego _____

   _____

   _____

   _____

   Peter and John _____

   _____

   _____

Exploring God's Word

Hebrews 13:17 *Obey those who rule over you, and be submissive, for they watch out for your souls, as those who must give account. Let them do so with joy and not with grief, for that would be unprofitable for you.*

5. Why do you think it would be unprofitable to grieve the authorities over you?

_____
_____
_____
_____
_____

6. How are we taught submission to God through submission to His delegated authorities?

_____
_____
_____
_____
_____
_____
_____
_____
_____
_____

7. How does this verse differentiate between obedience and submission?

_____
_____
_____
_____

Personal Application

_____
_____
_____

Isaiah 1:19–20 *If you are willing and obedient, You shall eat the good of the land; But if you refuse and rebel, You shall be devoured by the sword.*

8. How will God eventually deal with those that are not willing and obedient?

_____

9. Why is it not sufficient to be obedient? Why is submission important?

_____

_____

_____

Personal Application

_____

_____

_____

1 Chronicles 28:9 *As for you, my son Solomon, know the God of your father, and serve Him with a loyal heart and with a willing mind; for the LORD searches all hearts and understands all the intent of the thoughts.*

10. According to David, why is it fruitless to serve God simply with your actions and not your heart?

_____

_____

_____

11. God desires the correct attitude with action. How do we sometimes fail to obey even when we have a submissive heart?

_____

_____

_____

_____

_____

_____

Personal Application

_____

_____

_____

Daniel 3:16–18 *O Nebuchadnezzar, we have no need to answer you in this matter. If that is the case, our God whom we serve is able to deliver us from the burning fiery furnace, and He will deliver us from your hand, O king. But if not, let it be known to you, O king, that we do not serve your gods, nor will we worship the gold image which you have set up.*

12. Why is this type of disobedience acceptable to God?

_____

_____

_____

_____

_____

13. What kind of guarantee do we have that God will deliver us from affliction if we obey Him?

_____

_____

_____

_____

_____

14. If there is no guarantee, then why should we follow the example of Shadrach, Meshach and Abed-Nego and obey even until death?

_____

_____

_____

_____

Personal Application

_____

_____

_____

1 Peter 3:1–2 *Wives, likewise, be submissive to your own husbands, that even if some do not obey the word, they, without a word, may be won by the conduct of their wives, when they observe your chaste conduct accompanied by fear.*

15. In an age of feminism, how does this verse speak truth?

_____

_____

_____

_____

16. In what ways does a submissive spirit help bring salvation to unbelievers:

_____

_____

_____

Personal Application

_____

_____

_____

Exposing the Truth

17. Sometimes, like children, we obey God with our actions but fall into sin because of the stubbornness of our hearts. And like children, we too must learn to change our attitudes and submit to the authority of God in our lives before we can grow as children of God. Why do so many Christians fail to learn this attitude of submission and stay in a childish state of spirituality?

_____

_____

_____

18. In each of the following areas, what role does fear play in our failure to submit to authority?
Spiritual Life _____

_____

Church Life _____

_____

Personal Relationships _____

_____

I have grieved upon hearing stories of women who took the command of unconditional submission and applied it to encompass unconditional obedience as well. I've heard cases as perverse as believing husbands who demanded their wives to watch lewd adult videos with them to provide sexual excitement, and the wives yielded because they thought they didn't have Scriptural recourse. I know of husbands who demanded their wives be dishonest for them, and they did. I've heard of husbands who forbade their wives from attending any church service, and the wives actually stopped attending. These directives are not to be obeyed because they violate Scripture.

Let's go further. I know of cases of husbands beating their children or wives, and the wives covering for their abuse. In other instances children were sexually molested, and the wives did nothing. This is a violation of every premise on which God establishes authority, and women in these situations need to understand that God would never want them to stand back and do nothing. If a husband is involved in life-threatening behavior, a wife should separate herself and the children from him and not return until she is sure there has been complete repentance.

John Bevere, *Under Cover*, pp. 137–138.

Applying the Lesson

To conclude this session, answer the questions that were posed at the beginning of this study:

Is obedience unconditional?

What if I don't agree with my leader's decisions?

What if authority is making bad decisions?

What if authority tells me to do something wrong?

Where do I draw the line?

Applying these truths to your life may be difficult and require a good deal of repentance and prayer. However, as you endeavor to turn your heart toward God, He will strengthen you and give you the hope to continue on your journey.

Checking Your Cover

Conclude with prayer, beseeching the Lord to:

Bring your heart to a place of submission

Give you the strength to be obedient to the authorities over you with an attitude that is pleasing to God

Help you know where to draw the line in obedience and avoid sin.

Video Script for Lesson 7
Obedience and Submission

Hebrews chapter 13. Now I want to say this. This is a very, very important session tonight. Submission probably causes the greatest amount of confusion among believers than about anything else I know. I hear questions constantly along these lines. Is obedience unconditional? What if I don't agree with my leader's decision? What if authority makes a bad decision? What if authority tells me to do something wrong? Where do I draw the line? In these next three video sessions we will answer every one of these questions because the Word of God has specific wisdom for every one of them. The first thing I want to do is, I want to talk about the difference between obedience and submission.

Hebrews the thirteenth chapter, we're going to read from verse 17. Paul says, under the inspiration of the Holy Spirit, *"Obey those who rule over you, and be submissive, for they watch out for your souls."* So you can see he is obviously, specifically targeting church authority in this Scripture. Are you seeing this? And *"Those who must give an account: Let them do so with joy not with grief, for that would be unprofitable for you."* Now isn't it interesting? Who will it be unprofitable for? The leader? Or will it be unprofitable for you? For you—isn't that amazing? Now I want to say this again. Even though he's specifically targeting the church leaders, this spans the borders as well. But I want you to notice that we are told to do two distinct things in this verse. Number one: we are to obey those who rule over us. And number two: we are to be submissive to those who rule over us. Are you with me? Now this is where many get confused. They lump the words obedience and submission together and there is a difference. Now, I want to say this—that we can obey but not necessarily be submitted. Now I remember when I first learned this is when I was serving in a very large church in the southern part of the United States as the administrative assistant to the pastor.

There were many, many decisions that would go by my desk that he would make because I reported directly to him and his wife, and it was staff of about 450 people. There were many times that I saw things that I just thought were wrong. And let me backtrack just a little bit further. When I first started working for him, I remember the first couple of weeks—I had taken a several thousand dollar a year pay cut as an engineer for Rockwell International to go work for this church and made under $20,000 a year. But it was a joy because I remember the first couple of weeks—I was sitting in the parking lot picking up groceries for them and crying thinking, "God, why are they paying me? I should be paying them." I was so grateful for the opportunity to be able to serve. And this lasted for about a year. Then the honeymoon started wearing off. And all of a sudden I started seeing the flaws in the personality of the pastor. Now how many of you know if you look close enough you'll find flaws in anybody? Amen. Amen. And I remember I started seeing him make decisions that I thought, "Well you know, that's not right, that's not right, I don't know if he should do that." And you know one day God spoke to me. He said, "Did I put you in that position or him in that position?" I said, "Lord, you put him in that position." He said, "That's right," and He said, "I'll show him things that I don't need to show you. And I'll not show you on purpose to see if you'll follow him as he follows me." Then later on the Lord made this very clear to me he said, "Son, if I intended for every believer in the body of Christ to just hear from me," he said, "I would not have put authorities in their lives. The very fact that I put authorities in their lives means that I speak to people through those authorities." I developed a negative attitude. I'd been at the church for about four years, or actually three-and-a-half years, I'd been the executive administrative assistant, and I went through a time period where for six months I didn't get anything from what he preached. Now let me say this, this is one of the greatest preachers in the United States in the 1980s. And I went, "I remember when I first started attending the church I would be in awe with the wisdom of God that would come out of this man of God's mouth." And I remember this six month period just thinking constantly, "I'm not getting fed, I'm just not being fed." And I remember I was at dinner one night with another couple who worked for the executive staff as well. And the husband worked on the executive staff and so did I. The husband and the wife and my wife and I were all sitting around the dinner table going, "You know, we're just not getting fed anymore in the church." And they said, "You know, we're not getting fed either." And the husband and the wife and myself started going off on this thing and my wife kept quiet the whole time. And we all looked at each other and we said, "You know, we just really believe that God's getting ready to send us off in our own ministries. That's why we're not being fed, our time here is coming to a close." And so we all agreed on that and basically finished our meal and had our time together and I left. Well, a couple of days later I was in prayer and the Holy Spirit spoke to me in that prayer closet referring to that night because I'd been making that statement constantly, "I'm not being fed." And the Holy Spirit said to me, he said, "The problem is not with your pastor. The problem is with you." And I said—well you know, whenever God brings correction to you, you know you kind of think—"Lord do you have the right person?" But you know what I've learned? If we're going to be like Jesus—because the Bible says we're going to be like Him—we're going to behold Him, we're going to be just like Him right? If we're going to be just like Jesus when He comes back, than one of us has got to change. It's not going to be Him. So what that means is most of the dealings of God in my life are going to be corrected. Good preaching. So the Lord spoke to me he said, "The problem is not with your pastor. The problem is with you." I said, "Lord, what do you mean?" And the Lord spoke to me and he said, "Son, what did I say in Isaiah 1:18–19?" And I recited the verse back to him, I knew it from memory. I said, "It says, 'If

you're willing and obedient, you'll eat the good of the land.'" And the Lord spoke to me and he said, "Son, there's your problem right there." I said, "Lord, I am obedient. I do everything I'm told to do." And the Spirit of God spoke to me and said, "I didn't say, 'If you're obedient, you'll eat the good of the land.' He said, "I said, 'If you're *willing* and obedient, you'll eat the good of the land.'" And he said, "*Willing* deals with your attitude, and your attitude stinks." That's exactly what the Spirit of God said to me. He said, "I said, 'If you're willing and obedient, you'll eat the good of the land.'" He said, "The reason you're not being fed is because your attitude stinks." He said, "Change your attitude and repent," and he said, "You'll start being fed." Well, I repented right there in that prayer closet, I remember right where I was, I remember the exact place to this day. I can still see myself praying. And I remember the next Sunday morning I walked back into that church same seat, same pastor, same series of messages, same church. Heaven opened up that morning and I sit there and all I wanted to do is cry because I kept thinking, "What have I missed for six solid months, all because of my attitude?" Submission deals with your attitude, obedience deals with your action.

David said to his son in 1 Chronicles 28:9, he said to him *"As for you my son Solomon, know the God of your father, and serve Him with a loyal heart and with a willing mind; for the LORD searches all hearts and understands all intent of the thoughts."* Now if you look at Hebrews 13 again it says in the NIV, *"Obey your leaders and submit to their authority."* I want to say this—we can be submissive in our attitude and not necessarily be obedient. Remember the son that the father came to in the parable that Jesus told? He said, "Son, go work in my field," and the son said, "Sure Dad, I'll do it," and yet he didn't do it. Jesus said, "He did not obey the will of his father." Now of course the other son said, "No, I won't do it," but yet went and did it. And of course he did the will of the father. But let me tell you what the father would have loved to have had is a submitted son with a submitted attitude who obeyed his father. That's what God really desires—not only for us to obey, but to have a willing, submitted attitude in our obedience. So not only does God say, "Obey, those who rule over you," He also says, "Submit to those who rule over you." The reason is, there is a difference. Submission deals with our attitude; obedience deals with our actions. Now the question is, where do we draw the line? Where does it finally come to the place that we don't obey an authority? I want to make this statement to you tonight. The Bible teaches unconditional submission. But the Bible does not teach unconditional obedience to authority. There is only one time—and I want to emphasize this—one time that we are told not to obey an authority, and that is when an authority tells us to do something directly against what is written in the written Word of God. That is the only time that we are told not to obey. If your pastor tells you to wear blue socks with purple pants and a pink shirt up on the choir—if that's what he wants, that's what we're going to wear and we're going to do it with a happy attitude. There is no sin in wearing blue socks with purple pants and a yellow shirt, are you with me? Because I have found that 99% of the problems that people have obeying is not when leaders tell them to sin but just telling them things they don't want to do. I said this in an earlier session, I'm going to say it again: Submission does not mean "I submit as long as I agree." Submission doesn't even begin until there's disagreement. Only time we're not to obey is when we're told to do something contrary to the written Word of God.

Nebuchadnezzar, king of Babylon, he was a man that God called His servant. Another incident that shows that God appoints all leaders, because Nebuchadnezzar was the one who literally tore up Israel and Judea, all right? But he took some of the Hebrew people back with him and some of their names were Daniel, Shadrach, Meshach, and Abed-Nego—you're all very familiar with them. But there was a decree made by Nebuchadnezzar that the people were to bow down to his idol that he had erected whenever they heard the sound of musical instruments. Whenever musical instruments would play, the people were to bow down to the idol. Well the

king said that, but when the musical instruments were blown, Shadrach, Meshach, and Abed-Nego did not bow down to the idol, they stood. When this was told to the king, they were immediately brought to him. Nebuchadnezzar questioned them and said, "Why didn't you bow down when the musical instrument was played?" Shadrach, Meshach, and Abed-Nego responded with this. This is out of the New Living Translation, Daniel 3:16-18, Shadrach, Meshach, and Abednego replied, *"Oh Nebuchadnezzar, we do not need to defend ourselves before you if we are thrown into the blazing furnace. But God whom we serve is able to save us. He will rescue us from your power, your majesty, but even if he doesn't, your majesty can be sure that we will never serve your gods or worship the god's gold statue you have set up."* Now do you notice they spoke with him with respect? When you address a king as "your majesty" you are giving him great honor. Notice that they do not say to him "You jerk, you think I'm going to bow down and worship your idol?" That would be not obeying and also not being submissive. But the Bible teaches us unconditional submission. Even if an authority tells us to do something contrary to what you are, we are not to speak to them like they are bunch of jerks. Are you with me? We are to speak with respect. The result of this was Nebuchadnezzar had them thrown into the fiery furnace—you all know the story. There was a fourth man and Nebuchadnezzar clearly saw that God did deliver them and God brought them out of the furnace and honored the men greatly. Are you with me?

Now look at 1 Peter 3. Now Peter, in this chapter, shows us that submission deals with attitude in addressing wives with unbelieving husbands. Look at what he says, chapter 3:1: *"Wives, likewise, be submissive to your own husbands, that even if some do not obey the word, they, without a word, may be won by the conduct of their wives."* Now it's really sad to say this, but I have found that there are actually some believers, some quote "believing husbands" that are harsher on their wives than on some unbelievers. It's a very rare exception, but it's out there. But Peter is making the statement that "Wives, you are to be submitted even to unbelieving husbands." Now in another verse in Scripture, back over in Titus, wives are told to obey their husbands. So again, not only are they told to obey, but they are told to submit. Look at what Peter goes on to say, verse 2: *"When they [begin] to observe your chaste conduct accompanied by fear."* Here is the submission. Are you seeing this? *"Do not let your adornment be merely outward—arranging the hair, wearing gold, or putting on fine apparel—rather let it be the hidden person of the heart, with the incorruptible beauty of a gentle and a quiet spirit, which is very precious in the sight of God."* So in other words, Peter then describes what a submitted wife is like. A submitted wife has an attitude of reverence, peace, respect, and she speaks with respect to authority. Now I bring this up because of this. I get really grieved when the obedience and submission issue is brought to an unhealthy and ungodly and unscriptural extreme. Are you with me?

I'm going to actually read out of this book because I want to make sure I cover every point so that you get it. "Like most, I have grieved when I have heard stories of women who took the command of unconditional submission and applied it to encompass unconditional obedience as well. I have heard cases as perverse as the believing husbands who demanded their wives to watch lewd adult videos with them to provide sexual excitement and the wife yielded because she thought she didn't have any scriptural recourse. I know of husbands who demanded their wives to be dishonest for them and they did it. I have heard of husbands who have forbade their wives from attending any kind of church services and the wife actually stopped attending. These kind of directives are not to be obeyed as they violate Scripture. God tells us not to forsake the assembling of ourselves. God tells us not to steal, to lie. When the phone rings in the house and the husband says to the wife, 'Tell him I'm not home,' she can say 'Honey, do you want me to just tell him you don't want to take the phone call because I'm not going to lie. You know I love you, you know I'm submitted to you.' She can handle it like that, if she speaks with

respect, but she's not going to disobey the Word of God, the written Word of God." Are you here?

Let's go further, "I know cases where husbands beat their wives and children out of abuse and the wife covered for the abuse. There are others where children were sexually molested and the wife did nothing. I actually know cases of people like this. And the reason they did nothing is because they believed they were supposed to be obedient to their husbands. This is a violation of every premise on which God establishes authority. And women in this position need to understand that God would never want them to stand back and to obey and do nothing. If a husband is involved in a life threatening behavior such as this, a wife should separate herself and her children from him and not return until she is sure that there has been complete repentance." Even David, a warrior and a man of strength, did not hang around the palace when Saul was throwing javelins. All right? He left and lived in the wilderness but never lost his reverential attitude towards Saul's authority. And I'm going to be talking about that in two sessions in great depth. He respected the authority on Saul's life and respected the anointed of the Lord all the way to his [Saul's] death and I'm going to go through that in detail. So let me tell you this, folks, do not take the command of God for unconditional submission and pervert it to unconditional obedience. I want to say this again. The only time we are not to obey, and the reason Shadrach, Meshach, and Abed-Nego did not obey, is because it violated the second commandment which says, "You shall not bow down to any other gods."

Now I want to actually show you tonight that God actually blesses people when they don't obey authority, when authorities tell them to sin. I want to show this. Go to Exodus chapter one. Exodus the first chapter. Are you there? Verse 15, chapter one. *"Then the king of Egypt spoke to the Hebrew midwives, of whom the name of one was"*—boy, I'm not even going to try it, let's just say Jane and the name of the other was Lisa. (The Theologians love it when I do this.)— *"And he said, 'When you do the duties of* a midwife for the Hebrew women, and see them on the birthstools, if it is a son, then you should kill him; but if it is a daughter, then she shall live.'" Now Verse 17 says, "But the midwives feared God"—I love that— "And did not do as the king of Egypt commanded them, but saved the male children alive." They did not obey authority because authority told them to violate, I believe it's the eighth commandment of the ten commandments which they hadn't gotten yet, but they hadn't violated the Word of God which is "Thou shall not kill." Are you seeing this? Watch what God did to these midwives because they didn't obey this command to sin. Verse 21: "And so it was, because the midwives feared God, that He provided households for them." God actually rewarded them not obeying the authority's command telling them to sin. Are you seeing this?

All right go with me to Acts 4. Actually seeing right there that God will literally bless when you don't obey when an authority tells you to sin, but you keep a respectful, submitted attitude. In Acts 4—are you there? I'm going to look at the eighteenth verse. The Sanhedrin called them, and them is Peter and John, and they "commanded them not to speak at all nor teach in the name of Jesus." Verse 19: "But Peter and John answered and said to them, 'Whether it is right in the sight of God to listen to you more than to God, you judge. We cannot but speak the things which we have seen and heard.'" Jesus gave a commandment and he said, "Go into all the world and preach the gospel to every creature." It is written in our Bibles. These men told them not to do what Jesus said they were to do. Peter said, "Whether we obey God or you—please—you judge."

I want you to see what happens as a result of them obeying the word of God. Verse 33: "And with great power the apostles gave witness to the resurrection of the Lord Jesus [Christ]. And great grace was upon them all." God blessed them with great power and great grace. Now I want you also to see the attitude that the disciples took towards the Sanhedrin who commanded them not to teach or preach in the name of

Jesus. Go to Acts 23. You saw that they did not obey this command, but yet I want you to see their submission to the Sanhedrin because, folks, you must understand the Sanhedrin were not only the spiritual leaders, they were the governmental leaders. The high priests were literally like our senators today. Are you getting this? They were not only the pastors of your church, they were your senators. Are you with me? Because when Rome conquered a territory, they would allow the conquered territory to continue to govern themselves under their supervision. Are you with me? So here we are in Acts 23:1, "Then Paul looking earnestly at the council"—this is the Sanhedrin— "and said, 'Men and brethren, I have lived in all good conscience before God until this day.'" Verse 2: "And the high priest Ananias commanded those who stood by him to strike him on the mouth." Now Paul didn't like that very much. Verse 3: "Then Paul said to him, 'God will strike you, you whitewashed wall! For you sit [in judgment] according to the law, and do you command me to be struck contrary to the law?'" Now look at verses 4 and 5 carefully. "And those who stood by said, 'Do you revile God's high priest?'" Now look at Paul's response. "Then Paul said, 'I did not know, brethren, that he was the high priest; for it is written, 'You shall not speak evil of a ruler of your people.'" Notice Paul was penitent of the way he spoke to that one who was in authority, even though the apostles' position was, "Will not obey their command to not preach or teach in the name of Jesus." Notice the respect the apostles took with that same council.

Daniel the sixth chapter, and look at Verse 3 actually. "Then this Daniel [actually] distinguished himself above the governors and satraps, because an excellent spirit was [within] him." Don't you just love that? Then "the king gave thought to setting him over the whole realm." Wow! This is a Hebrew young man in the Babylonian empire. Verse 4: "So the governors and satraps sought to find some charge against Daniel concerning the [good] kingdom; but they could find no charge or fault, because he was faithful; nor was there any error or fault [found] in him." Folks, let me tell you something. You are walking the life that God has called you to walk when the outsiders—the unbelievers—cannot find fault in your life. That is what the Bible commands us in the New Testament. Amen. So you know what these guys do? They say, "We don't want this Hebrew kid ruling over us." So they came up with a law that they knew he wouldn't be able to obey. They came up with a law that if anybody was to petition any other God other than the king, they were to be thrown in the den of lions. That's what verses 4–10 talk about.

Well, I want you to notice Verse 10: *"Now when Daniel knew that the writing was signed."* Isn't this wonderful the way the Bible writes? When he knew they signed that corrupt law, watch this, *"he went home. And in his upper room, with his windows open toward Jerusalem, he knelt down on his knees three times that day, and prayed and gave thanks before his God, as was his custom since his early days."* Why did Daniel do this? Because Psalm 55:17 says, *"Evening and morning and at noon I will pray, and cry aloud, and He shall hear my voice."* Daniel did what the written Word of God says. When the king was told about it, Daniel was brought before him. Because the king signed the decree he was very sad about it. Now he would have to put Daniel in the lion's den. He did. Daniel was in the lion's den all night. You notice from your Sunday school classes the result was the lions did not touch Daniel. The king was delighted to see it because he saw that God had absolutely delivered Daniel and blessed him for not obeying the king's decree. So then the king put the evil men in and the evil men who came up with the law were immediately consumed, them and their families even before they hit the bottom of the den. Isn't that amazing? Now I want to say something. It didn't always turn out this way.

Go to Hebrews chapter 11. Go to Hebrews the eleventh chapter, you will see something that is most powerful. Hebrews 11 is the Hall of Fame of Faith, is that not true? Yet let me show you some of those who got put in the Hall of Fame of Faith that didn't do what some of us today think are feats of faith. But they did do what God calls a great feat of faith and that is obedience. Watch this. Verse 35: *"Women received their dead raised to life again. Others were tortured, not accepting deliverance, that they might obtain a better resurrection. Still others had trials of mockings and scourgings, yes, of chains and imprisonment. They were stoned, they were sawn in two, they were tempted, were slain with the sword. They wandered about in sheepskins and goatskins, being destitute, afflicted, tormented—of whom the world was not worthy."* Are you seeing that there were times when people did make the decision to obey God but the reward wasn't a natural reward? Are you with me? Let me tell you the reward is great in heaven because that's what Jesus said. Isn't that right?

An unknown Roman wrote about the believers of his day, this is what he said. This is an unknown Roman back in first or second century and this is what he said. He said about the believers, "They obey the prescribed laws and at the same time they surpass the laws by their lives." Isn't that powerful? "Those who hate them are unable to give any reason for their hatred." In other words, the believers in the early church obey the laws but yet, by their lifestyle, they surpassed the laws. That's what that Church did when they went to that city and said, "We're buying you that mask." They said "We're going beyond this tax law, we want to bless." That's what blows the world away, that's when the world really sees Jesus in us. There are no gray areas. I made it very clear that if authority tells us to do something that is directly contrary to the written Word, we're not to obey their command.

Let me give you an example of a gray area. Let's say you work on the staff of a ministry and the pastor tells you he does not want you praying for people on phone counseling calls. I have heard people say this before. "Well, that pastor is not doing what God desires. God wants us to pray for people, and if they call I'm going to pray for them." You are in rebellion. The reason is, you are being paid to type, data entry, or file, or something else, not to pray for people. Because you represented that ministry incorrectly and you are not submitting to the authority over that ministry. That is not an example of a pastor telling you to do something that is not in the written Word of God. You see, there are no gray areas in this thing, folks. We are talking about directly going against, violation of the will and holiness and Word of God. Are you seeing that? That is the only time we are not to obey.

Session Eight

What if Authority Tells Me . . . ?

*"The king's heart is in the hand of the LORD,
like the rivers of water; He turns it wherever He wishes."*
Proverbs 21:1

Summary for *Under Cover,* Chapter 12

Anyone who has been under authority understands the difficulties that arise when you feel a decision of the leader is inappropriate. Often, we question the leader's ability to lead or we complain that his methods of leadership are faulty. We are left a grumbling and complaining people much like the Israelites that were led out of Egypt by Moses.

When we come under conflict with a leader and begin to question his ability, we are, in actuality, questioning God. The Israelites grumbled against Moses for their lack of food and comfort, not understanding that Moses was under the guidance of God. They thought they could separate God from those He put in leadership. In reality, their complaints were against the Lord, and as a result, they were punished.

When we begin to understand and believe that all authority is from God, we can begin to see how the hand of God moves in every event. No matter what the leader's personality or actions might be, the Lord is still in control and ordaining that person to that position. If we allow an attitude of arrogance or self-righteousness to creep into our lives, we can fail to see God's will being worked out in all things. It is only through submission to God's authority that we can be submissive to earthly authorities.

Even a leader's bad decision leaves us no right to treat them with contempt or to complain against their authority. As Christians, we are to always pray and give thanks for those in leadership over us. Out of a spirit of submission and respect we can do what is right in the sight of God.

Notes from Chapter 12 (Video Session 8)

_____

_____

_____

_____

_____

_____

_____

_____

_____

We've all encountered people who are dissatisfied with the leaders over them. They complain about ineffective techniques or unwise decisions and how they negatively affected their lives. They complain they were promised certain things by leaders, but they are still waiting for those things to happen. In fact, things seem to be

going backward. They are certain their pastor has missed it and now reason that his authority is separate from God's. This reasoning opens the door to complaining, which eventually manifests itself as insubordinate behavior. It is only a matter of time before they're flirting with deception and they're lured away from the authority of God placed over them for growth and protection.

John Bevere, *Under Cover*, p.142.

Warm-Up Questions

1. What different responses do people give to a leader's bad decision? Why?

_____

_____

_____

2. What effects does complaining against a leader have on those under his authority?

_____

_____

_____

3. In your experience, what has been the most effective way of helping a leader see a mistake in his or her judgment?

_____

_____

_____

Teaching by John Bevere

Watch video session 8 on the tape.

Teaching Review

1. Briefly describe the Israelites response to Moses as their struggle for freedom became more and more difficult:

   _____

   _____

   _____

2. Describe Esther's method of persuading the king to change his decision:

   _____

   _____

   _____

   _____

3. Why was Esther's method appropriate?

   _____

   _____

   _____

> It's not our responsibility to make calls on leadership decisions or even to judge the results after the fact. The One who put that person in authority will. If the Israelites had been allowed to judge Moses' decisions, he would have come out on the short end of the stick, and they would have returned to Egypt.
>
> John Bevere, *Under Cover*, p. 147.

Exploring God's Word

Exodus 16:8 *The LORD hears your complaints which you make against Him. And what are we? Your complaints are not against us but against the LORD.*

4. How did the children of Israel fail to see God's authority in Moses?

_____

_____

_____

_____

_____

5. Because of Israel's lack of vision, they continually fell into unbelief. How does our complaining against authority mirror the Israelites and keep us in unbelief?

_____

_____

_____

_____

_____

_____

_____

_____

Personal Application

_____

_____

_____

Luke 12:48 *For everyone to whom much is given, from him much will be required; and to whom much has been committed, of him they will ask the more.*

6. How will God judge those that have been placed in authority?

_____

_____

_____

_____

7. Why is it important that we seek out positions of authority with great humbleness?

_____

_____

_____

_____

Personal Application

_____

_____

_____

Proverbs 21:1 *The king's heart is in the hand of the LORD, Like the rivers of water; He turns it wherever He wishes.*

8. How does this verse confirm that God is in control of all the events of our lives?

_____

_____

_____

9. How does the knowledge that God is in control of the hearts of our leaders bring us peace of mind?

_____

_____

_____

_____

Personal Application

_____

_____

_____

2 Corinthians 2:9 *For to this end I also wrote, that I might put you to the test, whether you are obedient in all things.*

10. Why do leaders sometimes ask us to obey even when we do not understand?

_____

_____

_____

_____

_____

11. What benefit is there for us to learn submission and obedience as a first reaction?

_____

_____

_____

_____

Personal Application

_____

_____

_____

Exposing the Truth

12. As the children of Israel were being led out of Egypt and into the Promised Land, they often fell into unbelief and sin. In *Under Cover*, John writes, "Those men and women thought their insubordination was against Moses and not in any way connected to God. They thought they had successfully separated the two. They lived by reasoning instead of by the principle of obedience. Those who walk by the limited reasoning produced by sight and circumstances find themselves on the path of folly." How do we sometimes fall into the trap of reasoning as the Israelites did? What is the result of this behavior?

    _____

    _____

    _____

    _____

13. People often limit their submission and obedience to those with whom we agree. John says, "To resist delegated authority is to resist God's authority. We should not take upon ourselves the pressure to discern beforehand whether leaders are right or not. Nor should we judge after the fact. This is not our burden, but God's. He alone knows and can change hearts as He so desires." How does this statement

conflict with the independent mindset of our culture?
How do you react to this?

_____

_____

_____

_____

_____

14. Those under authority sometimes feel they have the
right to express their opinion concerning a leader's
actions or behavior. John continues in *Under Cover* by
writing. "You have to earn the right to speak into a
leader's life. You accomplish this through loyalty,
integrity, and faithfulness. Not everyone has the right
to speak into a leader's life in this manner." How does
each of the following characteristics allow a person to
speak into a leader's life appropriately?

Loyalty _____

_____

_____

_____

Integrity _____

_____

_____

_____

Faithfulness _____

_____

_____

I have an agreement with the people who work for me. If I make a decision they believe is uninformed, they can petition me once, or if new facts surface that may aid in the decision, they can petition me again. When they petition, it is important that they have carefully thought it through and they present it in such a way that helps me to see what they wish to communicate. I have often changed a decision when I've seen new information. However, if they petition me, and I stay with the original decision, then we move forward in agreement. If we move forward in unity, and I am wrong, God still protects us. He will protect me as well as those under me if we acted out of integrity of heart. David said, "Let integrity and uprightness preserve me, For I wait for You" (Ps. 25: 21).

John Bevere, *Under Cover*, p. 156.

Applying the Lesson

In this session, John has discussed some important questions in regards to obedience. Respond to each of the following "what if . . ." questions.

What if I discern that my leader is not making a very good choice? Should I still obey him knowing that he is headed for misfortune?

_____

_____

What if my leader has been negatively influenced into making a terrible decision?

_____

_____

What if we aren't discerning, but are sure that authority is making a bad decision? What if we have concrete evidence the leader was influenced by an evil report?

_____

_____

What if a leader makes a decision before having all the facts?

_____

_____

What if authority tells me the opposite of what I felt led to do in prayer?

_____

_____

Checking Your Cover

Conclude this session by praying that God will:

Help you know the true nature of submission and obedience

Have the faith to follow God's delegated authority even when you do not understand

To always remain humble in your attitude

Video Script for Lesson 8
What If Authority Tells Me . . .?

We've all encountered people who are dissatisfied with their leaders, correct? They complain about ineffective techniques or the unwise decisions that they think their leaders are making and how it negatively effects their lives. They complain, I've heard this constantly, they complain that they were promised certain things by leadership but they are still waiting for it to happen. Right? In fact, things seem to be going backwards. They are certain their pastor has missed it and now reason that his authority is separate from God. This opens the door to complaining which eventually manifests itself in insubordinate behavior. It is only a matter of time before they're flirting with deception and lured away from the authority God placed over their lives for their protection. Are you with me?

Now if you really want to see a leader that looked like he was taking people backwards, let's talk about Moses. All right? God is the one who raised up Moses, right? The descendants of Abraham had been tormented by Pharaoh for four hundred years and God appears to Moses on the mountain and says, "You the deliverer, you the man," right? Here's the signs. Go tell the pharaoh, "Let my people go." Moses comes down from the mountain, before he goes to Pharaoh he first of all stops and speaks to the children of Israel. Look what he does, look at verse 29 of chapter four in Exodus. *"Then Moses and Aaron went and gathered together all the elders of the children of Israel. And Aaron spoke all the words which the Lord had spoken to Moses. Then he did the signs in the sight of the people."* Now look at verse 31: *"So the people believed."* Everybody say, "They believed." "They believed." Now watch. *"And when they heard that the Lord had visited the children of Israel and that He had looked on their affliction, then they bowed their heads and worshiped."* Can you imagine what was going on in that room? There's a multitude of leaders because they're all relatives, right? And let

me tell you something. They've been promised all their life that God is one day going to send a Deliverer. But you know what, their daddy heard about him and he died and never saw him. Their grandfather heard about a deliverer but He died, he lived his whole life as a slave and never saw the deliverer. Their great-grandfather had heard about it, but he died. And now here they are looking at God's appointed deliverer. They are pinching themselves going, "Whoa, God is really going to deliver us." And they worship, right? Can you imagine the praise and the worship that erupted out of this? Now watch. Moses leaves them—goes right to Pharaoh and tells Pharaoh exactly what God told him to say on the mountain, *"Thus sayeth the Lord, 'Let my people go.'"* You know what Pharaoh looks at him and says, "So the people aren't busy enough, huh? So they need some more work, right, Moses?"

Now I'm going to read to you out of the New Living Translation how Pharaoh responded to him. Look up at me and listen. *"To which Pharaoh responded, 'Who is the Lord that I should obey his voice and let Israel go? I do not know the Lord nor will I let Israel go. Why do you take the people from their work?'"* So the same day Pharaoh increased their hardship. He angrily decreed to his slave drivers, "Load them down with more work, make them sweat." Now you've got to understand the life of a Hebrew was: they got up at sunrise, went to the brick pits, worked all day long, came home and basically collapsed only to get up the next day and do the same thing. And got nothing for their labor except a slum. No longer would straw be provided already for the overwhelming tally of bricks the Israelites were required to produce each day. They would have to glean by night and labor by day. So, now you can't go home and collapse, you've got to go out to the field and get the straw because they're not giving it to you anymore. Are you getting this? The total number of bricks could not diminish even though the straw would no longer be provided. The Hebrews scattered throughout the land searching for straw. The slave drivers were brutal. Backed by their whips, they harshly demanded, "Meet your daily quota of bricks just as you did before." They beat the Israelite foremen in charge of the work crews. "Why haven't you met your quotas either yesterday or today?" they demanded. So the Israelite foremen went to Pharaoh. Now listen to this. And pleaded with him. "Please don't treat us like this," they begged. "We are given no straw but we are still told to make as many bricks as before. We are beaten for something that isn't our fault. It is the fault of your slave drivers for making such an unreasonable demand." But Pharaoh replied, "You're just lazy. You obviously don't have enough to do. If you did you wouldn't be saying, 'Let us go' and offering sacrifices to your Lord. Now get back to work. No straw will be given to you, but you must still deliver the regular quota of bricks." Since Pharaoh would not let up on his demands, the Israelite foremen could see that they were in serious trouble. And as they left Pharaoh's court, now listen to this, they met Moses and Aaron who were waiting outside for them. Then they said to Moses, "May the Lord judge you for getting us into this terrible situation with Pharaoh and his officials. You have given him an excuse to kill us."

So now Moses is the hero when he has the meeting with them. But he goes and preaches the Word of the Lord to Pharaoh, and his preaching brings greater hardship on their life. So what do they do? They get so angry when they see that it's all because of Moses' preaching. They look at him and say, "May the Lord judge between you and us." They called divine judgment on Moses. They are now separating Moses' authority from God's. Are you seeing this? They think, "Look at what you have done to us." Now God finally does deliver them, right? Let me tell you though, before he does deliver them, you know what the Bible says five times? One, two, three, four, five times. It says this, "The Lord hardens Pharaoh's heart and he did not let the children of Israel go out of the land." The more God hardened

Pharaoh's heart, the harder it got for Israel. But God finally, miraculously, delivers them, correct? They come out of Egypt, they're excited for a short time, only to find out they are brought to a land that is vast all right, it's a big land, but it's got no bread, it's got no crops, it's a wilderness. And they think, "You promised us land flowing with milk and honey." Now they're furious with Moses because now they have brought them out of Egypt. First of they were backed up by the Red Sea and thought they were going to be killed. Now they get through the Red Sea and they have nothing to eat, and nothing to drink for three days in the wilderness. And they think, "You know Moses, we had food in Egypt, we had meat pots, we had fish pots, we had vegetables. We don't have anything out here. We thought Pharaoh was harsh. You're sadistic, you're killing us. You brought us out here to starve." Don't you remember they said all these things? "You have brought this entire assembly out here to starve us to death. You're cruel." So now you know what they say? "Let's raise up a leader and go back. At least under Pharaoh we had something to eat and at least we were going to live, this guy has brought us out here to kill us. He thinks he's a god."

Are you beginning to get this, folks? I mean pastor Moses wasn't doing a very good job. If they were to judge his leadership abilities by his results, he would have come out way short. Are you with me? And all he was doing was what God told him to do. It was not Moses, it was God that was orchestrating these circumstances. Because they get out in the middle of that desert and I want you to go to Exodus 16. They are just furious with him. Exodus 16, look at verse two. *"Then the whole congregation of the children of Israel complained."* Everybody say, "Complained." "Complained." Would you look up at me? Complaining is a form of rebellion. Complaining says to authority, "I-don't-like-what-you're-doing-and-if-I-were-you-I-would-do-it-differently." That's why God hates it. The whole congregation of the children of Israel complained against who? *"Against Moses and Aaron in the wilderness."* But look what Moses goes on to say in verse eight.

And Moses said, *"This shall be seen when the LORD gives you meat to eat in the evening, and in the morning bread to the full; for the LORD hears your complaints which you make against Him. And what are we? Your complaints are not against us but against the LORD."* Moses made it very clear, "You know who you are really complaining against." Now the children of Israel said they were complaining against Moses and Aaron. And Moses made it real quick, he said, "You know who you really complain against. It's not me, it's God." They didn't have the guts to complain to God, but they had the guts to complain to their leader. Are you with me? If Moses would have been judged by them at this point because you know what? He brought them three days into the wilderness, they had nothing to eat or drink and they finally came to Marah. When they came to Marah there was finally some water. They were so excited and they were saying, "Okay, maybe things are going to turn around." They find out the waters in Marah were bitter and they couldn't drink them. They had had it. They said, "We're going back." Are you with me?

If Moses would have been judged according to their standard, he would have been a failure as a leader. That's what so many people today judge their pastors and other leaders that God's puts over their lives. God orchestrates things in their life, maybe kind of tough, difficult situations and they think, "The whole fault is my leader." It's not the fault of your leader. Do you think he's that powerful? To ruin your life? Joseph said to his brothers, "It wasn't you that sent me here it was God." And Joseph's brothers said "We're going to kill him and keep him from the call of God in his life." Nobody gets you out of the call of God in your life. No man, woman, child, or even leader can keep you from the call of God in your life. The only one that can keep you from the call of God in your life is you. The children of Israel got offended with their leader and complained. It kept them from the promised land. That's the only one who can get you out of the will of God. No leader can keep you from the will of God in your life. If you get ahold of this you're going to get free.

But somebody says, "Well, what if I discern? If I was the children of Israel I would be more like Joshua." Well, don't be so quick to say that and I have to remind myself of that. Because it's real easy when the books are written and the story's over to look back and say, "I wouldn't have done that." Because somebody says, "Well, you know I would have been discerning like Joshua." Let me tell you something. Joshua was not obedient because of his discernment, he was obedient because he understood the principle of submission and obedience. That's why he had true discernment, that's why he realized Moses was God's sent man. There are people today constantly in church saying, "I discern, I discern, I discern," but many times it's just a criticalness. Anybody can be critical, all you have to have is two eyes and a carnal brain and you're critical. But they say, "This is discernment." That's not discernment at all. Are you with me? Now what if you say, "Now, listen. What if I discern that my leader is not making a very good choice? Should I still obey him, knowing that he is headed for misfortune?" Okay, are you with me? "Should I still do that?" Well, when I was youth pastor and that pastor made the decision to cancel our youth home groups that I'd worked on for seven months, there was another element in there. There was an administrator that was out there to get me. His son was in my youth group and he didn't like what I was preaching, so he started a campaign to get me fired. And so what happened was, when I went into that meeting I thought that what he had done was that he had twisted the ear of my pastor, my senior pastor, to give him information that helped him make a bad decision. For that reason, I was still unwilling to yield to my pastor's authority and I argued with him for 20 minutes in that meeting. But let me show you something that God showed me shortly after that.

Look at Proverbs 21, I want you to go there. Look at Verse 1: *"The king's heart is in the hand of the LORD. Like the rivers of water; [God] turns it wherever He wishes."* Now you know what the Bible says, right there, is that the person who is in authority over you, the king, that's the person in authority. His heart's in the hand of the Lord and God can turn it any way He desires. God doesn't say, "The king's heart is in my hand as long as he's not in a wrongly influence or as long as he behaves a certain way." He says, "The king's heart is in my hand no matter what." Now I know that brings up a real question in you. What if we're not just discerning, what if we really, really know that authority is making a bad decision? What if we have concrete evidence that the leader was influenced by an evil report? Is there no recourse, can't we do something to help? The answer is absolutely, "Yes."

If you look at the life of Esther. Esther was queen to the Persian king. There was an evil man named Haman who wanted to kill all of the Jews. He came up with a decree that every single Jew should be slaughtered on a certain day. Esther was queen and Haman did not realize that she was a Jewish lady. Mordecai, Esther's uncle, comes to Esther and says, "Esther, you have got to go before the King." But Esther says, "Mordecai, if I go before the king and he doesn't point his scepter at me, my head comes off." Mordecai said, "But Esther, you've been brought into the king for such a time as this." Esther makes the decision, goes before the king, when she does the king has seen her with favor and points his scepter at her. And says, "Esther what do you request of me?" And Esther says, "Please come to a banquet." The night before the king comes to the banquet, the scribe is reading to the king all the chronicles. And in the chronicles, the king is told about a man named Mordecai who saved the king's life. The king said, "Did I do anything to reward him?" And the scribe said, "No." The king went to Haman and said, "Haman, what should I do?" And Haman thought the king was talking about him. And Haman said, "You should honor him and put him on your best horse and parade him around the whole city." And so the king says, "Good, I want you to do it and you be the one to lead him. I want you to lead Mordecai around." Now he's furious about this, right? But Haman thinks, "All right, he's going to be killed." But what God is doing is God is already preparing the heart of the king for when Esther approaches

him. So on a second banquet, Esther comes before the king and the king says to Esther and Haman's there, "Esther, what is it that you want?" Now listen to what queen Esther says, this is out of the New Living Translation, listen to this: *"And so queen Esther replied, 'If your majesty is pleased with me'"*—now, remember, she is speaking to her husband— *"'and wants to grant me my request, my petition is that my life and the lives of my people will be spared. For my people and I have been sold to those who would kill, slaughter, and annihilate us. If we had only been sold as slaves I could remain quiet, for that would have been a matter too trivial to warrant disturbing the king.'"* That's Esther 7:3–4. Can you see the way she spoke to him? She doesn't look at her husband and say, "You jerk. Don't you realize this guy misinformed you and now you are killing a bunch of innocent people including me, your wife?" That's not the way she speaks to him. She speaks with a submitted heart and she petitions him knowing that he doesn't have all the information. And when he sees it, he says, "Forget the Jews and put Haman to death." The very thing that Haman devises of them, that's what happens [to him]. But I want you to notice that Esther did approach the king because she knew that he did not have all the information. But she spoke with respect.

This was totally different than what I did when I was sitting before my pastor and arguing with him for 20 minutes about the home groups. Are you seeing the difference? I have a policy with my staff. I tell my staff, "If you see that I don't have information on a decision, you may come to me and petition me and give me that information one time. If more information comes up after that, come back and petition me again, that's fine. But once I give a decision, we're going that direction and we're all going to go together in one heart, in one mind, in one accord, whether I've made a mistake or not."

Well, what if a leader's making a decision before he has all the facts? Here's another incident. David with Saul, remember this? David goes to Saul, they're fighting the Philistines. The giant Goliath comes out for 40 days and David goes to the king and says, "I'll kill him." And the king looks up and says, "You'll kill him?" Now listen, David then petitions the king and entreats him as a father. Everybody say, "Entreats him as a father." "Entreats him as a father." This is the way you address authority, you speak with respect, you address them as a father, you never rebuke a father. David didn't look at Saul and say, "Come on, Saul, where's your faith? Don't you have any more faith than this? God gave me the paw of the lions and the bears, this giant's nothing." That's not what David said, he spoke with great respect and said, "Saul, O king, the Lord gave me the paw of the lion and the paw of the bear, I know he'll do the same thing." And Saul saw the faith, God turned his heart, and the king said, "Go get him." Are you with me? Are you seeing this?

All right, now I want to come to the big one, this is the one I want to spend some time on. What if authority tells me the opposite of what I felt to do in prayer? Are we on the same page, are we all together on this one? What if authority tells me to do the opposite of what I was shown to do in prayer? How do we handle that? Let me go back to the party for a minute. And remember I told you this morning God spoke to me and told me to do it? Remember I even told you that God gave me the plan on how to do it, how to choose the leaders, to train the leaders? And I had even told my pastor in the parking lot and eight months later—after eight months of work— he came into a pastors' meeting and said, "Gentlemen, the Holy Spirit has shown the direction of the home church is not to have home groups. I want you to cancel all your home groups." And I argued with him for 20 minutes. I was so passionate. Number one because I thought he was wrongly influenced, and number two, God had spoken to me in prayer. That's why I fought with my pastor so intensely. But now let me tell you something, folks. God tests us. Do you know what a test is? That is when God tells you to do something that he doesn't intend for you do, but he tells you do it just to see if you'll do it. Genesis 22:1 says this. God tested Abraham. Right? How did he test him? He said, "I

want you to take your son and I want you to go three days journey to Mount Moriah and I want you to offer him up as a sacrifice." You know what the Bible says, early in the morning Abraham rose up and went. He didn't wait three or four months, he went immediately. Abraham went all the way to the place where he lifted up the knife, was ready to run the knife through, and the Angel of the Lord stopped him and said, "Stop. Now I know you fear God because you didn't withhold the most valuable thing in your life I know that you'll obey Me in everything."

In 2 Corinthians 2, look what Paul said to the Corinthian church. Now Paul was an authority in this church. He was the senior pastor in this church. To be very Scriptural about it, he was the apostle over this church and Paul wrote this letter and look what he said in verse 9. 2 Corinthians 2:9 he said, *"For to this end."* Everybody say, "To this end." "To this end." Now would you look up at me please? What does it mean when somebody says, "To this end"? He's saying, "For this purpose, the whole reason I told you to do this"—watch this— *"For to this end [or for the whole reason I told you to do this] I also wrote that I might put you to the test, whether you are obedient in all things."* In other words, what Paul is saying to them is, "I gave you a command in the first letter to do something. And I gave you that command for one reason, to see if you would do it." Because Paul gave a very difficult command and that in itself carries something. If we're able to do the most difficult thing God asks us to do, then that means that we'll do anything. Those parties to me represented eight months of work. To me they represented the success of our youth ministry and they also represented young people coming into the kingdom of God which I was so passionately wanting to see. But God said, "I want the thing that is the most important thing in your ministry—the thing you've worked the hardest on—I want you to give it up," and he spoke it through my pastor. Why? Because I believe God told me to do it in prayer because he knew he would tell my senior pastor a few months later to tell all of us not to do it because God wanted me to see if I would recognize his voice in the voice of my senior pastor. God did it for one reason and that was to test me. God did speak to me. He did tell me to do it but he fully knew what was coming down the road. He wanted to see if I would give up Isaac. It was the most important thing in the youth ministry and the Lord knew if I would submit to His authority on that issue I would submit to Him on anything else. And the area he was testing me at that particular time was delegated authority. I had already gone through another test on His direct authority a couple years earlier. I fully believe this folks, God will test you in both areas of your life. He will test you on His direct authority and He will ask you for the thing that He actually promised you and you waited for. Because let me tell you something. God did not tell Abraham to put Ishmael on the altar. "Ishmael is what you birthed in the flesh." God said, "I want Isaac, the very thing I promised you, and you waited 25 years for, and you love very much." Then he tests us with delegated authority to see if we see His authority in the delegated authority.

In Numbers 30. I want you to notice the second verse. *"If a man makes a vow to the LORD, or swears an oath to bind himself by some agreement, he shall not break his word; He shall do according to all that proceeds out of his mouth."* Would you look up at me? Do you know how important it is to God that when we make a vow, we keep our vow? I want to show you actually—put your marker there. I want to show you Deuteronomy 23, go there real quick. Let me show you how important it is to God. Look at what verse 21 says. God says, *"When you make a vow to the LORD your God, you shall not delay to pay it; for the LORD your God will surely require it of you, and would be sin to you."* Everybody say, "Sin." "Sin." *"But if you abstain from vowing, it shall not be sin to you."* Verse 23: *"That which has gone from your lips you shall keep and perform, for you voluntarily vowed to the LORD your God what you have promised with your mouth."* Do you see how serious it is?

If you look at Ecclesiastes 5 it says, *"Do not be rash with your mouth, And let not your heart utter anything hastily before God. . . . When you make a vow to God, do not delay to pay it; For He has no pleasure in fools. Pay what you have vowed—better not to vow than to vow and not pay [it]."* Now do you see how serious a vow is to God? Do you see this? Say, "Amen," if you do. "Amen."

I want you to see something. Go back to Numbers 30 and I want to show you something most interesting. Numbers chapter 30 are you there? Look at verse 3. *"Or if a woman makes a vow to the LORD"*— Now remember how important the vows are— *"and binds herself by some agreement while in her father's house in her youth, and her father hears her vow and the agreement by which she has bound herself, and her father holds his peace, then all her vows shall stand, and every agreement with which she has bound herself shall stand."* Verse 5: *"But if her father overrules her on the day that he hears, then none of her vows or agreements by which she has bound herself shall stand; and the LORD will release her, because her father overruled her."* Do you see the importance that God puts in delegated authority? The vow that is so important God says, "When she makes the vow and her father overrides it, the Lord will not hold her to it because her father's overruled it." He goes on to say in the next several verses, if that woman ever gets married and she makes a vow and her husband hears the vow, if on the day that she makes the vow he overrules the vow, she shall not be held accountable for that vow, she's released. When God entrusts His authority to somebody, he doesn't take it back.

I'll never forget the day when the Spirit of God, I was in prayer and He said, "Son, you must understand when I give authority I am not like some who takes it back when I don't like the decisions people are making." He said, "Because if I was that way, I would have jerked the fruit right out of Adam's hand before he ate it and said, 'What do you think you're doing? You're going to cause suffering to come on all of humanity. And you're going to cause My son to have to come and have to die for this.'" He let him eat it because God said to Adam, "You rule the garden." He gave him authority in that garden and God did not override the authority which He gave to Adam. When God makes a man, a husband over a wife, he does not overrule that authority. If that husband says, "That vow is overruled," then the very vow that is so important to God, God says, "She's released." If you want to know the truth, it's the exact same way with all authority. If your pastor comes to you and says this and this and this. Let me tell you something. You can just say, "All right Lord, this is what my pastor has said, I am submitted to your authority. If he's not saying what's right then Lord that's between you and him. But as far as, Lord, my relationship with you, I'm obeying your delegated authority and you'll never be able to say to me I didn't obey." That's the kind of attitude we've got to have. Unless, I'm going to say it one more time, unless authority tells you to do something that is contrary to the written Word of God. That is the only time we are not to obey.

Session Nine

Unfair Treatment

The LORD is near to those who have a broken heart,
And saves such as have a contrite spirit.
Psalm 34:18

Summary for *Under Cover,* Chapter 13

God desires communion with us. It is for this sole purpose that we were created. However, sin has come into the world and turned our hearts from God. We are now content to find satisfaction and fulfillment in the things of this world. We no longer seek the face of God. We turn to our own desires and live in the darkness that we have allowed to come into our lives.

God, however, was not content to let us stay in the darkness. He has never ceased doing everything to bring us back to Himself and to the light. And for this purpose, He allows trials in our lives to break us of sinful and dangerous habits. Many men and women throughout history have experienced God through trials and have been cleansed of the sinfulness that separated them from God. David, in the psalms states many times that it is a broken heart that God desires—the heart humbled before God.

Often, our conversion takes place under the authority of leaders that God has placed in our lives to help change us. Sometimes these leaders are good and compassionate, while at other times they are harsh, even cruel or wicked.

Whatever the condition of their heart, God places them and uses them for good in each individual's life. The Lord never allows any spiritual harm to come to those that love Him. He only asks that we have the faith of a child to trust and obey Him in every situation. He takes care of all our needs.

The Bible gives us the example of David under the leadership of King Saul. Once the favorite subject of the king, David was eventually forced to flee for his own life. Saul was bent on killing David out of jealousy. However, David always remained submitted and loyal to Saul. Even though he was being unfairly treated and had every earthly right to retaliate against Saul, David never sinned against God's anointed king. He understood that all authority on earth has been ordained by God and to question it is not the place of man.

It was through his trials with Saul that David learned to trust the Lord for his life and all his needs. We too can learn through the trials that God allows us in our lives. As we endeavor to seek the will of God, see how His hand moves in every situation of our lives.

Notes from Chapter 13 (Video Session 9)

_____

_____

_____

_____

_____

_____

_____

Allow me to illustrate. A warhorse is not fit for service until his will is broken. Though he may be stronger, swifter, and more gifted than all the other horses in the stables, he cannot serve until he's broken. He will stay in the stables while less gifted horses go to war. To be broken does not mean to be weakened. It has to do with submission to authority.

In the horse's case, his master is the rider. If the horse is successfully broken and trained, he can be trusted in any and all circumstances. In the heat of the battle as the bullets or arrows fly, he will not flinch. While swords and axes are wielded, he will not retreat. While guns are raised and cannons shot, he will not deviate from his master's desires. He will stay in firm submission to his master, no matter who he is. He will bypass any attempt to protect or benefit himself in order to fulfill the commands of the rider.

This breaking process is uniquely accomplished in each individual in accordance with the prescription of the Lord Himself. He is the only One who knows when the process is truly complete, and you are prepared for the manner of service He desires to bring through you. Each new level brings another round of breaking.

John Bevere, *Under Cover,* p. 161.

Warm-Up Questions

1. What is your first reaction when you are treated unfairly by an authority in your life?

_____

_____

_____

2. How do you usually respond when you see someone in a situation that is unfair? Why do you react this way?

_____

_____

_____

3. How do you view hardship and suffering in your life?

_____

_____

_____

Teaching by John Bevere

Watch video session 9 on the tape.

Teaching Review

4. How is the word "harsh" defined in the Greek dictionary?

_____

_____

5. According to 1 Peter 2:21, what is a Christian's calling?

_____

_____

6. What three things does suffering unfair treatment from leadership accomplish?

_____

_____

_____

_____

7. Why didn't Jesus defend Himself when He was accused at His trial?

_____

_____

_____

8. How many times did David spare Saul's life? What does this tell us about David?

_____

_____

_____

_____

We must keep before us that it is for the ultimate purpose of good that God brings us through unfair treatment at the hands of authorities. He uses it to set us up for a blessing. Peter continued his exhortation: "Do not repay evil with evil or insult with insult, but with blessing, because *to this you were called* so that you may *inherit a blessing*" (1 Peter 3:9, NIV, emphasis added).

The blessing may not consist of natural things, although many times it can; rather, it comes in more important areas, such as Christlike character, advancement of the kingdom, or eternal rewards. When we submit to God's authority, no harm can come to our spiritual well being. Peter made it clear by asking, "And who is he who will harm you if you become followers of what is good?" (1 Peter 3:13). The context of this statement is to follow Jesus' personal example.

John Bevere, *Under Cover*, p. 175.

Exploring God's Word

Psalm 51:16–17 *For you do not desire sacrifice, or else I would give it; You do not delight in burnt offering. The sacrifices of God are a broken spirit, A broken and a contrite heart—These, O God, You will not despise.*

9. Why do we sometimes try to offer to God what He does not want?

_____
_____
_____
_____

10. According to this Scripture, what is it that God desires?

_____
_____
_____
_____

11. How is our offering more appropriate when we offer God what He desires rather than what we want to offer Him?

_____
_____
_____
_____

Personal Application

_____
_____
_____

1 Peter 2:18–21 *Servants, be submissive to your masters with all fear, not only to the good and gentle, but also to the harsh. For this is commendable, if because of conscience toward God one endures grief, suffering wrongfully. For what credit is it if, when you are beaten for your faults, you take it patiently? But when you do good and suffer, if you take it patiently, this is commendable before God. For to this you were called, because Christ also suffered for us, leaving us an example, that you should follow His steps.*

12. How does this verse call all Christians to behave toward authority?

_____

_____

_____

_____

_____

13. When we suffer unjustly, how are we to respond? Whose example are we to follow?

_____

_____

14. What does suffering unfairly teach us about the nature of Christianity?

_____

_____

_____

_____

_____

_____

_____

Personal Application

_____

_____

_____

Romans 12:19 *Beloved, do not avenge yourselves, but rather give place to wrath; for it is written, 'Vengeance is Mine, I will repay,' says the Lord.*

15. Why is it difficult to turn from revenge when we are treated wrongly?

_____

_____

_____

_____

_____

_____

_____

16. How is God a much more righteous judge than we are?

_____

_____

_____

Personal Application

_____

_____

_____

1 Peter 3:9 *Do not repay evil with evil or insult with insult, but with blessing, because to this you were called so that you may inherit a blessing.*

17. How does God enable us to overcome our natural inclination for vengeance when we are mistreated?

_____

_____

_____

_____

_____

18. How does God reward us when we refrain from evil?

_____

_____

_____

Personal Application

_____

_____

_____

Exposing the Truth

19. Think about your own experiences with authority. Have you ever experienced any unfair treatment? How did you react to the situation? Was this what you would consider a Christ-like response? If you could react differently, what would you have done?

_____

_____

_____

_____

20. In the *Under Cover* series, John says, "The breaking process is uniquely accomplished in each individual in accordance with the prescription of the Lord

Himself. He is the only One who knows when the process is truly complete, and you are prepared for the manner of service He desires to bring through you. Each new level brings another round of breaking." Why does God continually bring us to new levels of faith and humility in order to accomplish His will in us? Will we ever complete the process of transformation?

_____

_____

_____

_____

_____

_____

_____

21. The Scriptures show us the life of Christ and what He had to endure while He remained on earth. In what ways did Christ suffer unfair treatment from each of the following people and what was His response to each?

The Jewish religious leaders _____

_____

Response _____

_____

_____

The Roman officials _____

_____

Response _____

His own followers _____
They failed to understand.

Let me give you another example of one who is armed. A crucial part of airline pilot training is the use of flight simulators. In these simulators pilots are confronted by almost every flight emergency they might face. In the safety of this setting, they hone their response skills until they can successfully face them. This preparation arms them for emergencies. If something happens on an actual flight, the pilots do not panic-they respond, assisted and guided by extensive training. Even though the passengers may panic and give way to shock and hysteria, the pilots remain calm and in full control. Investigators who review black box tape recordings from crashes are amazed by the calmness of the pilots. There is usually no panic in their voices even up to the moment of impact. They were armed!

John Bevere, *Under Cover*, p. 176.

Applying the Lesson

Many churches today play a major role in promoting social causes around the world. They promote the rights of individuals and minorities in order to gain an equality that is many times lacking. This championing of social causes can sometimes, however, lead to inappropriate attitudes regarding authority. It is important for the church to remain Christ-like even when trying to fight against the evils of social injustice. How does your local church both care for the needs of those being unfairly treated and remain in submission to authorities that can be careless or even harsh?

_____

_____

_____

_____

_____

Checking Your Cover

Conclude this session by praying that God will enable you to be Christ-like as you continue to learn humility, patience, and long-suffering.

Video Script for Lesson 9
Unfair Treatment

Now I want to say this as you turn there and we get ready to go here. God has a goal for us. Everybody say, "God's got a goal for us." "God's got a goal for us." Now the goal may not be too much fun, it may not be comfortable, it may not be nice as far as your flesh comfort goes, but it is very good for us. And you know what that goal is? To break us. Everybody say, "Amen." "Amen." Now let me give you an example of what brokenness means because you know what? So many times brokenness has been mistaken for weakness and brokenness has nothing to do with weakness. Can you say, "Amen"? "Amen." You can have a horse that is more powerful, more gifted, stronger, jump higher, run faster than any other horse. But if it's not broken when wartime comes, it's sitting in the stables. The reason is those horses that are broken when they ride into battle, the guns are firing, the swords are being wielded, and that horse stays steady on course and only moves at the nudge of his master who is the rider. He is completely submitted to that rider, therefore he is a broken horse. That is exactly what God desires for us. David said it like this in Psalm 51:16–17. *"For You do not desire sacrifice, or else I would give it. You do not delight in burnt offering. The sacrifices of God are a broken spirit, a broken and a contrite heart—These, O God, You will not despise."* Amen.

I want to read now from [1 Peter 2:13]: Peter says, *"Therefore submit yourselves to every ordinance of man for the Lord's sake, whether the king as supreme, or to governors, as to those who are sent by him for the punishment of evildoers and for the praise of those who do good. For this is the will of God, that by doing good"*—Everybody say, "Doing good." "Doing good."— *"you may put to silence the ignorance of foolish men—as free, yet not using liberty as a cloak [for wickedness], but as bondservants of God. Honor all people. Love the brotherhood. Fear God. Honor the king."* We've talked about that much in previous lessons, right? I want to move to the next verse tonight. Verse 18: *"Servants,"* now let me say it to you like this—employees, students, church members, civilians—are you getting the drift? *"Servants, be submissive to your masters"*—employers, bosses, teachers, coaches. Are we on the same page, we're just modernizing this all right?— *"with all fear."* Everybody say, "All fear." "All fear." Folks, can I say something to you? Basically, what I've been preaching to you the last eight sessions and what I'm going to continue preaching to you is the fear of God. When we fear God, we recognize his authority. Now watch this. Verse 18: *"Servants, be submissive to your masters with all fear, not only to the good and gentle"*—we love good and gentle leaders, don't we?— *"but also to the harsh"?* Wait a minute. Some people don't even know this verse exists. *"Employees, church members be submissive to your employers with all fear not only the good and gentle but also to the harsh"?* Now some of you are thinking, "Well maybe the New King James is just a little bit strong here with that word." So I thought that too. So I went back to the original and I found out that the Greek word for the word "harsh" is the Greek word *skolios*. In the Thayer's *Dictionary* it means this: crooked, perverse, wicked, unfair, and forward. Are we together on this? Now listen to what *W. Vine's*, who is an expert in Greek New Testament words says. *Vine's* says it is tyrannical for unjust leaders, tyrannical masters. Now are you familiar with tyrants? Peter is telling us to be submissive not only to the good and gentle, but to tyrants? Now how many of you know that God is not a child abuser? Now when I read a verse like this I've got to say God, "What's the wisdom in this one?" Well, God always picks out the perfect leaders for us in order to bring us to a place of growth and maturity and brokenness.

You know I want to read this to you out of the New

Century Version. *"Not only to those who are good and kind, but also to those who are dishonest."* The Contemporary English Version says, *"Do this not only to those who are kind and thoughtful, but also to those who are cruel."* In the New American Standard it says, *"Not only to those who are good and gentle, but also those who are unreasonable."* Are you getting the drift on this one?

Now I'm going to tell you this, Peter's words get absolutely more uncomfortable before they get easier. So I just want to brace you for this, okay? Because look at verse 9. Out of the New Living Translation he goes on to say this, *"God is pleased with you when, for the sake of conscience, you patiently endure unfair treatment."* Everybody say, "Unfair treatment." "Unfair treatment." Now all of us are familiar with unfair treatment. God says it is actually commendable, it is wonderful in His sight, He absolutely delights when His people endure unfair treatment. Now unfair treatment is when you were treated wrongly when you did what was right. You do good and you get mistreated for it. Isn't that true? Now I remember, we had a situation where my oldest son, he was seven years old, and Austin, his younger brother who was four years old at the time, got something that Addison felt that he should have gotten and he thought the thing was totally unfair. So he just looked at his mom, kind of stomped his foot down a little and said, "Mom, that's not fair!" And Lisa turned around and looked at Addison and said, "Addison, life's not fair." And Addison looked up at my wife as if to say, "You're my mom? What do you mean life's not fair?" And she said, "Addison, was it fair that Jesus did absolutely nothing wrong yet He hung on the cross bearing your punishment and your judgment?" He looked at her and said, "No, it's not fair." She said, "Life's not fair the way you think fair is fair." She said, "But it's just." Amen. Amen.

Now I want you to notice this, look at verse 20 now. He goes on to say, *"For what credit is it if, when you are beaten for your faults, you take it patiently?"* In other words, all he's saying there is when you do what's wrong and get punished for it, you get treated hard for it. Don't think like you're going to get persecution that's going to give God glory. You're going to get what you deserve is what he's saying. See there's two kinds of persecution. There's persecution we bring on ourselves and there's persecution for righteousness' sake. Persecution we bring on ourselves is usually from unwise behavior. Correct the behavior and that persecution stops. But the persecution for righteousness' sake is what God loves. When we take it right. Are you with me?

Now watch what he goes on to say watch this. Verse 21: *"For to this you were called."* Everybody say, "This is my calling." "This is my calling." You know we're always talking about that. What are you called to do? What has God called you to do? Everybody listen, "This is your calling." Isn't this fun tonight? Aren't you glad you came? It's all going to make sense in a few minutes. *"For to this you were called, because Christ also suffered for us, leaving us an example, that you should follow His [foot]steps."* Now I want to read this out of the *Amplified Bible.* Look up at me please and listen. *"For even to this you were called it is inseparable from your vocation. For Christ also suffered for you leaving you His personal example so that you should follow in His footsteps."* What is our calling folks? To handle unfair treatment correctly. Jesus left us His personal example. Everybody say, "His personal example." "His personal example."

I want to show it to you, go over with me please to Mark's gospel, the fifteenth chapter. Now while you're turning over there. Let's ask a question here tonight. What good does handling or suffering unfair treatment accomplish in handling it correctly? Number one: it makes room for God's righteous judgment. Number two: it develops the character of Christ. And number three: our submission under this treatment glorifies God. Let me show you what I'm talking about. In Mark's gospel the fifteenth chapter, I want you to look at the third verse. Jesus is brought before Pilate and in verse 3 it says, *"The chief priests accused him of many things, but He answered nothing."* Now would you look up at me? I want to explain this situation to you. The chief priests, as I explained to you in the previous video lesson, back then were the governmental leaders as well as the religious. Jesus is in the highest court in the land, there is no higher court. If you want to modernize this, He's in the Supreme Court. He's already been accused in a lower court and has now been brought to a higher court. He is standing before the Roman governor and this Roman governor has the power to condemn Him, the power to put Him to the cross, or the power to put Him in the dungeon, or into hard labor. These men, that are governmental leaders like the senators of his country, are speaking about Jesus in this judgment seat before this judge absolute, total, complete lies. There isn't a shred of truth to what they are saying. Are you with me? But yet Jesus is not answering them back. Now the question we have to ask is, "Why isn't He answering them back?" The reason we're going to see in 1 Peter is, is that He is committing His case to the hands of God.

I want to share with you something. I was in a situation one time when an authority in my life was not treating me right. And I kept frantically defending myself and even at times felt like vindicating myself. And the Spirit of God gave me a vision one day. And He said, "Son, as long as you are defending yourself, this is what I'm doing." And I saw the Lord standing with His hands behind His back, He could do nothing. The moment I stopped defending myself I saw God involved in my situation and the Lord said, "Do you want me to defend you or do you want you to defend you?" I said, "God, I want you to defend me." He said, "That's good." Amen. Can you agree? The moment you justify or defend yourself you yield to your accuser as judge. Amen. You forfeit your spiritual right of protection for he rises above you in the realm of the Spirit. When you get what I'm saying in this very lesson today into your spirit, it's going to free you. Now Jesus answers nothing. Notice verse 3 again. *"And the chief priests accused Him of many things, but He answered nothing."* Everybody say. "Answered nothing." "Answered

nothing." So He's totally silent. They are speaking complete lies. Why? Because Peter said He left His case in the hands of God who always judges rightly. Now watch this, verse 4: *"Then Pilate asked Him again, saying, 'Do you answer nothing? See how many things they testify against You.'"* Verse 5: *"But Jesus still answered nothing, so that Pilate marveled."* Everybody say, "Pilate marveled." "Pilate marveled." This is a Roman governor, he has sat in this judgment seat many, many, many times before. Men stood before him accused. And these men, if they were accused, were going either to slave labor, or they were going to the dungeon, or they were going to a criminal's execution death. And Pilate had watched time, after time, after time, men frantically defending themselves. Giving answers to the accusations, defending themselves, trying to keep judgment from coming on their lives. Yet he is watching this man who he happens to know is a good man. Because Pilate knew He was delivered to them through envy. Pilate is marveling, he knows these guys are speaking lies to him, yet He's not defending Himself. Why? Because He left His case in the hands of God who judges righteously.

I remember when Addison was nine years old, my oldest son. He was coming home from school night after night, he was in a Christian school, and for some reason, he had this one particular teacher that just had it out for him. And this teacher was after him. If five kids were talking in the class, Addison would be singled out and yelled at by this teacher. He would come home in tears many nights. This man was extremely hard on him, he sent a note home about him that went on his permanent record. Addison had been a good student up to then. I mean the kid's made I don't think a handful of Bs in six years. The kid has been a phenomenal student. But this teacher was out to get him. And so one night he comes home for dinner. And Addison's sitting at the dinner table and he said, "Mom and Dad, I don't know what to do." He said, "We were in line today, the teacher's back was to us, two kids standing behind me were talking and giggling," and he said, "the teacher started turning around, and as he turned around, they shut up. And he pointed me out and yelled at me in front of the whole class." And now the tears were running and Mom got him and she says, "Oh, son." And he's just going, "I wasn't even talking." And I said, "Well, Addison," I looked at him and I felt compassion for my son. I said, "Son, what did you do when this teacher did this to you today?" And he said, "Dad, I looked at him and said"—and you could see the frustration in his eyes. He said, "I looked at the teacher's eyes, 'I wasn't talking, it wasn't me, it was them.'" I said, "Now son, is this the way you always respond when he corrects you?" He said, "Yes, especially if he's not right." Well I said, "Son, that's not right," I said, "it's wrong." I said, "I've got a question for you. Do you want to do this God's way or do you want to do this your way?" And I began to explain to him and I read to him these verses of Scripture. And I showed him how Jesus did not defend himself and the reason Jesus gave us His personal example. The reason He didn't defend himself was because He left His case in the hands of God because He wanted God to judge Him. Are you with me?

And I said, "Now son, let me share something with that happened with me. You were a little, tiny boy, you're were about one-and-a-half or two years old, let me share something with you. Remember back when I was a youth pastor? There was the office manager of the church, he was out to get me. He was a man that was above me. It was me, and then I reported to him, and he reported to the senior pastor of the church. And this guy was out to get me. He had released a memo campaign that employees would come up to my wife saying, 'Why doesn't he just put your husband's name on it?' The reason he had done this is because he had a fifteen-year-old boy in my youth group. And I was preaching in this youth group messages of holiness and purity in the fear of God. And one night his fifteen-year-old son after a service came up to my wife just weeping and said, 'How can I live the holy life that pastor John is preaching when this is going on at my home, this is going on, this is going on, and this is going on?' And my wife was horrified. My wife basically ministered

to him and kind of just left the mom and dad part alone; but she thought, my goodness this is my husband's boss. Well, when that happened, the man set his eye against me, he started the memo campaign. And I'm telling you, he started separating the senior pastor and I. He started telling the senior pastor things about me that I don't believe were true. And he started telling me things about the senior pastor that I don't believe were true. He started putting information in both of us trying to put a wedge between us. And I went for four months without meeting the senior pastor. I wasn't able to get in. For some reason he would meet with me. And so I remember one night after a youth service four of the young kids came up to me and said, 'Pastor John, we're so sorry that you're being fired. We can't believe it.' I said, 'Excuse me? Well, who said it?' They said so and so. I went to him. 'Who told you this?' They said so and so. Well, I traced it to four kids and finally traced it back to this office manager's son. I said, 'Where did you hear this?' He said, 'From my dad.' So I went to the office manager and I sat down in his office with him. And I said, 'Listen, your son told some other kids in the youth group that I'm being fired.' And I said, 'What is up?' And he said, 'Oh, John I'm so sorry, you know I was just repeating to my wife at home what the senior pastor's saying about you and my son happened to hear it and that's what happened. I'm just saying what he's saying.' Well, now for the next two months I didn't know if I was going to be fired or what was going to happen. I had left an engineering job, I'd been in the ministry for over four years, and I didn't have a 'Plan B'. And I had a wife and I had a little child to feed. And my wife is just sitting there going, 'What is going on?' I said, 'I don't know.' Well it kept getting worse and worse and worse until finally a decision was made to fire me. A final decision was made to let me go. And I remember the senior pastor got up on the Sunday morning and told the church of 7,000 people, he said a decision has been made, there's going to be a big change in the youth group. I want to meet with all the youth on Tuesday night. The two brothers of the pastor told me, they said, 'John, you're fired. This was it.' And I remember, I was to walk into his office on Monday morning and I was to meet with him and the office manager and one other senior associate pastor and that was when they were going to fire me. And I remember walking into that office because all weekend my wife said, 'What are you going to do?' I said, 'Nothing.' I said, 'God sent me here, He's going to have to be the one who vindicates me.' I said, 'I'm not doing a thing.' And she said, 'All right.' I walk into the pastor's office, the pastor's sitting there alone, the office manager is not there, the other senior associate's not there. And the senior pastor said, 'John, God sent you to this church, I'm not letting you go.' He said, 'Why does this man want you fired so bad?' I said, 'I don't know.' He said, 'Well, make it right.' I said, 'I don't know what I'm doing.' He said, 'Just make it right.'"

"Well I remember about a month later, I had some written evidence of the way this man was operating because he was not only trying to get rid of me, but he was also trying to get rid of the praise and worship leader, and one other pastor. And I got some written, documented evidence of what this guy was doing. And I thought, 'Great!' And the senior pastor had said to me in that meeting, 'Now, I want doors open between you and me.' So I could then make an appointment and bypass. And I thought, 'Okay, I've got documented evidence of how this man's working. I'm going to bring it to the senior pastor.' And I remember making an appointment with the senior pastor and the morning I was to meet with him, I was in prayer saying, 'Okay God, how am I supposed to share this?' For 45 minutes I'm like, 'Okay Lord, tell me how am I supposed to say this?' Yet there's no peace. And I remember after 45 minutes I looked up and I screamed, 'Lord, you don't want me to show this to him do you?' And the peace of God went whoosh. And I thought, 'I don't understand it.' And I tore it up and threw it away. I thought, 'You know, I was thinking I'm doing this not only for me but for the other people, but really later I knew who I was doing it for.' You understand what I'm saying?"

"Well, about a month later I was outside praying

because I love praying outside. And I was outside praying on the church grounds and I remember an hour before the office was opened, seeing this office manager drive up in his Cadillac. And he pulls up into his parking spot and the Holy Spirit speaks to me and He says, 'Matthew chapter eighteen, I want you to go to him and apologize to him.' I said, 'Lord, what? Me apologize to him? He needs to apologize to me, he's been trying to fire me.' And the Lord spoke to me and that's all He said. And so I prayed about something else. I started praying for world missions real quick. That's the truth. And after about 20 minutes of absolute dry prayer and God's presence nowhere to be found. I said, 'Lord, what are you saying right now?' And the Lord said, 'Matthew eighteen, I want you to go to that man and apologize to him.' I said, 'Father I don't understand this. This makes no sense.' Well, the Lord began to minister to me and I saw what was going on. And I remember walking into my office and calling him and saying, 'I need to meet with you. Would you meet with me?' He said, 'Sure.' So I went to his office and I sat down with him and I said, 'I want to apologize to you.' I said, 'I was out in prayer this morning and the Spirit of God showed me something. I had been very critical and very judgmental of you and I am wrong.' And he looked at me and said, 'I forgive you.' Then we just had a few minutes of conversation, that's all I said. I didn't say, 'But you've done this and you've done that.' I said, 'I have been critical,' period. I walked out of the office. Well, his attacks against me subsided. And I remember six months later, I was out of town for one weekend. And everything this man had done got exposed. It was so severe they could have thrown him in jail like that. He could have been prosecuted. I had no idea it was that severe. The pastor had mercy, he did not prosecute, but he immediately fired that man that weekend. And when I came back from out of town he was already gone and his desk cleared out."

"I remember a year-and-a-half later, seeing him in the airport and when I saw him I remember I walked up to him, put my arms around him, and I could honestly look into his eyes and say, 'How are you doing?' Because I had already gone and I had already apologized to him. But you know the interesting thing is? The very pit he had dug for me he himself had fallen into."

I told this story to my young son, Addison, at nine years old. I said, "Son, this is what happened." I said, "Now son you can choose to do this God's way and let God defend you with your teacher, or," I said, "you can keep justifying yourself." And he said, "But Dad what if the teacher's wrong?" And I said, "Has your way worked so far?" He went, "No." I said, "Let's do it God's way." He said, "You know what I'm going to." So the next day he sat down with his teacher, he made an appointment with him. He apologized to his teacher for challenging his authority constantly. The teacher was blown away. The end of the next week, Addison got from that teacher student of the week award. And at the end of the year, that teacher gave a reward to the most outstanding student in his class the entire year. Do you know who got it? Addison got it. Now it works for a nine-year-old boy, how much more will it work for us? Are you seeing this?

Go back to 1 Peter 2. Let me show you this. 1 Peter 2:21: *"For to this you were called, because Christ also suffered for us, leaving us an example, that you should follow His steps."* Everybody say, "He left me His personal example." "He left me His personal example." *"'Who committed no sin, Nor was deceit found in His mouth who, when He was reviled [or accused, He] did not [accuse or] revile in return; when He suffered, He did not threaten, but committed Himself to [His father] who judges righteously."* Would you look up at me please? David is a young man that learned the same thing. David was brought into Saul's palace. He was made his armor bearer, he became good friends Saul's children, he ate at his table. David had been prophesied by the prophet that he was going to be the next king of Israel. And everything was going just right for David. But all of a sudden one day they come back because David is Saul's armor bearer and the women are singing songs. Saul has slain his thousands and David his ten thousands. Now Saul is

throwing spears at David trying to pin him to the wall, making him a decoration in the castle. And so David eventually has to leave the castle. For 16 years, David is running from wilderness to wilderness. Saul gets three thousand of the finest warriors of Israel. They go to the wilderness of Engedi because they heard David was there. They go into the cave to minister to themselves, I believe they were taking a bath or going to the bathroom or something, but they have to take off their armor. When they did, David's men looked at him and said, "This is it, David. God has given you your enemy. Look at what he has done. He's got no armor on. Let's go kill him. God is vindicating you." David said, "God forbid that I touch my master." Right? And so you know what David does? Because in the heart of every person that has a cruel leader they think somebody lied to him and told him I'm in rebellion or I want something of his. So David's constantly thinking, "How can I prove I'm not in rebellion to my leader?" So David goes and cuts a little piece of the robe off. And he goes a great distance and Saul comes out and David says, "My father, my father." In other words, "Saul, why aren't you being a father to me?" He said, "I could have killed you right there. If there was rebellion in me—I was even encouraged to do it. But I want you to know there's no rebellion in me. I am not out after your throne or ministry." And Saul goes, "Oh David, you're righteous, more righteous than I." And Saul leaves and David thinks, "Sheoo! I've finally proven my innocence to him. I've proven I'm not in rebellion. He'll probably send somebody to bring me back."

But two chapters later, just two chapters later, Saul hears he's in the hills of Hakilah and Saul brings the same three thousand soldiers out to kill him. Now can you imagine the devastation in David when his leader is now coming out to kill him and he has already proven there's absolutely no rebellion in him? He now realizes, "This man is out to kill me no matter what, no matter if I'm innocent or if I'm guilty. He is a wicked man." Are you following me? Now listen carefully, Saul comes into the place where David is, into the area where he's at. And the

Bible says that the Lord put Saul, Abner, and all three thousand soldiers into a deep sleep from the Lord. And David knew it. So David goes to his men and goes, "Who will sneak into Saul's camp with me?" And God picks the perfect guy, Abishai, blood-thirsty, he's Joab's little brother. Do you understand? And Abishai says, "I'll go." David says, "Let's go." So they sneak all the way to the center where Saul is lying down and Abishai gets the spirit and says, "All right, David, just give me the word. I'm going to run it through and he'll never get up again." He's waiting for David to say something, but he's not saying anything. He looks and says, "David—David, come on—just give me the word." And David doesn't say anything. So he looks at him and he says, "Wait a minute—David, David, David. This man murdered 85 ministers, their wives and their children in cold blood because they gave you a sword and they gave you some food. He murdered 85 of God's priests in cold blood, and their wives and their little babies. Come on, just give me the word." David doesn't say anything. "So David, this is self defense. He's trying to kill you and if you don't defend yourself, he'll kill you. This will stand up in any court of law. Just give me the word." And David's not saying anything. "David, don't you know, God sent the prophet to anoint you, you're going to be the next king of Israel. Why do you think God would put this whole army into a deep sleep? He is delivering our nation from this man who's killing people, innocent people and destroying our nation. He's delivering us." David still doesn't say anything. Abeshi looks at him and says, "Why aren't you telling me to do this?" And David looks at Abishai and says, "Don't touch him, because who can stretch out their hands against their leader and remain guiltless?" And you know what David said? He said, "Let God judge between him and me." He left his case in the hands of him who judges righteously. He walks out of the camp. To remain a man or woman after God's heart, you must leave your case in the hands of God's own heart. Why does God say, "Handle unfair treatment correctly"? Why does He tells us to rejoice and not to defend ourselves? Because he said, "If you don't, I will. If you get this in your spirit, you get it in your life." Let me tell you something, God never loses any cases He seeks to defend. It may not be as quick as you want it or the way you want it, but it will come.

Session Ten

Self-Inflicted Judgment

I beseech you therefore, brethren, by the mercies of God,
that you present your bodies a living sacrifice, holy,
acceptable to God, which is your reasonable service.
And do not be conformed to this world, but be transformed by
the renewing of your mind, that you may prove what is that
good and acceptable and perfect will of God.
Romans 12:1–2

Summary for *Under Cover,* Chapter 14

Not every one responds to leadership like David did. Too
often we delight in seeing defects in our authorities, and
then feel justified to throw off restraint. But our response
to the sins of others, especially those who are leaders, is
one of the greatest indicators of our spiritual maturity.
This being the case, God often uses the faults and mistakes
of authorities in our lives to expose the true condition of
our hearts.

As we see those in authority over us fail to maintain
integrity, we are faced with a choice. We can either
criticize and belittle them for their transgression, or we
can maintain respect for their position and recognize God's
authority on their lives. What we choose to do will
enlighten us to the condition and attitude of our hearts. A
heart that is dedicated to divine authority will refrain from
judging any authority that has failed. A heart that does not

recognize God's ordinance will be critical and complain against that authority's lack of character.

Noah's sons experienced this when they found their father drunk and naked in his tent. Shem and Japheth maintained respect for their father and would not disgrace or criticize him for his actions. However, Ham failed to recognize this authority and was cursed by Noah for his disrespect. Noah's failure brought to light the true condition of Ham's heart. We, too, see what we truly believe when our leaders fail.

Too often our own pride hinders us from keeping a right attitude concerning God's ordained authority. We exalt ourselves in our own eyes and criticize others for their lack of faith or morality. God would have us humble ourselves before we invite calamity into our lives. It is God that humbles the proud and exalts the weak. As we begin to convert our minds and our hearts, God will reward us for the respect we show to those in authority over us.

Notes from Chapter 14 (Video Session 10)

_____

_____

_____

_____

_____

_____

_____

_____

_____

_____

I understand that a movement within the Church called discipleship got out of hand in the 1970s, and submission to leaders teetered out of balance. People were asking pastors about whether they could go on vacations, buy a specific car or other major item, or marry a certain individual. I wasn't involved so I don't know exactly how far overboard it actually went, but some who were involved said that it ended up being unscriptural.

This movement and other abuses of leadership caused a rebound in the opposite direction. Because spiritual authority had been abused, people opted to despise it. This spawned some extreme free agents and spiritual vagabonds who ran from church to church, convention to convention, and conducted their prayer meetings and birthed their own churches often because they couldn't find a pastor perfect enough to submit to. This mentality contributed to the secret power of lawlessness that Paul warned would occur in our day.

John Bevere, Under Cover, p. 187.

Warm-Up Questions

1. Write down the names of three leaders that have in some way failed to maintain their position and describe what that failure was:

Leader	Failure
_____	_____
_____	_____
_____	_____

What was your reaction to each of the leader's failure?

Leader   Failure

_____   _____

_____   _____

_____   _____

2. In what ways does our society contribute to the lack of respect for authority?

_____

_____

_____

Teaching by John Bevere

Watch video session 10 on the tape.

Teaching Review

1. How did each of the following men react to the failure of the authorities in their lives?

Ham _____

Shem and Japheth _____

_____

David _____

_____

2. According to Romans 13:1–2, how does a person bring self-inflicted judgment on themselves?

_____

_____

3. Define giftedness.
   Giftedness is _____

   _____

4. What is the difference between giftedness and authority?

   _____

   _____

   _____

   _____

   _____

   _____

Exploring God's Word

Matthew 5:44 *"But I say to you, love your enemies, bless those who curse you, do good to those who hate you, and pray for those who spitefully use you and persecute you."*

5. How does this verse contradict our natural inclinations?

   _____

   _____

   _____

   _____

6. In what ways does this verse apply to our attitudes concerning authority?

   _____

   _____

   _____

   _____

7. How will this type of Christian response to persecution help heal us of a critical heart?

_____

_____

_____

Personal Application

_____

_____

_____

Ephesians 4:11–12 *He Himself [Jesus] gave some to be apostles, some prophets, some evangelists, and some pastors and teachers, for the equipping of the saints for the work of ministry, for the edifying of the body of Christ.*

8. Under whose authority are all the offices of the church ordained?

_____

9. For what purpose has the Lord initiated these positions?

_____

_____

10. How then should we view the people that fill these positions within our churches?

_____

Personal Application

_____

_____

_____

Romans 12:3 *For I say, through the grace given to me, to everyone who is among you, not to think of himself more highly than he ought to think, but to think soberly, as God has dealt to each one a measure of faith.*

11. What happens when an individual begins to think too highly of himself?

_____

_____

_____

12. How can we think soberly according to our faith?

_____

_____

_____

_____

_____

13. Why is humility a key characteristic of a godly leader?

_____

_____

_____

_____

Personal Application

_____

_____

_____

Romans 16:17–18 *Now I urge you, brethren, note those who cause divisions and offenses, contrary to the doctrine which you learned, and* *avoid them. For those who are such do not serve our Lord Jesus Christ, but their own belly, and by smooth words and flattering speech deceive the hearts of the simple.*

14. How are we to interact with those who cause rebellion within the body of Christ?

_____

_____

_____

_____

15. What are rebellious people ultimately serving?

_____

_____

_____

16. Who is most easily deceived and why?

_____

_____

_____

Personal Application

_____

_____

_____

Exposing the Truth

17. Self-inflicted judgment visits us according to our response to the treatment we receive from authorities. Everyone will experience unfair treatment at one time or another. You simply have to decide how you will

react to the situation. You can either react out of self-preservation and attack the one who has mistreated you or you can act out of Biblical standards and recognize God's authority in every leader. For each of the following situations, write down both a natural reaction and a Christ-like reaction:

You were criticized at work for something you did not do.

Natural Reaction _____

_____

Christ-Like Reaction _____

_____

_____

_____

You have not received credit for a job well done.

Natural Reaction _____

_____

Christ-Like Reaction _____

_____

_____

You catch a leader in immorality.

Natural Reaction _____

_____

Christ-Like Reaction _____

_____

_____

_____

Others are jealous of you because of your status or position.

Natural Reaction _____

_____

_____

Christ-Like Reaction _____

_____

_____

_____

Applying the Lesson

As you look over your responses to the situations above, consider what your reactions would be. Do you react more out of pride and self-preservation or do you try to be like Christ, recognizing God's authority with humility? Write a brief statement dedicating yourself to acting as Christ does. Commit to learn humility, respect and compassion for all those in authority.

_____

_____

_____

Checking Your Cover

"Father in heaven, give me the strength to be like Christ in all my thoughts and actions. Through your Holy Spirit, guide and direct me as I am under authorities that You Yourself have ordained. Teach me to treat all that comes to me throughout the day with peace of soul, confident that Your Will governs all. Humble my heart Lord so that You can mold me into a compassionate and loving person,

full of faith and the Holy Spirit. I love You and desire to please You, Lord. I give myself to You. Amen"

Video Script for Lesson 10
Self-Inflicted Judgment

In this lesson I want you to open your Bibles to Genesis 9 and also, while you're at it, find Romans 13. Put a marker in Romans 13. And let's go to Genesis the ninth chapter. It is sad but not everyone responds to leadership like David did. We talked about that in the last session. Too often we delight in seeing defects in our authorities. Now listen carefully. Then we feel justified to throw off restraint. But our response to the sins of others, especially those who are leaders, is one of the greatest indicators of our spiritual maturity. This being the case, God often uses the faults or the mistakes and even sins of authorities in our lives to expose the true conditions of our heart. We see this clearly in one of Noah's sons.

Noah was the one who built the ark. After the flood, Noah took up farming. One time—I guess out of depression maybe, the fact that he was the last father on the earth. I mean that could be kind of lonely, you understand that?—Noah got drunk on some of his produce. He got so drunk, he went into his tent and completely uncovered himself, he was stark nude. His youngest son walks in, whose name is Ham, and when Ham sees his dad he goes, "Uhh," and he walks out and he tells everybody. Now, everybody at that time was just Shem and Japheth, but he told them. You got it? And he goes out and he says, "Guys, Dad is drunk as a skunk and naked as a jaybird." Now Shem and Japheth, when they hear about that, put a garment on their shoulders. And they walk into the tent backwards refusing to look at their father's nakedness. They do not want that image in their minds. They walk in backwards and they cover him up. They do not want the women and the children knowing about it and they walk out. They cover their father. Are you with me? Ham uncovers him, Shem and Japheth cover him. Now watch what happens. The next morning, Noah wakes up and he realizes what his youngest son had done and Noah pronounces a curse on Ham's youngest son Canaan. And listen to the curse he pronounces. Look at verse 24: "*So Noah awoke from his wine, and knew what his younger son had done to him. Then he said: 'Cursed be Canaan; A servant of servants, He shall be to his brethren.' And he said: 'Blessed be the LORD, The God of Shem, And may Canaan be his servant. May God enlarge Japheth, And may he dwell in the tents of Shem; And may Canaan be his servant.*" A curse is pronounced on Ham's youngest son and that curse goes from generation to generation. Are you with me? Now isn't it interesting? The very curse that Ham thought he was going to bring on his father ended up coming on him. Remember in our earlier video lesson we found out that rebellion is witchcraft? It is a curse, isn't that right? The very thing he thought he was going to do. Why does he want to dishonor his father? Because then if his father tells him to do something that he doesn't want to do, then he doesn't necessarily have to obey him. If you don't like what your authority tells you to do, if you can discredit your authority in your eyes, then you don't have to obey him, you can cast off restraints. Noah's the one that sinned, Ham was the one that was right, but you can 100% right and still be wrong. Ham was 100% accurate in what he reported, yet he was wrong. Why? Because he dishonored his authority.

Somebody who has a rebellious heart will rejoice when their authority falls. If you ever find a mistake that somebody in authority over you makes or a sin or some kind of failure, if you ever find joy, or "They got what they deserve" in your heart; you don't have the heart of God. Compare that with David. What does David do when Saul finally gets judged by God? He sings a love song about Saul. Ham took joy in what happened with his father. He didn't have the heart of God.

Romans 13, I want to read it again. This is our foundational Scripture for the entire *Under Cover* sessions. Verse 1—Let's read it carefully. *"Let every soul be subject to the governing authorities. For there is no authority except from God, and the authorities that exist are appointed by God. Therefore whoever resists the authority resists the ordinance of God."* Now watch this carefully. "And those who resist will bring judgment on themselves." Isn't that amazing? They bring judgment on themselves. Folks, I have spent—in the entire 1980s—I worked for two major ministries. One ministry had 450 employees on their staff. The other one had about 150 employees on their staff. I worked for these ministries for years. I want to tell you something tonight. I'm going to tell you something that never ever failed to happen. In all the years and even afterwards, every single person that left those ministries complaining about their pastor, complaining about the leadership that the pastor appointed, griping about it, angry about it, even if they were mistreated, I've seen judgment come on their lives. It's manifested in the areas of financial problems, sickness, hardships, it never fails. And it seems that they're never able to find a stable job afterwards. However, I saw people on those staffs mistreated. I saw them absolutely mistreated. They were let go when it was somebody else's fault and false reports got to them and they were not treated right. They didn't have a chance to be able to report it right. And you know what? They stayed sweet. I'd go to them afterwards and they'd say, "You know what? I love Pastor and this is a decision, I submit to it to him. And I just love him." And I never heard them complain. And you know what? I watched every single one of those people, I watched God promote them. And I have kept up with many of them as much as 13 years later, and I have seen their lives just do nothing but be blessed and steadily progress in their call of God in their life. It has never, ever, ever failed. Not once. I have never seen a person leave complaining and not repenting of their complaining. Bitter, angry, and yet not go through some form of hardship. The Bible says, "Those that resist the authority bring judgment on themselves."

Go with me to the book of Numbers please. Numbers 12. Are you there? All right. In Numbers 12, we read in verse 1, *"Then Miriam."* Now I'll ask a question. Who is Miriam? Moses's sister. Can I add this? His big sister. Are we on the same page for those of you that have siblings? All right. What else is Miriam? She is a prophetess. And a matter of fact, she's not a self-appointed prophetess like we see some self-appointed prophets and prophetess running around in the Church today. God called her a prophetess. Her prophecy is still written in the Bible, isn't that right? Right? So we are talking about a heavy hitter here, right? *"Then Miriam and Aaron."* Would you look up at me. Who's Aaron? Moses's brother. Can I add this? His big brother. Who else is Aaron? He's high priest, right? So you know folks, we're talking about two pretty heavy hitters here in the camp, okay? These are people high up in position, right? *"Then Miriam and Aaron spoke against Moses."* "They criticized him" another translation says. *"Because of the Ethiopian woman whom he had married; for he had married an Ethiopian woman."* Moses marries this woman from Africa. Now I'm going to say something, please listen to me all the way through. Is what he did technically right? No. God did not want them to marry outside because he was trying to preserve Abraham's seed. He said in Deuteronomy, he actually said to Moses' own mouth, *"Your wives will turn your heart away from me."* Are you with me? Now, I want to make this very clear. God was preserving his seed in the Old Testament, but you've got to take every truth in the Old Testament and run it through the cross. The cross will either change it, it will delete it, or leave it the same. Are you with me? Example, take praise and run it through the cross, it leaves it the same. Take prophecy and run it through the cross, it revises it. Take this principle and run it through the cross, and it deletes it. Because Paul says to us clearly there is neither Jew, there is neither Greek, there is neither Black, there is neither Asian, there is neither Indian, "for you are all one in Christ Jesus." There is nothing wrong today with a Black man marrying an Asian woman, or an Indian man marrying a Chinese woman. Are you with me?

Nothing wrong, I think it's great. Amen. Because we're one big family. Technically back then what he did was a little wrong, wasn't it? Now the question I want to ask is what fueled their criticism? What fueled them to speak against Moses?

Verse 2: *"So they said, 'Has the* LORD *indeed spoken only through Moses? Has He not spoken through us also?' and the Lord heard it."* Now would you look up at me? What fueled them was the fact that God had spoken through them before. Well I say so because Miriam's prophecy is still in the Bible. Aaron was the spokesman that gave the Word of the Lord to the Pharaoh, isn't that right? I mean God had gifted these two people, but here's where they went wrong folks. They allowed the gifting of God in their life to elevate themselves above the authority.

See let me make an explanation to you. If you go to 1 Corinthians 12. Now just listen to me and I'll just tell you about this, you can look it up later. If you go to 1 Corinthians 12:4, you will find out that the Bible says that *"There are diversities of gifts, but the same Spirit."* What are some of the gifts? Healings, prophecy, tongues, interpretations of tongues. You go over to Romans you find other gifts are giving, mercy, leadership, right? There's all kind of gifts, right? Are you with me? The Bible *says "There are diversities of gifts, but the same Spirit."* The Holy Spirit is over the gifts. Are you with me? But the next verse, verse 5 in 1 Corinthians 12 says "There are diversities of offices but the same Lord." That shows us that Jesus the Lord is over the offices. If you look in Ephesians 4 it says He himself, Jesus himself gave some to be apostles, prophets, angels, pastors, and teachers. Now you must realize the authority of the kingdom of God. Everybody say, "The kingdom of God is the kingdom." "The kingdom of God is the kingdom." "It is not a democracy." "It is not a democracy." The authority of the kingdom flows from the Father down through Jesus. Didn't Jesus say, "All authority is given to me in heaven and in earth?" Therefore the authority flows right down through Jesus. It goes right through the offices, not through the gifts. So here's the common

thing that happens. This person's in a pastor's church and he says, "You know this pastor's got only three hundred people in his church. My company's got 5,000 people, I need to help him. Well, he won't receive my help, he doesn't know what he's doing," he starts criticizing the pastor. He's allowed the gifting in his life. Yes, he's got a gift of leadership, God put it in him. And he's doing quite well in the business world. But what he does is he allows the gift of leadership to elevate himself above the authority God put him under.

Let me give you another example. Pastor's in the church and you know what, there's another person in the church and they prophesy and the words came to pass. They laid hands on a few sick people and they got healed. They laid hands on another person and they fell over. Wow! And they say, "You know what? My pastor doesn't prophesy, speak in tongues, lay hands on the sick, and he doesn't knock people over like I do." So now, all of a sudden, they are elevating themselves above the authority that God put them under. Are you with me? This is exactly what fueled Miriam and Aaron. They thought, "Okay, he did the wrong thing marrying this Ethiopian gal and so now he's blown it. God's talked through us, we've been Mr. and Mrs. Perfect, so obviously now we've got something to say. We now become over Moses." Now they never would have probably said that, but they are elevating themselves by their behavior of criticism. Who are you to criticize another man's servant? Who are you to criticize God's servant? You have no place. It's not even your—I relieve you from the pressure of it tonight—It's none of our business. Isn't that wonderful? And everybody always sitting there stressing about, "Ohhh-how could God handle this person or that person or this person-ohhh." You know what? You're stressing over something that's none of your business. And you're treading on dangerous grounds. So they said, *"Has the Lord indeed spoken through Moses? Has He spoken though us also? And the Lord heard it."* Let me tell you something, folks. God hears what you're whispering to one another. He hears what you're saying around the dinner table. Hey listen, don't come to your pastor and say, "Why aren't my kids submitted?" when you're criticizing your pastor or your boss at the dinner table at home. The Lord heard it.

Now look at [Numbers 12] verse 3. *"(Now the man Moses was very humble, more than all men who were on the face of the earth.)"* Now that's God opinion, that was not Miriam and Aaron's opinion at that point. They thought that he had just gotten a little too big for his britches. Let me tell you something, folks. Look up at me please. True humility does not mean to act like a wimp or religious, this weird religious stuff. True humility, let me tell you something. People who walk in true humility many times are mistaken for people that are arrogant. What did David's big brother say to David? I know the pride that's in your heart. Hey, God said, "He's a man after my heart." But he didn't say, "I'll kill him, give me his head I'll cut it off." He said, "He's full of pride." No, it was a man after God's heart. Humility is when you're completely, totally submitted to the will of God and you're obedient to Him. That's humility. *"(The man Moses was humble more than all the men on the face of the earth.)"* Verse 4: "Sudden." Everybody say, "Sudden." That's the way judgment comes, it comes suddenly, unexpected, bamm. Are you with me? And you know what's really scary? Is that you'll keep talking away, talking away, talking away, thinking God's not taking notice of this. This is what happens with people when they start to sin. And I'm talking about sinning with their mouth. When they start talking about leaders over them. They think—well you know, they kind of look for the lightning bolt on the first criticism. And they feel the conviction of the Holy Spirit, but nothing happens and they think, "Okay, I guess God's not upset with that." So then they feel freer the next time, see? And the conviction's not so hard because there's a veil of deception. Amen.

"Suddenly, the LORD [came and] said to Moses, Aaron, and Miriam, 'Come out, you three, to the tabernacle [for a] meeting.' So the three came out." Now can't you just see them walking out and Miriam's elbowing

Aaron saying, "Get ready, Aaron, he's marrying this Ethiopian chick, God's now going to make you the man. He blew it. This is it,"? And you know what, they're feeling self-justified the whole time they're walking out, right? Are you with me? So now watch this. Watch this, verse 5. *"Then the LORD came down in the pillar of cloud and [He] stood in the door of the tabernacle, and [He] called Aaron and Miriam, and they both went forward."* They think, "Okay for our time, man." Verse 6: *"Then He said, 'Hear now My words: If there is a prophet among you, I, the LORD make Myself known to him in a vision. I speak to him in a dream. Not so with My servant Moses; he is faithful in all my house. I speak with him face to face, Even plainly, and not in dark sayings; And he sees the form of the LORD. Why then?"*—Read this carefully, bold face, highlight it in your Bible— *"Why then were you not afraid to speak against My servant Moses?"* Watch this folks. *"So the anger of the LORD was aroused against them, and He departed. And when the cloud departed from above the tabernacle, suddenly Miriam became leprous, as white as snow. Then Aaron turned toward Miriam, and there she was, a leper. So Aaron said to Moses, 'Oh, my lord! Please do not lay this sin on us, in which we have done foolishly and in which we have sinned. Please do not let her be as one dead, whose flesh is half consumed when he comes out of his mother's womb!' So Moses cried out to the LORD, saying, 'Please heal her, O, God, I pray!'"* Now watch this. *"Then the LORD said to Moses, 'If her father had but spit in her face, would she not be shamed seven days? Let her be shut out of the camp seven days, and afterward she may be received again.'"* Let me tell you something, it was certain, it was severe. Amen.

Now I want to say this. There are times people have fallen under certain judgments because of speaking against authority. And you know what? They get their act together afterwards. You'll never find Miriam doing anything wrong again in the Scripture. Now that's the good news because even when God brings judgment, in judgment He looks for mercy. Now let me tell you, she was shut up from the camp for seven days. But you know, what's really neat is her attitude was really changed and her behavior changed. But you know what? This isn't always the case. Because I can tell you about another group of guys. As a matter of fact, we're real close to there right now.

Go over to Numbers 16. It didn't turn out that way for them. They received eternal judgment. Everybody say, "Eternal judgment." "Eternal judgment." Numbers 16, look at verse 1. Are you there? *"Now Korah"*—now I'm going to make this very clear to you. Look up at me. Everybody say, "Korah." "Korah." Korah was a Levitical priest. You got it? He's the guy that's going into the holy place that the other people were not allowed to go to. Heavy guy here, folks. *"Now Korah the son of Izhar"* (here we go with these names), *"the son of Kohath, the son of Levi, [the son of Dathan]"*—excuse me— *"with Dathan and Abiram the sons of Eliab and On the son of Peleth, sons of Reuben, took men;"* Wow, that's a job getting through that. Verse 2: *"and they rose up before Moses with some of the children of Israel, two hundred and fifty leaders of the congregation, representatives of the congregation, men of renown. They gathered together against Moses and Aaron, and [they] said to them, 'You'"*—now watch this— *"'You take too much upon yourselves, for all the congregation is holy, every one of them, and the LORD is among them. Why then do you exalt yourselves above the assembly of the LORD?'"* Would you look up at me? They came against Moses. They said, "Moses, you take too much upon yourself. You've made yourself a prince and a leader over us." Well, let me say this to you, folks. The kingdom of God is not a democracy. In a democracy, leaders are elected. If you've got some talent, you've got some friends with money, you can get elected. Got it? Not so in a kingdom. Leaders are appointed. Everybody say, "Appointed." "Appointed." Say it again. "Appointed." The Bible says very clearly in Romans 12, I think it's verse 3 that every man—listen— *"Let no man think more highly of himself than he ought to think."* Are you with me? Because God goes on to say in Hebrews 5:4 concerning appointment—Everybody say, "Appointment." "Appointment." He says, *"And no man takes this honor to himself."* You do not aspire to

be a leader. Let me tell you. Most people in leadership in the body of Christ really don't want it, to be honest with you. I'm being truthful with you. I have looked at my wife before and I said, "You know what? God has said, 'You've written your last book. I want you to sit down.'" It would be wonderful to go up and rent a ski lift and just witness to people as they come by. Or just go out and play golf and witness to people on the golf course or just go serve somebody. To be very honest with you. I mean when you really have been put into a place by God—to be honest with you—it's not something your flesh is passionate for. It's something your heart burns for because you want to please God. But it's not something you sit there and say, "Oh wouldn't it be fun to do that?" Uh-uh. And I find people who are aspiring and wanting to have aspirations and uh—what's the word I'm looking for—very ambitious, are people that do no have the heart of God. Or they're not ready for the call, okay? They're still not broken yet. Are you with me?

The Bible very clearly says, *"No man takes this honor to himself."* And you know what it says in verse five in this chapter of Hebrews? *"So also Christ did not glorify Himself to become High Priest."* Even Jesus didn't put himself in this position. Are you with me? Now put your marker right there and go over to Romans 1. Let me show you something here. Romans the first chapter. I need to talk to you about appointment. Everybody say, "Appointment." "Appointment." Remember Jesus made the statement, *"Many are called, few are chosen."* The word chosen and appointment are very similar. What he's literally saying is, "Many are called, though only a few are appointed." Why are only a few appointed? Because few pay the price in obedience to be chosen. Are you with me? God has a call on every one of us and listen. Many of us are actually called by God's five-fold ministry. What do I mean by five-fold ministry? These are your eldership positions in the church. But you know what? Not everybody is going to walk in those five-fold ministry positions. Because many will not pay the price to be able to be chosen by God and be appointed into that place.

Because the Bible is very clear that every man or woman must be tested before they are appointed.

When the apostle Paul got saved because, let me show you this. Let's take Paul as an example. Romans the first chapter, are you there? In Romans 1, Paul makes an interesting statement. He says in chapter 1:1— *"Paul, a bondservant of Jesus Christ, called to be an apostle, separated to the gospel of God."* Everybody say, "Called." "Called." "And separated." "And separated." When he was separated, was when he was appointed. Now let me talk about that separation. When Paul first got saved, he had a passion, he preached Jesus. Got himself into a little trouble, had to be let down in a basket. But then what he did was he spent years serving in the church, I believe in the ministry of helps. As a matter of fact, one of my Bible school teachers actually shared that he had served almost 11 years in the helps type of ministry. But then at one point in his home church. Everybody say, "Home church." "Home church." You don't get appointed by the prophetic ministry group that's meeting down by the beach in the nice hotel. God appoints people by your home church when elders have watched you serve and live before him. Say, "Amen." "Amen." Alleluia. Isn't that nice? So now listen to me. I'm going to be rough because so many people are getting hurt. I'm going to get a little rough right now on that okay? I hope you understand. So Paul served and at one particular time, obviously he had been faithful because the Bible says, "Let them first also be tested, and after they have been tested, let them be appointed." He had obviously been faithful and was appointed in the church of Antioch as a teacher. Everybody say, "Teacher." "Teacher."

Now go with me please to Acts 13 and let's see this. He's already served in the ministry of helps then he was obviously appointed as a teacher. And we know he was appointed as a teacher, write this down from 2 Timothy 1:11: Paul says that he was a teacher of the Gentiles—excuse me—an apostle and a teacher sent to the Gentiles. Everybody say, "Teacher." "Teacher." Now look at this, Acts 13:1. *"Now in the church that was at Antioch."* We're talking about the local New Testament church. *"There were certain prophets and teachers."* Are you seeing this? Now look at who some of the prophets and teachers were: *"Barnabas, Simeon who was called Niger, Lucius of Cyrene, Manaen who had been brought up with Herod the tetrarch."* So we see that Saul and Barnabas are either prophets or teachers and we know from Paul's own mouth in 2 Timothy 1:11 that he was a teacher, right? Watch this. *"As they ministered to the Lord and fasted; the Holy Spirit said, 'Now separate to Me Barnabas and Saul for the work to which I have called them.' Then, having fasted and prayed, [they] laid hands on them, they sent them away."* Verse 4: *"So, being sent out by the Holy Spirit"*—it was the Holy Spirit who ordained them in front of their local New Testament church where they had served. That is God's way. That is a way of God because then the elders of the Church can watch that person, see how he handles rough situations, see how he handles criticism, see how he handles unfair treatment, see how he handles other character things. And they can say, "Yes, God can speak to their hearts," they're witness with him and say, "Yes, Lord, I've seen the evidence. Yes, we can lay hands on him." Are you with me? Then you're sent out by the Holy Ghost. That is how I was ordained into the ministry. My pastor after me serving as youth pastor faithfully. And I told my pastor, I said, "If I'm here 'til Jesus comes, this is where I'm staying." I said, "God will have to talk to you before I leave." I said, "He'll have to show you." And I remember God showing my pastor in a vision that I was called to travel and preach. He came into that pastors' meeting with 11 pastors and said, "Gentlemen, the Holy Spirit showed me last night, one of you is called to travel all over and that's you, John Bevere." And 11 months later, he laid hands on us and he sent us forward. Are you seeing? It was the Holy Ghost who sent him. Now Paul knew he was called as an apostle but it wasn't until he was ordained and sent forth, right?

Now, let me show you something about Moses. Go over with me to Acts 7, this is most interesting. In Acts 7, look at verse 22. *"And Moses was learned in* all the wisdom of the Egyptians, and was mighty in words and deeds." Notice he was mighty in words. Isn't it interesting? After God got through with his breaking process, he says, "I can't even talk." Verse 23: "Now when he was forty years old"—watch this—"when he was forty years old, it came into his heart to visit his brethren, the children of Israel. And seeing one of them suffer wrong, he defended and avenged him who was oppressed, and struck down the Egyptian." Verse 25: "For he supposed that his brethren would have understood that God [delivered] them by his hand, but they did not." Now watch this, keep reading. Verse 27: "But he who did [this to his neighbor] pushed him away, saying, 'Who made you ruler and judge over us?'" This was a Hebrew man— Moses tried to avenge him and he pushed Moses away and said, "Who made you a ruler and a judge over me?" He said the exact same thing that Korah said. But you know what? There was no judgment for that guy. You want to know why? Because Moses hadn't been appointed yet. The authority of God wasn't on him.

But if you go back over to Numbers 16, go over there. I want you to see what happens with Korah. Verse 12: "Moses sent Dathan and Abiram the sons of Eliab, but they said, 'We will not come up.'" Verse 23: "So the LORD spoke to Moses, saying, 'Speak to the congregation, saying, "Get away from the tents of Korah, Dathan, and Abiram."'" Moses rose and went to Dathan and Abiram, and the elders [of Israel] followed him. And he spoke to the congregation, saying,

'Depart now from tents of these wicked men!'" Man this guy's a Levitical priest! And notice the term that Moses used. He is a "wicked man." Why? One reason he rose up against the authority that God put over him. And you know what's really, really scary? Is he still thought he was serving God. Because he said, "Moses, all the congregation's holy." He still thinking he's serving God. Watch this. "'Touch nothing of theirs, less you be consumed . . .' So they got away from around the tents of Korah, Dathan, and Abiram; And Dathan and Abiram came out and stood at the door of their tents, with their wives, their sons, and their little children. And Moses said, 'By this you shall know that the LORD has sent me to do all these works, for I have not done [any of] them of my own will. If these men die [of natural death, or] die naturally like all men, or if they are visited by the common fate of all men, then the LORD has not sent me. But if the LORD creates a new thing, and the earth opens its mouth and swallows them up with all that belongs to them, and they go down [to the pit alive,] then you will understand that these men have rejected the LORD.'" And you know what happens? The words no longer come out of his mouth. The whole earth opens up and these men are swallowed in it. And you know what's really amazing? The next day, this is how contagious rebellion is. The whole congregation rises up and says, "Moses, you killed the men of the Lord." Do not make friends with a rebellious person because it is like a contagious disease. Can you say, "Amen"? "Amen."

Session Eleven

Odds and Ends

*For I know the thoughts that I think toward you,
says the LORD, thoughts of peace and not of evil,
to give you a future and a hope.*
Jeremiah 29:11

Summary for *Under Cover*, Chapter 15

God establishes all authority, but it comes in many shapes
and sizes. The same type of authority that one experiences
in the work place is not the same type that they will find at
home. Learning how to separate the types of leadership and
how to be submissive to each accordingly will enable a
person to be submissive in appropriate ways. God wants us
to understand how to obey Him properly. Responding to
the authorities He has established in His wisdom and
discernment are necessary for this understanding.

The Family

Before any other types of authority were ever established,
God ordained the family. He initiated the husband as head
of the family and commanded the wife to be submissive to
her husband. This order reflects the divine relationship
between Christ and the Church. Just as Christ cares for the
Church and the Church is led by Him, so too, husbands
care for and lead their wives in faith and submission to
Christ. It is only by living in this perfect way that
marriages can be godly. All other attempts at domination

or rebellion lead to broken marriages and unhealthy relationships.

Children too are given instruction to obey and honor their parents. Obedience is an action that is required of children. Respect and honor are attitudes learned by children as they grow. There is no room for a rebellious child in the Christian home. God makes it clear that He hates rebellion and that those who practice it will be judged severely.

Social Authority

Throughout Scripture, the Lord makes it clear that we are bondservants to Christ. Because of this, we can begin to see all authority as Christ's authority. With this understanding, our work and social behavior should be done as unto Christ Himself. We work hard and are honest because that is what God desires of us. We avoid gossip and stealing because it would displease the Lord. We should work as though all of our work and behavior is unto God and for the salvation of the world. As we do this, we win unbelievers to God and bring honor and praise to our savior.

Notes from Chapter 15 (Video Session 11)

_____

_____

_____

_____

_____

_____

_____

> Before there was church, civil government, or social authority, there was family. Its function is the most crucial because the health of the other three depend on it. You can have defects in other arenas of delegated authority, and the family can remain independently strong. But you cannot have broken family order without its affecting the others. Authority in the family is an essential foundation for the others.
>
> John Bevere, *Under Cover*, p. 194–195

Warm-Up Questions

1. What role do your parents play in your life today?

   _____

   _____

   _____

2. How did your parents deal with rebellion in the home? If applicable, how do you deal with rebellion in your home?

   _____

   _____

   _____

3. Why does God tell wives with unbelieving husbands to submit to their authority? What is accomplished by this submission?

   _____

   _____

   _____

Teaching by John Bevere

Watch video session 11 on the tape.

Teaching Review

1. Place the following in order of authority as God has ordained:

   The Children   The Father   The Lord   The Mother

   _____

   _____

   _____

   _____

2. When is acceptable to disobey one's own parents?

   _____

   _____

   _____

3. List several ways that Christ treats the church:

   _____

   _____

   _____

4. How are husbands to treat their wives in the same way?

   _____

   _____

   _____

I have warned my children to guard themselves from any form of rebellion. The most deceptive or subtle form is complaining. It despises authority by inadvertently saying, "I don't like the way you are leading me, and if I were you, I would do it differently." This insults leadership. Can you see now why complaining contributed to the children of Israel being kept out of the promised land? Their complaining communicated their contempt toward God, even though it was directed toward Moses. In essence, they told God He wasn't doing it right, and they would lead differently.

Honoring our parents brings the wonderful promise of a long and good life. I would rather choose life than judgment. This must be settled in our hearts.

John Bevere, *Under Cover*, p. 201.

Exploring God's Word

Matthew 10:37 *He who loves father or mother more than Me is not worthy of Me. And he who loves son or daughter more than Me is not worthy of Me.*

5. How does this verse call us to make a difficult decision?

_____

_____

_____

_____

6. Why does God require that we love Him more than anyone else?

_____

_____

_____

_____

_____

Personal Application

_____

_____

_____

Mark 3:31–35 *Then His brothers and His mother came, and standing outside they sent to Him, calling Him. And a multitude was sitting around Him; and they said to Him, "Look, Your mother and Your brothers are outside seeking You." But He answered them, saying, "Who is My mother, or My brothers?" And He looked around in a circle at those who sat about Him, and said, "Here are My mother and My brothers! For whoever does the will of God is My brother and My sister and mother."*

7. How did Jesus react when His own family wanted to keep Him from doing God's will?

_____

_____

_____

_____

_____

8. What did He mean by saying whoever does the will of God is His family? How does that affect us today?

_____

_____

_____

_____

_____

_____

_____

Personal Application

_____

_____

_____

_____

> **1 Peter 3:1–2** *Wives, likewise, be submissive to your own husbands, that even if some do not obey the word, they, without a word, may be won by the conduct of their wives, when they observe your chaste conduct accompanied by fear.*

9. How can God use a wife's conduct to win her lost husband?

_____

_____

_____

_____

_____

_____

_____

10. Why do words and lectures often have little impact on the unsaved?

_____

_____

_____

_____

Personal Application

_____

_____

_____

Colossians 3:22–24 *Bondservants, obey in all things your masters according to the flesh, not with eyeservice, as men-pleasers, but in sincerity of heart, fearing God. And whatever you do, do it heartily, as to the Lord and not to men, knowing that from the Lord you will receive the reward of the inheritance; for you serve the Lord Christ.*

11. How do we sometimes fail to please God with our hearts even when our actions are correct?

_____

_____

_____

_____

_____

12. Why is a heavenly reward so much more valuable than an earthly reward?

_____

_____

_____

13. If we obey as to the Lord, what will our reward be?

_____

_____

_____

_____

Personal Application

_____

_____

_____

_____

Exposing the Truth

14. In *Under Cover,* John writes, "Before there was church, civil government, or social authority, there was family. Its function is the most crucial because the health of the other three depend on it. You can have defects in other arenas of delegated authority, and the family can remain independently strong. But you cannot have broken family order without it affecting others." For each of the three areas of delegated authority, describe the affects that occur as the family structure is compromised.

The Church _____

_____

_____

_____

_____

_____

_____

Civil Government _____

_____

_____

_____

Social Authority _____

_____

_____

_____

_____

_____

_____

15. John quotes Watchman Nee as writing, "What a risk God has taken in instituting authorities! What a loss God will incur if the delegated authorities He institutes misrepresent Him! Yet, undaunted, God has set up these authorities. It is much easier for us to fearlessly obey authorities than for God to institute them. Can we not then obey them without apprehension since God Himself has not been afraid to entrust authority to men? Even as God has boldly established authorities, so let us courageously obey them." What part does trust play in our ability to obey God's delegated authorities?

_____

_____

_____

_____

_____

_____

Applying the Lesson

Submission to authorities comes on many levels. In order to apply what we have learned, we must be able to recognize our own weaknesses. For each of the following areas, evaluate yourself and recognize where your weaknesses are and what you need to change. Once you have determined your needs, dedicate yourself to being like Christ and submitting to authorities as unto the Lord.

Family _____

_____

Church _____

_____

Work _____

_____

Civil Government _____

_____

Checking Your Cover

Conclude this session asking that God will enable you to:

> Have a Christ-like heart and attitude
>
> Be able to see your own mistakes and confess them
>
> Endeavor to change and please God with all your thoughts and actions.

Video Script for Lesson 11
Odds and Ends

What I want you to do is go with me, please, to Ephesians the fifth chapter. Let me say this while you are turning. I want to first of all talk about the family. Find Ephesians and, actually, Colossians. Ephesians 5 and Colossians the third chapter. So you're in Ephesians 5, and then Colossians the third chapter, and what we're going to do is talk about family authority. And we see Ephesians 5:23 says, *"For the husband is the head of the wife, as also Christ is the head of the church; and He is the Savior of the body. Therefore, just as the church is subject to Christ, so let the wives be to their own husbands in everything."* Everybody say, "Everything." "Everything." Go over to Colossians 3:20. It says, *"Children, obey your parents in all things."* Do you notice with the wives it said, "in everything" and "in all things," right? *"For this is well pleasing to the Lord."* Now I want to make this statement; There is a divine authority structure in the home. There is the husband, there is the wife, there are the children. The husband is the head of the home, the wife is the head of the children, or she and her husband both are the head of the children. The wife is to submit to the husband as the church submits to Christ. Amen. That is what God said, not chauvinistic men. Can you say, "Amen"? "Amen." And God says that for one reason, and that is protection. Amen. Now I want to say this. When God says "all things," He means "all things." And when He says "to their own husbands," He means "their own husbands." The wife is not to submit to somebody else's husband. She submits to a pastor because he's over the pastoral things of the church. She submits to a civil authority over civil things. She submits to her job authority over job things. But when it comes to the home, she is submitted to the husband. Amen.

Now the only exception—and the children are the same way—the only exception is when your parents or your husband tells you to do something that is contrary to the written Word of God. Can you say, "Amen"? "Amen." I have an example of that in my own personal life. When I got saved in college and filled with the Holy Spirit, God dealt with me for months about the call of God to the ministry. I didn't want anything to do with the ministry because every preacher I met was weird and his kids were weird. And I thought you ended up in Africa in a shack and you had no shoes. So my idea of ministry was not very good. And one day the Spirit of God came on me, October of 1979, and the Spirit of God said—I was in the church of 2,000 members—the Spirit of God came on me, I started crouching down in my seat. I felt like all 2,000 people were looking at me, that's what happens when God comes on you. And the Spirit of God said to me "I have called you to preach. What are you going to do about it?" And I'll never forget I said, "If I end up in Africa with a shack and no shoes or I have a smelly house with weird kids, I don't care, I'll preach." Thank God that's not true. I learned later that that's not what His will was. Amen. Amen. But now let me say this to you. When I came home and told my parents they were not real happy. I was raised Roman Catholic—altar boy for many years—and when I told my Catholic mom, "God has called me to preach and I'm going to Bible School." She basically said, "Over my dead body." Now that changed a little while later and she just basically looked at me she said, "If you go to Bible School, you are on your own. We will not cover a thing." Well," I said "that's fine. But God's calling me to preach. I've got to do what God is calling me to do."

And you know what? It's interesting, Jesus went through the same thing. The Bible says this in Luke 2:51, I'm reading out of the *Amplified*. It says, *"Jesus went down with them, His mother and father, and came into Nazareth and was habitually obedient to them."* Isn't that beautiful? This is the *Amplified*

Bible. *"He was habitually obedient to them."* Isn't that something? But now watch, once he went into the ministry. He came to a place they didn't like too much, what did he have to say? Did you realize that? I'm going to read to you, I think this is out of the Amplified. Just listen, look up at me. This is out of Mark's gospel, chapter 3. Listen to this. *"And when those who belonged to Him, His kinsmen"*—in other words, his family— *"heard it they went out to take Him by force. For they kept saying, 'He is out of his mind, beside himself, and deranged.'"* That's what His family said about Him. *"Then His mother and His brothers came standing outside, they sent word to Him calling for Him."* In other words, "We want to talk to You, son." *"And the crowd was sitting around Him, and they said to Him, 'Your mother, Your brothers, and Your sisters are outside asking for You.' And He replied, 'Who are My mother and My brothers?' and He looked around to those who sat in the circle about Him. And He said, 'See here My mother and My brothers. For whoever does the things God wills is My brother, sister, and mother.'"* That is Mark's gospel chapter three, verses 21, 31—35.

Now let me say this: Jesus had to obey the Father. Because they wanted Him to do something contrary to what the Father had spoken. And with us it's the written Word of God. Are you with me? He is the Word of God. All right? Now the good news is this. Obviously because of His obedience to the Father, they got straightened out. Because you find Mary in the upper room and she got filled with the Holy Spirit. The wonderful thing is my mom and dad were very, very upset. I didn't get invited even to some of the parties. Because they thought I'd preach to everybody, and you know what? After years went by, my mom looked at me and she said, "Son, you are a changed man." Because I was a very selfish young man before I got saved. And I remember I had the privilege, when my dad was 79 just two years ago and praying with him to receive Jesus. And so now my mom and dad, they read our books, they pass out our videos, give books to neighbors, and what's happened? They are really turned on to what God has been doing. So this is what happens when you

choose to obey—God will reward you. If your parents tell you to do something that is contrary to the Word or your husband. Are you with me? But that is the only exception. I have said it over and over and I'm going to keep saying it.

Now let's go back to the norm. God's says in His Word that if we obey our parents and honor them, that it will go well with us. Remember that? *"It is the first commandment with a promise. That it might go well with you and that you will live a long life."* Everybody say, "Might go well with you." "Might go well with you." I learned that it doesn't go well with you the hard way. And I wish I didn't have to. However, when I graduated from college, I went to Dallas, Texas and I worked as an engineer for Rockwell International. And I remember when I went down there, the Lord led me to a very powerful church with about 6,000, 7,000, or 8,000 members. And I remember after being there the first night, I had met the leader, or one of the leaders, in the single's ministry. And he needed a roommate as well. And so we got to talking together at the restaurant where all the singles met after the service. You know what singles do. And he said, "Man, let's room together." And I said, "That sounds great. We'll save a lot of money." So I remember calling my dad the next day. Now remember, my dad was not born again yet. And I said to my dad, "Dad, I've got great news. I'm going to save hundreds of dollars a month. I met a guy who's one of the leaders in the singles ministry in the church and we're going to get an apartment together." My dad on the other end of the phone said, "Son, don't do it." He said, "You don't know him." I said, "Dad, he's born again. He's a leader in the ministry. Come on." And I kind of, you know, went back and forth with my dad for several minutes. And finally, I just thought, "He doesn't understand. He's not saved yet. I'm praying for him," and I hung up. So I remember, we went up and we got the apartment. And I remember we went to get the rental truck to get his furniture and he said, "Oh man, I forgot my checkbook. Do you mind covering the deposit for the rental truck?" I said, "No problem, one hundred fifty dollars." Then I remember when we moved in the apartment he said, "I forgot my checkbook do you mind covering the deposit for the apartment?" No problem, another one hundred fifty dollars. Then I remember the first month went by and he didn't pay the rent. I ended up paying the rent. I paid his phone bill. I paid the electric bill. The second month went by. I paid his rent, I paid his phone bill, I paid the electric bill. He didn't have a car, he borrowed my car. Many times he'd bring it back about 8:00 in the morning and I had to be at work at 7:30. Every morning he brought it back and the car was filled with smoke. And I remember one morning and he brought it back and I had a huge dent on the side of my car and the devil kept saying, "Walk in love, walk in love." So the devil will really use things on a young believer if they don't understand and try to get them to do some goofy things. Are you with me? Yes, we're supposed to walk in love, but that doesn't mean you rely on somebody that is living in this kind of a lifestyle. Now he kept saying he was witnessing to people and this. But I remember one time I got up at 4:00 in the morning to go to the bathroom and there's the guy sitting in my living room, in my apartment, with a can of beer and a cigarette, looking at me like, "What are you doing here?" And you know I was living in pure and absolute hell and torment—it seemed like hell—I'm sorry, I don't ever want to belittle hell. I was living in torment for two months. And I remember, after two months, I remember I discovered the man was a homosexual. I was one of the last person's to find out about it. It did not go well with me. When I found out that he was a homosexual, I had the locks changed on the apartment and had him kicked out in 12 hours. Let me tell you something. He was shortly found out by the youth pastor and he was immediately released from the church. But I'm going to tell you this. It did not go well with me. So I was in prayer. And I said, "God, how did you let this happen to me? My first two months out of college. How could I go through two months of this? Why did you let this happen? Why didn't you warn me?" And the Lord said, "I did warn you." I said, "No you didn't." And the Lord said, "I did too, I spoke through your father." I said, "What?" And the Lord said, "He's your father." And I said, "But he's not born again and he doesn't understand these things." And he said, "I never said the heart of the king is in my hands as long as he's born again. I said he is the authority in your life." I said, "But Lord, I went to college, I graduated, I'm working as an engineer, I'm 22 years old. What do you mean, does he still have to be an authority in my life?" And the Lord spoke to me and showed me how in Genesis the [second] chapter, God ordained it right from the beginning. *"Therefore a man shall leave his father and mother and be joined to his wife."* The very last blessing of permission that a parent gives to his child is when he says to his child, "You may marry that person." Once they marry that person they are released unto the authority line that is established. That's why God says, "A man shall leave his father," because he establishes the *new* authority in that home. Once that man marries, now the parents are no longer in authority, they are just to be honored. A new authority line is established. Do you see this? And God spoke to me and he said, "Son, I was speaking wisdom right out of your dad's mouth and you weren't listening." And I remember I saw that so clearly. You know I really saw this in action when I asked my wife to marry me. Because I went to my wife's father and I asked him, I said, "I would like your daughter's hand in marriage." And you know what he said? He said, "I'll give you my blessing." I went back to Lisa at the time and I said, "Great! Your dad gave me his blessing." She said, "What?!" She said, "My dad doesn't like you." She said, "He doesn't like any Christian. He doesn't want me around any kind of Christians. He told me at dinner he doesn't like you because you're a Christian boy." And I said, "Well, he gave me the blessing." Because I believe that God would speak blessing and will through her father, God turned his heart and he softened and he gave me that permission. It's exactly what Pastor Rob said a few minutes ago. "Where is your faith in God's authority in the leaders over you?" Amen. Are you with me? All right, alleluia. Are you enjoying this?

Now children—let's move on to the children. God

gives specific warnings to children, doesn't He? Let me read some of them, these are heavy hitters. Deuteronomy 27:16. *"Cursed is the one who treats his father or his mother with contempt."* Whoa! Cursed is the young man or woman who treats his father or mother with contempt? Did you hear that? Young people did you hear that? Now I remember when I was a youth pastor. I remember I had a single mother sitting before me one day with her teenage son. And I remember in that meeting, that teenager was talking to his mother with such contempt I couldn't believe it. I had to correct him many times. I'd say, "Young man, don't talk to your mother like that." And he was in my youth group. And I remember that at the end of the meeting, out of my mouth came out something that surprised everybody in the room, including me. I looked at that young man and I said, "Young man if you keep talking to your mother like this you're going to end up in jail." And I thought, "What did I just say?" And I remember after leaving youth pastor and I was launched and I started traveling—Two years later I came back to my home church. Well, I'd stayed in my home church for years afterwards. I remember being home one Sunday and the mother of this young man came running up to me after a Sunday morning service. She said, "Pastor John, Pastor John guess what? My son's in jail!" I thought how can you be so excited? And she reminded me of how I looked at him and said that if he didn't stop, he'd end up in jail. She said but, "Guess what? In jail he's giving his life radically to Jesus and he's preaching to all the prisoners and he's wanting more and more material because he's so radically in love with the Lord." And I said, "Well praise God. I'm sorry he had to go through the jail to get it, but I'm glad he's got it." It didn't go well with him. Are you seeing this? He treated his mother with contempt and it didn't go well.

Let me read another one to you Exodus 21:15. *"He who strikes his father or his mother shall surely be put to death."* Whew! Exodus 21:17: *"He who curses his father or his mother shall surely be put to death."* Aren't you glad that judgment isn't that today? Can you imagine all the young people in our youth groups being put to death? Now here's the serious thing. I'm not talking about this church. I'm serious, I'm not—because you know what? This is a hungry church. But you know what? I can't believe what I see in some youth groups today. I mean it just blows me away. Blows me away. But here's the thing. The judgment may not be stoning them today. Let me tell you, the spiritual thing that happens to them, the curse that comes on them is very severe. Because God's attitude about it does not change, folks. God does not like it when children treat their parents with contempt, or curse them. Are you with me?

It is very severe, in Deuteronomy 21:18–21. God says that *"If a man has a stubborn and rebellious son who will not obey the voice of his father or the voice of his mother, and who, when they have chastised him, will not heed them, then his father and his mother shall take hold of him and bring him out to the elders of his city, to the gate of his city. And they shall say to the elders of his city, 'This son of ours is stubborn and rebellious; he will not obey our voice; He is a glutton and a drunkard'. Then all the men of his city shall stone him to death with stones; so you shall put away the evil from among you, and all Israel shall hear and fear."* Pretty powerful, isn't it? Sobering isn't it? We need to teach our children how serious it is not to honor authority. Amen. Amen.

Ephesians 5:24 tells us that wives are to submit to their husbands in everything. Can you say, "Amen"? "Amen." Now, as I said, other men do not have authority over the wife, the husband does. Correct? My wife and I in the mid-1980s fell under an erroneous teaching in the body of Christ. And that teaching was this, that husbands and wives were equal in redemption and equal in authority. So we lived for a couple of years where there was no head of the home. We bought into this teaching. And let me tell you something. Our marriage was absolutely havoc, it was terrible. It was so bad that if my wife and I didn't have a covenant with God, we would have been divorced. And I remember one day looking at my wife, and were driving home from church, and I looked at her and I said, "Honey, I am the head of this home and I'm going to lead whether you follow me or not." And you know what? Peace started entering into my life from that point forward. But Lisa went a couple months later, she didn't think I was a very good provider, she didn't think I was responsible. So constantly at night she was waking me up saying, "What if this happens, what if that happens, what if this happens, what if that happens, what are you going to do?" And I kept saying, "Why do you keep planning for failure?" I said, "Don't worry about it, we'll pray. God will take care of it." And she'd get upset because I'd go back to sleep and she'd lay there and keep worrying. Well, the pressure got really bad with Lisa. Now listen, I'm not telling you anything that she's not said, she wrote it up in a whole book called *Out of Control and Loving It*. And one time she was in the shower about two months later after I made that statement to her. And she was going through the whole gamut again. She used to have to go in the bathtub and absolutely just soak herself in the bathtub to try to get her mind to calm down. And she was in the shower, and she was going through the whole thing again and the Lord spoke to Lisa in the shower. And He said to Lisa—I'm going to read it so I make sure I don't mis-do it. He said, "Lisa, you don't think John is a good leader." And she said, "No I don't, I don't trust him." And so God said to her, he said, "Lisa, you don't have to trust John, you only have to trust me." See God is the one that said, "Submit to your husband," not the husband. And if God says it, then you don't trust God because he's the one that said it. Amen, good preaching. Now watch this. He said, "You don't think John's doing a very good job as the head of this home. You feel you could do better." Then he said, "The tension and the unrest you're experiencing is the weight and pressure of being the head of the household." He said, "I've let you be the head of the household." He said, "It's a yoke to you, but it's a medal to your husband. Lay it down and the medal will come on your husband," that's what he said to her. Well she came out of that shower crying. I mean for the next two hours she couldn't stop crying. She said, "Forgive me, I didn't trust you, but I trust you now. God has told

me to submit to you, I submit to you, you are the head of this home." And you know what? I've got news for you, our marriage entered into a peace like we had never, ever, ever, ever known before. And today Lisa is traveling all over the world telling women this very thing. Because she found out there is bondage in rebellion, but there is liberty in submission. Can you say, "Amen"? "Amen." Alleluia.

Now let's talk about unreasonable husbands. 1 Peter 3:1—all right, go over there. 1 Peter 3. Now you're going to see something very interesting here. Verse 1 says, *"Wives likewise."* Everybody say, "Likewise." "Likewise." Now you've got to understand something here, folks. Likewise means he's comparing it to something he's just previously said. So can I read the whole thing? Remember we read verse 18. *"Servants, be submissive . . .not only to the good and gentle, but . . .the harsh."* Let me read the whole thing to you in context. This is out of the New Living Translation. *"You who are slaves* [or employees or whatever] *must accept the authority of your master. Do whatever they tell you not only if they are kind and reasonable but even if they are harsh. For God is pleased with you for the sake of your conscience. You have patiently endured unfair treatment . . .In the same way, you wives must accept the authority of your husbands even to those who refuse to accept the good news of the gospel."* So what he's saying is, "Wives, you too. If you've got husbands that are unreasonable, keep a submitted heart." Are you with me? Why? *"Because when they observe your chaste conduct and behavior, you can win them over to the Lord."* God said it is the wives' submitted attitude that is the greatest potential to win an unbelieving husband over to Jesus. Are you with me?

I remember when I was in the state of Minnesota and this woman sat down and she shared a testimony. I was staying in her house, she had a nice husband, a nice two sons. And she said, "You know John, my husband wasn't saved for years," and she said, "You know what I did? I put tracts by his workbench, I put Bibles on the coffee table, I put books right beside his bed, I always invited couples over where the husband's a real strong believer." She said, "I would slip, you know, tracts in little places that I knew where he was going to be." And she said, "One day the Holy Spirit spoke to me and said, 'How long are you going to hinder your husband's salvation?'" She said, "'What?' And the Lord said, 'As long as you keep trying to manipulate him into salvation with all your little tracts and Bibles and everything else,' He said, 'your husband's not going to come.' He said, 'Get rid of all of your tracts, quit inviting people over for the sake of getting the husband to preach to your husband.' And he said, 'Trust me and just submit to your husband.'" And you know what she told me? She looked at me, she told me—this was her telling me this, not him—she said, "Two months later, he gave his life to the Lord." And you know what? They have a wonderful marriage and they are in love with each other.

Let's go to social authority. Everybody say, "Social authority." "Social authority." What are social authorities? They are your jobs, your teachers, your coaches, et cetera, all right? This is a category that I chose to call it. And hear what the Bible says in Titus 2:9–10—I'm going to read to you out of the *Amplified Bible*—says this: *"Tell bondservants to be submissive to their masters, to be pleasing and to give satisfaction in every way. Warn them not to talk back or contradict. Not to steal by taking things of small value. But to prove themselves truly loyal and tiredly reliable and faithful throughout."* Are you hearing this? This is how God says we are supposed to be on the job. *"So that in everything they may be an ornament and due credit to the teaching which is from and about God our Savior."* Now I have sat and I have listened to bosses tell me about employees that work for them, they're believers and those bosses are bragging about those employees. I have listened to owners of companies say to me, "I have this guy in my company, my plumbing company. He has been the most faithful man. He has been the most trustworthy man. He has never cussed in nine years, when cussing is all everybody around him is doing. He's not done this, he's never stolen, he's always worked and made sure he's done his job right." I mean they

go on and on and I just think, "Oh thank God, what a testimony." That employee is literally getting the attention of the owner of that company because of his godly behavior. However, I have heard the opposite and it has broken my heart.

I remember sitting on an airplane. I was sitting next to this guy and I mean, man, we were having a blast. I mean we were having a great conversation. Huh? He was in a good mood, I was kind of you know, happy, chipping in with the conversation, talking about all kinds of things. We're in the flight, you know, we're just going away having a great time—you know, great conversation. So finally he says to me, "What do you do?" "Well, I'm a preacher, I work for God." And he says, "Arrrr." I thought, "Okay." Now we had already established a good enough rapport where I could just really pry in. And I said, "Well, it's obvious that somebody has kind of upset you when it deals with ministry." And he says, "You know," he says, "I'll tell you." He said, "I own the second largest cab company," and he named the city, "of this city." And he said, "I had an employee that worked for me and she was one of these born again ones, you know that . . ." And I said, "Oh no." And he said, "You know, she worked for me for two months—I think it was two months." And he said that she left. "And she said when she left me"—now this is back in the early '90s, back when the phone bills were big overseas okay?—"She left me," he said, "she left me with an $8,000 phone bill to her son in Germany and had taken some things from the office." And he said, "She was going around and preaching to everybody in our office." And I thought, "Oh my, my, my, my, my." And I thought—You know what? One man heard me talk about this and he offered to pay the $8,000 phone bill. I'm not kidding. One of our partners, heard me speak about this on the tape. So I contacted the company, but unfortunately the man passed away couple years later—But I thought what a sad testimony. Now this man won't even listen because of the lifestyle he saw through one of his employees. Listen to what the apostle Paul goes on to say, listen to this. *"Servants obey everything, obey in everything those* who are your earthly masters, your bosses. *Not only when their eyes are on you as pleasers of men, but in simplicity of purpose with all of your heart. Because of your reverence for the Lord."* Everybody say, "Reverence." "Reverence." *"Your reverence for the Lord and a sincere expression of your devotion to Him. Whatever may be your task, work at it heartily from the soul. As something done for the Lord and not for men."* Now you work your job and you're doing it for the Lord, you'll probably do a much better job than if you're doing it for your boss. But if you see the authority of God on your boss and you have the compassion of God for your boss, you'll work for him as if you're working from the Lord. Because Paul goes on to say, *"Knowing with all certainty that it is from the Lord and not from men that you will receive the inheritance which is your real reward."* The one who you are actually serving is the Lord's Christ.

Let me say this. That woman may never stand before a court for what she did on this earth. But one day she'll stand before the Lord. If she would have had the fear of God in her life, she would not have done those things. Are you with me? It's a very sobering thing. I know it's a very extreme case, but I think it makes a point.

In Matthew 23, Jesus says this. Verse 1: *"Then Jesus spoke to the multitudes and to His disciples, saying: 'The scribes and the Pharisees sit in Moses' seat'"*— of authority is what he is saying. *"'Therefore whatever they tell you to observe, that observe and do, but do not do according to their works; for they say, and do not do.'"* Can I read it out of the *Amplified?* Look up at me. *"Then Jesus said to the multitudes and his disciples, the scribes and the Pharisees sit on Moses' seat of authority. 'So observe and practice all they tell you,*

but do not do what they do for they preach and do not practice.'" So in other words, Jesus said, "Look beyond what they're living and look at the authority on them." Isn't that interesting? Because he said, "They are actually seated in that seat of authority."

Watchman Nee made a statement in his book called *Spiritual Authority* that I would like to read. He said, "What a risk God is taking in instituting authorities. What a loss God will incur delegating authorities if his institutes misrepresent him. Yet undaunted, God has set up these authorities." Now listen to this. "It is much easier for us to fearlessly obey authorities, then for God to institute them." In other words, God's taking a bigger risk, right? Can we not then obey them without apprehension since God himself has not been afraid to entrust authority to them? "Even as God has boldly established authorities, so let us courageously obey them. If anything should be amiss the fault does not lie with us, but with the authorities. For the Lord declares that every soul be subject to the higher powers. The obedient needs only to obey. The Lord will not hold us responsible for any mistaken obedience. Rather he will hold the delegated authority responsible for his erroneous act. Insubordination however, is rebellion and for this one under authority must answer to God." And you know what's amazing? You know what's really amazing? This was written by a man who was mistreated by authorities. False charges were brought against him by the Chinese and he was arrested in 1952 and there he stayed in prison until his death in 1972. He was mistreated by authorities and yet he still writes a whole book called *Spiritual Authority* telling how important it is for us to submit to authorities. Now there's somebody that's living what they preach.

Session Twelve

Great Faith

"And the apostles said to the Lord, 'Increase our faith.'
So the Lord said, 'If you have faith as a mustard seed,
you can say to this mulberry tree, "Be pulled up by the roots
and be planted in the sea," and it would obey you.'"
Luke 17:5–6

Summary for *Under Cover*, Chapters 16 and 17

The Christian life is a life of faith. We can believe in many theological truths, practice great morality, or participate enthusiastically in church activities; yet, the only characteristic in our lives that will matter is our level of faith. God grants us each a measure of faith and it is our task to grow and nurture what God has given us. So, how do we grow in faith? The greater our level of submission is to God and His delegated authorities, the greater our level of faith.

Because faith is a gift of the Holy Spirit, we cannot earn it or manipulate God into increasing it in our lives. However, we can and are commanded to increase in faith through obedience and true humility. It is our attitude to authority that determines whether or not we truly believe what God says is true. A person with faith understands the way God's hand moves and directs everything in creation. There is no hesitation to do the Lord's will whatever the case may be.

The Scriptures give us numerous examples of saints that increased in faith through obedience to God and His authority. Abraham, who is called the father of our faith, trusted and obeyed God and His promises. Because of his belief and faith in God, he was given a son at the age of one hundred. Not only was God's promise fulfilled, but when Abraham was tested once again, he did not falter in his faith but was prepared to offer his only son. Because of his unwavering obedience, God blessed him and his descendents forever.

As we learn to humbly obey the Lord in every area of our lives, we will begin to understand and see the reality of God in all things. The blindness of our eyes is healed through the sight that God bestows on us in faith. As we are under His cover, we become heirs to the kingdom of God and eternally sons and daughters. Let us live under His Cover!

Notes from Chapters 16 and 17 (Video Session 12)

_____

_____

_____

_____

_____

_____

_____

_____

_____

> The greatest faith Jesus encountered in more than thirty-three years on earth was not John the Baptist's or His mother Mary's. It was not from any of the children of Israel who received healings or miracles. It was not from any of the Twelve. It belonged to a Roman citizen, a soldier, one of Israel's conquerors. What made his faith so great? *Because he understood and walked in submission to authority.*
>
> John Bevere *Under Cover*, p. 214.

Warm-Up Questions

1. By what methods does the Lord most often impart faith into a person's life?

   _____

   _____

   _____

   _____

2. On the following line place an X where you feel your level of faith is:

   Unbelief   *True Faith*

   _____

   How did you determine your level of faith for the question above?

   _____

   _____

   _____

3. Describe someone you know that you feel has great faith.

_____ expresses great faith in the way

they_____

_____

Teaching by John Bevere

Watch video session 12 on the tape.

Teaching Review

4. What are three significant points related to increased faith?

_____

_____

_____

_____

_____

_____

5. Why did Jesus say the Roman centurion had the greatest faith?

_____

_____

_____

6. How are faith and obedient actions viewed in the Scriptures?

_____

_____

_____

Exploring God's Word

Luke 17:5–6 *And the apostles said to the Lord, "Increase our faith." So the Lord said, "If you have faith as a mustard seed, you can say to this mulberry tree, 'Be pulled up by the roots and be planted in the sea,' and it would obey you."*

7. According to this verse, is it important how much faith we have? Why or why not?

_____

_____

_____

_____

_____

_____

_____

_____

_____

_____

_____

8. Why does it only require a little faith to do great things?

_____

_____

_____

9. Who is it that is able to increase our faith?

_____

_____

_____

_____

_____

Personal Application

_____

_____

_____

Hebrews 6:11–15 *We desire that each one of you show the same diligence to the full assurance of hope until the end, that you do not become sluggish, but imitate those who through faith and patience inherit the promises. For when God made a promise to Abraham, because He could swear by no one greater, He swore by Himself, saying, "Surely blessing I will bless you, and multiplying I will multiply you." And so, after he had patiently endured, he obtained the promise.*

10. What two characteristics are required of a person to obtain the promises of God?

    _____

    _____

11. What has God promised if we stay patient and faithful?

    _____

    _____

    _____

Personal Application

_____

_____

_____

James 2:20–24, 26 *But do you want to know, O foolish man, that faith without works is dead? Was*

*not Abraham our father justified by works when he
offered Isaac his son on the altar? Do you see that
faith was working together with his works, and by
works faith was made perfect? And the Scripture
was fulfilled which says, "Abraham believed God,
and it was accounted to him for righteousness." And
he was called the friend of God. You see then that a
man is justified by works, and not by faith only . . .
For as the body without the spirit is dead, so faith
without works is dead also.*

12. What is the relationship between faith and works?

_____
_____
_____
_____
_____
_____
_____
_____

13. How is a man justified in his faith by his actions?

_____
_____
_____
_____
_____

14. How is faith dead when it is not accompanied by
    works?

_____
_____
_____
_____

Personal Application

_____

_____

_____

_____

1 Corinthians 13:2 *Though I have all faith, so that I could remove mountains, but have not love, I am nothing.*

15. Why does right belief never outweigh right practice?

_____

_____

_____

_____

_____

_____

_____

16. How does love justify a person more than faith?

_____

_____

_____

_____

_____

_____

_____

Personal Application

_____

_____

_____

Your destiny in God is before you. When you choose obedience, you choose to fulfill destiny. Nothing and no one can stop you. For years it looked gloomy for David, as with Joseph, as with Moses, as with Joshua, as with Hannah, as with Noah, as with Esther, as with the rest of the patriarchs. But remember, there is a hall of fame for those who fulfilled their destiny, and these listed here made it. God is looking for men and women in these last days to add to the list of patriarchs to be honored at the judgment seat of Christ. I pray we can be among those who fulfill the commission to bring glory to our wonderful Lord.

John Bevere, *Under Cover*, p. 224.

Exposing the Truth

17. In the *Under Cover* Series, John says, "The authority in which we walk is directly proportional to our submission to authority. The greater our level of submission, the greater our faith." Consider those whom you would describe as having great faith. What is their relationship to authorities and does this correspond with what John says? How can this statement be illustrated from Scripture?

   _____

   _____

   _____

18. Describe how each of the following individuals practiced both faith and obedience:
   Abel _____

   _____

Noah _____

_____

Joseph _____

_____

David _____

_____

19. In *Under Cover*, John writes, "To remain lowly in heart is to remain positioned for the rewards of obedience. To pride yourself in your own obedience is to position yourself for a fall, even though you've obeyed. This can spoil everything you adhered to. You could follow the counsel or word of God, yet by pride lose all you gained through obedience." How can God enable us to be humbly successful at obedience and avoid the snares of pride? Can this be done apart from the help of the Holy Spirit?

_____

_____

_____

Applying the Lesson

In this final session, take time to evaluate the progress you have made in understanding authority. In the following sections, list specific areas in which you have grown personally as well as communally.

Personal Growth

_____

_____

_____

_____

_____

_____

Now that you understand what God has for you, dedicate yourself to practicing this new knowledge and allow God to bless you abundantly.

Checking Your Cover

Heavenly Father, I purpose to submit to Your authority, and in doing so will submit to the family, civil, church and social authorities which You have placed over my life. Give me Your grace to not only desire, but to do Your good pleasure. I ask for a heart that delights in submission and obedience. I commit my life to my Lord Jesus Christ and forsake all manner of rebellion. In whatever way You have called me to glorify Your name I eagerly submit. Amen.

Video Script for Lesson 12
Great Faith

In this last session, I want to deal with the great rewards that come to those who submit to God's authority. To those who are "under cover." I remember when I was walking into my office one morning, it was a few years ago. I came into my office at 5:30 in the morning to pray like I had done so many mornings before and when I stepped into my office I heard the Holy Spirit speak to me like I'm speaking to you right now. And he said, "Turn to Luke's gospel, chapter 17 and read from verse 5." So I remember going over there and looking at verse 5 and I thought, "You know, I've preached out of here before." But you know what? Whenever God speaks to you like that, obviously you didn't get it all. Amen. As a matter of fact, we didn't get it all period. But you know, you just know he's going to show you something. Amen. So I read from verse 5: "*And the apostles said to the Lord 'Increase our faith.'*" Now look up at me. That's a good thing to ask for, don't you think? And I remember when I first got saved, I had only been saved for about two years, and I was sleeping in my apartment in Raleigh, North Carolina. And one night in a deep, deep, deep, deep sleep, I had found myself jumping up out of the bed and this came screaming out of my mouth— "I'm just looking for someone to believe." And I turned around and looked and there was my outline of my body covered in sweat and I thought, "Wow! God just spoke to me." This is my immaturity, I thought, "Lord, couldn't it be a little more profound?" And I remember going back to sleep and the next morning all I kept hearing was, "I'm just looking for someone to believe." Then all of a sudden it hit me. What grieved Jesus more than anything else in the gospel? Not what angered him. The Pharisees angered him. What grieved him more than anything else was people not having faith. And what pleased him more than anything else in the gospel? Is when people simply believed that what he said he would do, he

would do. The Bible is very clear that it says that without faith it is impossible to please God. I don't know about you, but I'm in the business and I want to please God. Amen. Can you say, "Amen"? "Amen."

Now the apostles cry out, "*Lord, increase our faith.*" Now you know what's amazing? What caused this cry for greater faith? Did Jesus just move a mountain? Did He just open up the eyes of somebody born blind? Did He just calm the sea? Did He just feed 5,000? Did He just raise somebody from the dead? No, you know what He did? He—look at him in verse 3. Look at this in verse 3— "*and He said*"— look at this: "*Take heed to yourselves. If your brother sins against you, rebuke him; and if he repents, forgive him. And if he sins against you seven times in a day, and seven times in a day returns to you, saying, 'I repent,' you shall forgive him.*" And the apostles [cried out] to the Lord, ['Lord,] increase our faith.'" Isn't it amazing? It wasn't the power of miracles, but when he said, "Walk in the character of God," that's what caused the cry to come. The apostles knew that faith and obedience were directly connected, something I was about to learn that morning.

Now let's read. The apostles said to the Lord "*Increase our faith.*" So Jesus responds to them. Verse 6: "*So the Lord said, 'If you have faith as a mustard seed, you can say to this mulberry tree, "Be pulled up by the roots and be planted in the sea," and it would obey you.'*" Now listen up. I was familiar with that. I knew that Jesus said in Mark 11:23 that "*whoever shall say unto this mountain, 'Be thou removed, and be thou cast into the sea.' And shall not doubt in his heart but believe those things which he says will come to pass. He shall have whatsoever he says.*" Amen. And I thought, "Boy! This is the same thing." He just pulled out a tree now not a mountain, but he's saying the same thing, right? So I was cool with that. I felt like I really had a handle on that. Jesus is also illustrating in this verse that faith is given to us as a seed. Everybody say, "Seed." "Seed." And how many of you know you can be given a pot of seeds, but if you don't go plant them, those seeds aren't going to grow? And it's your responsibility to plant them right? God makes them grow, but you've got to plant them. And so what Jesus is saying to them is, "Your faith is like a seed, but you better plant it and cultivate it so it grows." Amen. So that's what he's about to go on to say. Because look at this. Verse 7: *"And which of you, having a servant plowing or tending sheep, will say to him when he has come in from the field, 'Come in at once, sit down to eat'? But will [you] not rather say to him, 'Prepare something for my supper, and gird yourself and serve me until [I've] eaten and drunk, and afterward you will eat and drink'?"* Now, will you look up at me? This is where I always got baffled. I said, "You know Lord, this just doesn't make any sense. They ask about faith and you talk about having faith to move a mountain or a mulberry tree and you go straight from that to talking about protocol with a servant. This is like, 'Why did you just jump over it and talk about protocol with a servant?' It never made sense to me. You talk about this servant who's out there plowing the fields for his master and the master is definitely not going to say to him when he comes in, 'You eat.' He's first going to say, 'Prepare my food and make me something to eat.'" And I said, "Lord, I just don't get it." And I remember hearing the Holy Spirit that morning speak to me. And he said, "John, what is the ultimate purpose of hiring a servant to plow your fields and tend your flocks?" He said, "If you are a master, what is your ultimate purpose for hiring that servant to plow your fields and tend your flocks? What's the ultimate goal?" And I thought about it. And then I said, "I know what it's for, to put food on my table so I can eat." He said, "That's right. Would you have a guy out there tending your plants, tending your sheep, and then have him come in and have him feed himself and you starve to death?" I said, "That would be stupid." He said, "That's right." He said, "That man's job is to finish

it and complete it." Are you with me?

So watch what he goes on to say. Verse 9: *"Does he thank that servant because he did the things that were commanded him? I think not."* So now you notice we're talking about obedience. Are you seeing this? Verse 10: *"So likewise you, when you have done all those things which you are commanded."* Look up at me. Do you see that Jesus is talking about the faithfulness of a servant to his master, and completing the job? And then he turns it right around to us, and *"So likewise you, when [you've] done all those things which [you've been] commanded."* He turns around and talks about our obedience to God. Are you seeing this? What Jesus is saying is, "Guys you want to increase faith, this is how your faith increases. When you obey to completion. When you finish the job." Let me tell you something, folks. An unfinished job is just as bad as a job not started. Are you with me?

Now in saying this, he gives us three important points. Read verse 10. *"So likewise you, when you've done all those things which you are commanded, say, 'We are unprofitable servants. We have done what was our duty to do.'"* Jesus gives us three main important points here. Number one: there is a direct connection between faith and obedience to authority. Listen to me carefully. The more obedient you are the greater your faith becomes. Number two: faith increases when we complete what we are commanded to do. Point number three: an attitude of true humility is of the utmost importance to get us to finish the course. Let me try to get through all three in the short time that we have.

Point number one. There is a direct connection between faith and obedience to authority. Go with me, hold your places there, go with me to Matthew 8. Matthew the eighth chapter. Now I'm going to go through this quickly. I think this is something we should be familiar with. But in Matthew 8:5 as a matter of fact, let's just read it because you're going over there. Verse 5: *"Now when Jesus had entered*

Capernaum, a centurion came to Him, pleading with Him, saying, 'Lord, my servant is lying at home paralyzed, dreadfully tormented.' Jesus said to him, 'I will come and heal him.'" That's pretty good, isn't it? Verse 8: *"The centurion answered and said, 'Lord, I am not worthy that You should come under my roof. But only speak a word, and my servant shall be healed. For I also . . .'"*—now watch this carefully. Everybody say, "I also." "I also." In other words, he's saying that Jesus is what he is.— *"'For I also am a man under authority'"*—Do you notice he says under authority?— *"'having soldiers under me. And I say to this one, "Go," and he goes; and to another, "Come," and he comes; and to my servant, "Do this," and he does it.'"* Now watch this. *"When Jesus heard it* [Verse 10] *He marveled, and said to those who followed. 'Assuredly I say to you, I have not found such great faith, not even in Israel!'"* Do you know what is amazing? This is a Roman officer, he is a conqueror of the nation of Israel. And Jesus makes the statement, "I have not found this much faith, not in John the Baptist. I haven't found this much faith in my own mother Mary. I haven't found this much faith in my twelve apostles. I haven't found this much faith in anybody that's received any miracle from me. This is the greatest faith I have encountered in my 30 years of walking this planet is this Roman officer." Why did he have such great faith? Because the Roman officer looked at Jesus and said, *"I am a man under authority, having soldiers under me. And I say to this one, 'Go,' and he goes, this one, 'Come,' and he comes."* In other words, what he is saying to Jesus is this, "I report to the commander of the legion." You must understand that there was a commander of the legion. A legion was 6,000 soldiers, under that commander was 60 centurions, each of those centurions had 100 men under him. That man had 100 soldiers that reported to him, but he was submitted to the commander. That man was saying, "Because I am submitted to my commander, therefore I have my commander's backing and I have basically all of Rome's backing. So all I have to do is say one word and my soldiers jump. Because I am under authority, I have authority." Are you seeing this? And what he is saying is he says, "I also." Everybody

say, "I also." "I also." What he is saying to Jesus is, "Jesus I recognize You are under Your Father's authority. And I recognize that, just as I have authority in my military world because I'm submitted to the Roman authority, I recognize that You have authority in the spiritual world because You're submitted to Your heavenly Father's order of authority. So all You have to do is say one word and that devil has got to leave my servant. Just like my soldiers jump when I say one word." And Jesus marveled. He said, "I haven't found this kind of faith in all of Israel." What gave that man that faith? It was his understanding and living in authority. That is amazing.

Tie this in with what Jesus said to the disciples who desired to increase their faith. He said what? He said, *"You have faith as a mustard seed, you can say to the mulberry tree, 'Be pulled up by the roots and be planted in the sea,' and it would obey you,"* right? Notice that Jesus said all you had to do is speak a word, right? And the tree would obey you. Isn't that what the soldier said? "Speak one word and my" what? "I speak one word and my soldiers obey me. All you have to do is speak one word and that devil's going to leave my servant," right? Jesus said all you've got to do is speak one word and that mulberry tree is going to obey you, right? Who does the mulberry tree obey? The one who did the things that were commanded him. Are you seeing this? These guys are asking for increased faith. Jesus said, "You want increased faith? Those who do what the father has commanded, those who are submitted to the authority of the father. All they have to do is say one word and that mulberry tree will obey."

Point number two. Faith increases only when we complete what we are commanded to do. Look at the life of Abraham. Go to Genesis 22. Genesis 22. In Genesis the twenty-second chapter we read in verse 1: *"Now it came to pass after these things that God tested Abraham, and said to him, 'Abraham!' And he said, 'Here I am.' Then he said, 'Take now your son, your only son Isaac, whom you love.'"* Notice he let him get real close. *"'And go to the land of Moriah, and offer him there as a burnt offering on one of the mountains [that] I will tell you.'"* Now look at verse 3. *"So Abraham rose early in the morning."* The NIV version says, *"Abraham rose early the next morning."* There are people today that say, "You know, the Lord's been dealing with me about this for a couple months now," and they kind of laugh about it. They do not have the faith of Abraham. They do not have the fear of God that Abraham had. God gave him a three day journey. Why did he give him a three day journey? To give him time to think it over and turn back. God's going to give him time to really think this one through. But Abraham goes the three days and goes up to the top of the mountain, builds the altar, ties up his son on that altar. Now let me say this to you. His son was more important to him than even himself. It would have been easier for Abraham to put himself on that altar. That's how important Isaac was to Abraham. Yet Abraham lifts up the knife and he's ready to put his son to death and—watch what happens. Verse 12—The Angel of the Lord comes and he says in verse 12: *"Do not lay your hand on the lad, or do anything to him; for now I know that you fear God, since you have not withheld your son, your only son from Me."* Now the result of Abraham obeying to completion—look at what God says to him. Look at verse 16. *"And said: 'By myself I have sworn,' says the Lord, 'because you have done this thing, and have not withheld your son, your only son—blessing I will bless you, and multiplying I will multiply your descendants as the stars of the heavens and as the sand which is on the seashore; and your descendants shall possess the gate of their enemies. In your seed all the nations of the earth shall be blessed'"*—Watch this—*"'because you have obeyed [Me].'"* Would you look up at me please? God says all these things, "Your descendants will possess the gates of their enemy." Do you know what Abraham is called in Romans 4? He's called the father of faith. What was Jesus able to say years later to us? *"I will give you the keys of the kingdom [of heaven]"* and *"the gates of [hell] shall not prevail against [the church].'"* Why was Jesus able to say that? Because of the covenant of obedience of Abraham, God said, "Your descendants will possess the gates of their enemy."

Jesus was able to release that promise and his promise to us because of the obedience of Abraham.

Listen to what the Bible says, listen to this carefully. In Hebrews 6:11—12, we read, *"And we desire that each one of you show the same diligence to the full assurance of hope until the end,"*—Everybody say, "To the end." "To the end." In other words, until you complete what you're told to do— *"that you do not become sluggish [or lazy] but imitate those who through faith and patience inherit the promises."* And then he talks about Abraham. Folks, compare Abraham with Saul. Saul was told to kill the Amalekites, right? Every man, woman, and child and the animals. He did 99% of what he was told to do. What happened to Saul? We don't have the story about Saul that we have about Abraham. Abraham obeyed to completion, Saul didn't. Do you see the difference? I said, "Do you see the difference?" Now watch this. How many of us, like Saul, start out on fire with great enthusiasm, then when things get uncomfortable, difficult or results aren't as fast as expected, we disobey? Or others, they see an opportunity to benefit themselves while only slightly detouring from the directives of authority. All the while they justify it with religious purposes and reasonings, as Saul did when he spared the best sheep for the sacrifice to God. They were supposed to be destroyed according to the Word of he Lord. For if our obedience is not complete, our faith will not increase but rather dwindle. How many times have I seen people come into church as excited, passionate—they love the Word, but yet they go from church to church to church? They don't stay faithful in the position that they've been placed. They go from one position to another, they're not faithful in that position. And I watch these people and their lives as far as their calling and their life, and their ministry never really succeeds. Are you with me? Why? Because they have not obeyed to completion. And I have found that the greatest attack against us comes right before our harvest. I find that scripturally, and I find that has happened in my personal life. Why is that? Because the enemy doesn't want you to go up for that next level of faith. Amen.

Listen to what James says. I'm going to read to you out of James 2:20—26. Now I'm going to replace what James says—when he says, "works," I'm going to replace it with "obedient actions." Just listen to this. *"But do you want to know, O foolish man, that faith without [obedient actions] is dead? Was not Abraham our father justified by [obedient actions]?"* Notice he said he was justified by his obedient actions. Notice he equates his obedient actions with his faith because the Bible very clearly says Abraham was justified by faith. Are you with me? Abraham, our father, was justified by obedient actions *"when he offered Isaac"*—In another words, obedient actions and faith are one and the same— *"his son on the altar?"* Do you see that his faith was working together with his obedient actions and by obedient actions his faith was made perfect? *"And the Scripture was fulfilled which says, 'Abraham believed God, and it was accounted to him for righteousness.' And he was called 'the friend of God.'"* Do you see then that a man is justified by obedient actions and not by faith only? For as the body without the spirit is dead, so faith without obedient actions is also dead. So in other words, what the Scripture tells us very plainly is this: Faith is not faith at all unless there are corresponding obedient actions. You could tell me you've got great faith, you could talk the Word real good. You say, "But I've heard the Word and I've listened to the Word and my faith has grown because I hear the Word of God." But the Bible says, "If you hear it and don't do it, you're deceiving yourself. You don't have faith." Faith comes when we hear the Word and obey it to completion. When we're obedient even in the face of adversity. It is easy to obey God when the sun's shining and everything's going great. But when we really, really grow in our faith is when all hell seems to break loose and we're still walking in obedient actions because of what we heard the word of God say. Amen. Alleluia. If you look at the life of Abraham, it is a classic example of what happens when God tells you to do something in your life and you obey it all the way to completion. He's called the father of faith, Jesus is simply telling his disciples, if you simply do all that you're commanded to do,

that's how you can increase your faith. And that's going to give you the authority to just say one word to that mulberry tree and it will have to leave. Are you seeing this?

That is why Paul said to Timothy, *"Those who have served well as deacons obtain for themselves a . . . great boldness in the faith."* Why do they obtain great boldness in faith? Because they've obeyed all the way to completion. Man, if we could only really grasp this. You know what I find people are constantly doing? They're running from this place, to that place, to this place, to that place. Oh the wave's over here, the move's over there, the teaching's over here so good, and this and this and this. And they're moving, moving, moving, moving, moving, moving, moving. And you know what? They're not growing, they're getting a bunch of knowledge, but they're not growing. The Bible says, *"Those that are planted in the house of God shall flourish."* You know what happens to a plant every time you transplant it? It's roots start dwarfing. And you know what? The roots are the part you don't see. The faith is the part you don't see. It dwarfs. And then it becomes unfruitful and it eventually dies. When God gives you something to do, you stay with it until God—and God only—says it's time to go. You obey to completion. Let me tell you something. When God . . . I've been a Christian for over 20 years and I've lived in four states in those 20 years. I've been solidly a member of four different churches in those 20 years, in each state I was in. That God led me to those churches. I really have a hard time with people jumping from church to church. "Well, I don't like the way they're doing things over here, I'm leaving." Well, God's the one who told you to go, did He tell you to leave?

I'll never forget the time I did make the mistake of leaving one of those churches for two months. And I went to a friend of mine's church. And it got strained. And I remember coming back to my home church and the moment I put my foot in the door, God spoke to me and said, "I never told you to leave." I thought, "Wow! Isn't this amazing? You told me to come here and you never said to leave yet I left.

What an unwise decision." A third thing Jesus said. Look at this. Go back to Luke's gospel, chapter 17. The third thing he says, "*So likewise you, when you have done all those things which you are commanded, say, We are unprofitable servants. We have done what was our duty to do.*" Now do you notice the humility in that statement? "We're unprofitable servants, we've only done which is our duty to do." One thing Jesus is emphasizing here is what will keep your faith strong—what will keep you on course so that you can finish the race of faith—is that you maintain an attitude of humility. That's the way Lucifer felt. And that's why Paul comes along and says, "Hey, don't let it be a novice less you fall in the same condemnation as the devil." Listen carefully. "*To remain lowly in heart is to remain in position for the rewards of obedience. To pride our self in our own obedience.*" Now listen carefully to what's being said. To pride ourselves in our own obedience is to position ourselves for a fall even though we've obeyed. This can spoil everything you adhere to. You could follow the counsel or the Word of God in this entire 12 lessons that I've preached to you, yet lose everything by pride that you gained through obedience. If you look at the apostle Paul, in his life you will notice that he was a man that the older he got, the more humble he became. If you look at 1 Corinthians 9 you will find out that he said, "I am the least of all the apostles." Yet he did more labor than any of them. But he said, "It wasn't me, it was the grace of God in me." Now he wrote that letter in 56 A.D. Seven years later, or actually six years later, in 62 A.D. he wrote the Ephesians. And you know what he said to the Ephesians? He said, "*To me, who am less than the least of all the saints, this grace was given, [to me to] preach.*" Now he goes in the next six years from being the least of the apostles, bottom of the barrel. Remember you know there is this false humility stuff. You know what false humility is? Saying politically the correct things. It's when you say, "Oh, it wasn't really me, it was the Lord," when you're really saying, "But it really was, look at me." But it's the politically correct thing to say. That's just a lie. And how many of you know that you can't lie when you're writing the Scripture? When Paul

says, "I'm bottom of the barrel with all the apostles," he meant it. Six years later he says, "I am the least of every saint in the church." You can't lie when you're writing the Scripture. Amazing isn't it? That's Ephesians 3:7–8. Then you know what he said right towards the end of his life in 66 A.D.? Let me tell you something. You know when he made that statement? "I am the least of all the saints, I am less than the least." You know how far he was from his death? Five years away.

If I look at him, you know I look at Brother Summerall, how much respect I have for him. Brother Roberts, how much respect I have for him. But Brother Roberts is still with us. But let me tell you about Brother Summerall. Brother Summerall went home to be with the Lord when he was 83. It would be like Brother Summerall making that statement, "I am the least of all the saints. I am less of the least," when he 78 years old. Yet I saw him as a spiritual giant and I still see him as one. But yet Paul's opinion of himself is "I am less than the least of all the saints." And if you look at what he says right before he was beheaded, right around 65 A.D., a couple years later when he writes his letter to Timothy. He said, "*[Timothy], Christ Jesus came into the world to save sinners, of whom I am chief.*" He didn't say, "I was chief," he said, "I am." Yet he was the one who knew about the new creation realities. Paul never lost his attitude of humility. The thing about Moses was that he was the most humble man in all the earth. Could that be why God showed him his ways? Could that be why Paul had revelations more than anybody else to the point where it even baffled Peter? Because the Bible says in Psalm 25:9, the humble—God shows him His ways.

God showed Moses his Wisdom—what he was going to do before he did it. Why? Because he was a humble man. Humility deals with Christlike character. If you look at Jesus in Matthew 10—You know the rich young ruler came to Him Mark 10 and he said, "*Good teacher.*" And Jesus said, "*Why do you call Me good? Nobody's good but God.*" Well, of course He's good, He's the Son of God. But He doesn't boast in that characteristic. The only characteristic Jesus boasted in, the only characteristic He did was He said, *"Come and learn of Me. I am meek and lowly of heart."* He boasted in his humility. Can you say, "Amen"? "Amen." I said it earlier, I'm going to say it again: Humility does not deal with weakness, it deals with your complete submission and your absolute knowledge that you have nothing that God hasn't given you. There is nothing we have that God hasn't given us. Lucifer lost sight of the fact that even though he was beautiful and anointed, every bit of it was given by God. He lost sight of it. Are you listening young people? I said, "Are you listening?" Are you getting this? Alleluia.

Second Corinthians 10:5 Paul said, *"Refute all arguments, theories, and reasonings."* Everybody say, "Reasonings." "Reasonings." *"Refute all arguments, theories, and reasonings and every proud and lofty thing that sets itself up against the true knowledge of God. And we lead every thought and purpose away captive to the obedience"*—Everybody say, "Obedience." "Obedience"—*"of Christ."* Paul said, as believers what we are to do is forsake the principle of reasoning and embrace the principle of obedience. What Eve did, she forsook the principle of obedience and she embraced the principle of reasoning.

She took from the tree that looked good, but yet it was out [because] of her own judgment. Are you with me? The reason Paul says that we are to do this—two verses later he said— *"Punish every act of disobedience, once your obedience is complete."* What he is saying there is, "You will have the faith to deal with the evil forces and the acts of disobedience when your obedience is complete." Amen.

Song of Solomon 2:3–4 says this—Remember we started talking about a couple in the beginning of this course that got out from under cover? Remember that? By their disobedience? Let me read to you what the Song of Solomon says about those who are under his cover. *"I sat down under his [shadow] with great delight, And his fruit was sweet to my taste. He brought me [into his] banqueting house, And his banner over me was love."* Can you say, "Amen"? "Amen." His fruit is sweet when you're under his cover. How many of you want to eat sweet fruit? Stay under cover. Don't get out from underneath it. Everybody say it with me. "Stay." "Stay." "Under cover." "Under cover." Say this with me. "I'm going to stay." "I'm going to stay." "Under cover." "Under cover." Absolutely. God bless you. I hope you've enjoyed the course.

.